P9-CKA-393

Of Mice, Models, and Men

ANDREW N. ROWAN

Of Mice, Models, and Men: A CRITICAL EVALUATION OF ANIMAL RESEARCH

State University of New York Press

ALBANY

Published by
State University of New York Press, Albany

Printed in the United States of America

For information, address State University Press of New York Press, State University Plaza, Albany, N.Y., 12246

Library of Congress Cataloging in Publication Data

Rowan, Andrew N., 1946–
Of mice, models, and men

Bibliography: p.
Includes index.
1.Animals, Treatment of—United States. 2. Animal experimentation—United States—Moral and ethical aspects. I. Title.
HV4764.R69 1984 179'.4'0973 83–4986
ISBN 0–87395–776–8
ISBN 0–87395–777–6 (pbk.)

Contents

Acknowledgments

This book is the product of so many influences that I cannot possibly acknowledge all those to whom I owe some debt. For example, my parents, Bunty and Bertus Rowan, taught me the value and meaning of scholarly analysis and the careful weighing of very different arguments and positions. My teachers at Cape Town and Oxford Universities confirmed parental influences and gave me the solid grounding in biological sciences which was a necessary foundation for this book. Friends and colleagues in England, Europe, Canada and the USA have argued and discussed the issues with me and have helped me to understand both scientific and animal welfare viewpoints. Nevertheless, there are some whose names must be mentioned because of the extent of their support or because of specific advice given.

At the top of the list must come my wife Kathleen whose encouragement finally prompted me to sit down and start writing and then to keep at it. Second, I want to thank John Hoyt and Michael Fox for their encouragement and support. Third, I must thank Drs. Ted Friend, Frank Loew, Jan Moor-Jankowski, Bernie Rollin and Eve Segal for reading and commenting on certain sections of the manuscript. Finally, I would like to thank Patti Helmig for typing the manuscript and Dr. Susan Suarez, my editor at SUNY Press, for her help and support.

Foreword

In 1836, a young Quaker named W.E. Forster wrote to his friend Barclay Fox:

> I find my mother, supposing thee to have influence in scientific men, has been writing thee an epistle on cruelty. Don't let it bother thee; but if thou shouldst have a good and easy opportunity to preach to anybody upon these abominable living experiments, and let her know thereof, she will never be tired of holding thee up to the admiration of all the lads and lasses within hearing, and it will be a great kindness to her, at any rate, for she has been reading those dreadful things about galvanized frogs and impaled dogs, etc., till she is the same herself as if she had a continuous shock of galvanism about her.*

The use of animals in scientific research has been, and continues to be controversial despite the many gains in knowledge and in medical practice derived from it. Few aspects have engendered as much public interest and criticism.

Andrew Rowan has reviewed and evaluated historical and contemporary studies and data to provide an analysis of the principal arguments used by critics of the use of animals in research. In so doing, the reader is able both to note the sources of information and to examine the author's evaluation of it.

Scholarship requires a point of view which is open to informed criticism, and Dr. Rowan's book will receive its share. It represents,

* French, R.D. *Antivivisection and Medical Science in Victorian Society.* Princeton University Press, 1975.

however, a significant effort to bring objectivity into an area of increasingly emotional public debate.

Franklin M. Loew, Dean
School of Veterinary Medicine, Tufts University
Boston, Massachusetts
May, 1983

CHAPTER 1

Introduction

The Need for This Book

Over the course of the last hundred years, many books and articles have been written about the ethics of animal research. Authors both for and against animal experimentation have contributed to the argument (Smyth 1978; Lapage 1960; Pratt 1976, 1980; Dalton 1980; Leffingwell 1914; Vyvyan 1969, 1971; Diner 1979; Ryder 1975, Ruesh 1978). Smyth and Lapage who both defend animal experimentation, have discussed to a limited extent the context within which medical research on animals takes place. Few, if any, of the books arguing the opposite point of view have attempted to do so. This is a major defect because biomedical research is not isolated from the general social approval given to technological innovation and progress. For example, Jaggar, in a review of Pratt's (1980) book on alternatives to painful experimentation, comments:

> I want to turn now to what I see as the major weakness in Pratt's book: that Pratt's suggestions for alternatives to painful experiments on animals are presented piecemeal, on a case by case basis. His consideration of alternatives is not grounded on a systematic analysis either of the moral issues raised by animal experimentation or of the social and political context in which this research occurs. The latter failure is particularly important because the social context sets limits to the problems chosen for study, the research methods by which those problems are investigated, and ultimately, although I cannot argue this here, our very conception of science itself. Pratt's failure to consider the social context of animal experimentation has three consequences for his book. It deprives him of the basis for reaching any general conclusions about

> the justifiability of experimentation on animals. It leads him to underestimate the resistance his own proposals for alternatives are likely to encounter. Finally, it means that he does not see the need for alternatives that go far beyond those he recommends (Jaggar 1982, p. 276).

It is not difficult to criticize animal research. One can comb the literature and easily extract papers that are eminently worthy of criticism from the point of view of both scientific merit and animal suffering, as Diner has done (1979). However, such a book provides relatively little context. It is, therefore, always vulnerable to the counterargument that, if only the reasons behind the research had been described, then one would understand why the research was necessary and why it had to be done in precisely that manner. In the present book, a simple catalogue of painful experiments is avoided. As far as possible, generic criticisms are identified and then particular research papers are used only to typify a practice singled out for comment.

For example, there is widespread criticism from the viewpoint of animal welfare of the LD50 test, in which the lethal dose of a substance is calculated as the amount that would kill half the group of animals to which it is administered (hence the acronym, derived from *L*ethal *D*ose, *50*%). However, few of the critics have taken the trouble, until recently, to identify the reasons for performing the LD50 test or its historical basis. Instead, they criticize it simply for causing significant animal suffering, If they were to analyze the test in detail, they would find that there are also strong scientific arguments against it that support their position (see chap. 14). On the other hand, in some cases a detailed analysis of the basis for some seemingly useless animal research turns up good reasons for doing it. One may still decide that the research would entail too much animal suffering, but at least the decision is much more solidly based.

This book also attempts to meet the need for detailed rebuttal of some destructive misconceptions that have become entrenched during the last hundred years. For example, the terms *vivisection* and *antivivisection* have become so loaded with derogatory meaning that they should only be used with great care if one hopes for constructive dialogue. (I do use the term *antivivisection* here because it is still included in the names of some groups.) Nevertheless, researchers commonly label anybody from outside the research laboratory who criticizes animal research as an *antivivisectionist.* What this really means when explicitly translated is that such an individual has one or more of the following characteristics: antiprogress, anti-intellectual, antiscience, a misguided idiot, or a miserable misanthrope.

But when one carefully considers the meaning of *antivivisection*, one can see how unlikely it is that any sane person would be other than an antivivisectionist. Research scientists will readily admit that they would prefer not to use animals if it were not necessary. In other words, they would, in a perfect world, like to see the elimination of animal research. Therefore, their ultimate goal is the same as that of the most ardent abolitionist. Where the scientist, animal welfare advocate, and abolitionist differ is over the feasible *time scale* for the elimination of animal research and the vigor with which the goal should be pursued. On the other side, the term *vivisection* carries an equally vile set of implications and should also be discarded.

In fact, the derogatory implications associated with the use of these terms are part and parcel of the impassioned, but usually destructive, battles that have taken place in the past. A philosopher acquaintance, who was interested in the animal rights debate but not personally involved in it, told me of an experience he had when a friend persuaded him to address a group of research scientists on the ethics of animal research. When he entered the lecture hall on the appointed day, he was met with a wall of antagonism and animosity the likes of which he had not encountered in any other forum. On the other side, research scientists find themselves the target of virulent hate mail in which a death curse figures as relatively mild abuse. Whatever it is that causes otherwise normal and logical individuals to expose their unpleasant (human rather than bestial) natures, one thing is certain. Animals continue to suffer and human welfare is threatened while individuals indulge in the luxury of venting their spleen instead of seeking constructive progress.

Not infrequently, the animal welfare movement turns on itself in its frustration at being unable to achieve its goals. Thus, in 1982,, United Action for Animals (UAA) and Friends of Animals (FOA) lashed out at the Humane Society of the United States (HSUS), accusing it (wrongly as it happens) of collusion with the "forces of evil" to destroy a bill on alternatives that UAA had succeeded in having introduced in Congress. The bill was, in fact, gutted by Congress because the legislators could not accept its radical demands. In the ensuing internecine warfare, those medical research interests opposing any new legislation regarding laboratory animals watched in satisfaction as the actions of UAA and FOA clearly demonstrated to key congressional aides the deep divisions within the humane movement, and ultimately destroyed the slim chance of congressional action in 1982. Any discussion of the debate over animal research should also, therefore, include an analysis of the motivating forces that fuel the passions on both sides.

This book is divided into four parts. Part 1 provides the background for the critique of animal research, including a description of biomedical research (chap. 2); an analysis of the underlying attitudes and assumptions that cloud reasoned debate (chap. 3); a brief history of the debate (chap. 4); and an analysis of the number of animals used (chap. 5) and of the current theories on animal pain and suffering (chap. 6).

In the second section, some generic and specific issues in animal research are analyzed. Chapter 7 addresses the question of the training of scientists and the failure of the educational system to consider the ethical problems in a coherent framework. Chapter 8 covers primate research in the United States, a research area that appears to be particularly bound up with the bureaucracy of science. It thus affords a useful case study of how animal needs are frequently ignored as researchers jockey for position and prestige. Chapter 9 discusses behavioral research on animals and the interesting ethical paradox raised by such research. Either the animal is a good model for human behavior, in which case its high fidelity raises awkward, and ignored, questions regarding its ethical acceptability. Or the animal is a poor model, in which case one must question why it is used at all.

Chapter 10 deals with the battle over pound animals that has been fought during the last thirty-five years. It is an important issue for research in the United States since the idea of using pound animals jolted local humane societies out of their ostrich-like disregard of animal research and probably influenced the postwar reformation of the humane movement. In chapter 11, some of the generic complaints are discussed, including unnecessary animal research, undue animal suffering (in light of the proposed gains in knowledge), and inadequate anesthesia or care. Finally, chapter 12 introduces a modicum of balance by showing how some animal research has indeed led to benefits in health.

Part 3 (chaps. 13–17) deals exclusively with toxicity testing and its use in safety evaluation. The context of animal testing is discussed and some ideas are suggested for reform of current practice that could reduce our need for animal testing. Special attention, in separate chapters, is given to the LD50 and Draize tests, since they have been the focus, for advocates of animal welfare, of concerted criticism and campaigns in the past few years.

The final section deals with the background of the moral issues (chap. 18), the concept of alternatives (chap. 19), and a series of suggestions (chap. 20) for constructive action that would benefit the animals without harming future progress in biomedical knowledge or human health.

Issues not addressed

This brings me to one final point that must be touched upon. There are a number of individuals who actively oppose some or all animal research but who do not accept the basic assumptions of modern medicine. This book will provide them with relatively little of interest since its arguments and criticisms are placed squarely within the modern medical framework. Therefore, for the purpose of the present argument, it is assumed that the current level of biomedical research is necessary to improve human health and well-being.

Nevertheless, some counter positions have merit. Greater dependence on a preventive approach (doctors in ancient China were only paid as long as the patient was well) and a curb on chemical innovation and self-intoxication (e.g., cigarettes) could markedly reduce the need for animal research and animal testing. In fact, many critics of the modern health industry (e.g., Illich 1977) have argued variously that the pharmaceutical industry is not in business for our health; that doctors cause more disease than they cure; that the administration of drugs treats the symptoms and not the causes; that we should pay far more attention to preventive medicine; that the social and environmental aspects of health need to be stressed, as opposed to the mere absence of disease and pain; and other notions that may or may not be grounded on solid and detailed analysis.

This book does not deal with these issues—there is just not the space, nor do I have the knowledge. Another issue not addressed concerns the effect of animal research on society's approach to biology, nature, and health. Roberts (1980), for example, has argued that modern biology suffers from humanistic scientism. In other words, we conduct our research under the arrogant assumption that we can solve all our problems even if it involves a great deal of suffering on the part of other sentient beings.

She believes it is impossible to improve the human condition under these circumstances, since the evil of animal research will perforce prevent us from ascending toward the Summum Bonum (highest Good). She refers to her vision as theocentric humanism in which humankind strives toward a higher state of being. It is interesting to note that her philosophy is rooted in Neoplatonic ideas, and yet her argument directly contradicts that of Saint Augustine, who also drew heavily on Neoplatonism in rejecting the notion that humans had any duties toward animals.

Few people today are prepared to accept as realistic Roberts' vision of a new age of enlightment that would include a humane biology requiring neither human nor animal suffering (cf. Gurney 1982). There are also some serious flaws in her arguments, which detract from her message that animal research and true insight into matters biological are incompatible. On the issue of abortion, she accepts the existence of grey areas in which moral interests must be weighed and the interests of one being sacrificed to those of another. Admittedly, she sees this as an interim measure until a better solution is found, but it is not clear why similar difficulties are not recognized for animal research. Researchers argue that the interests of animals must be sacrificed for the sake of human benefits and, in some cases, the argument can be very compelling.

However, I do not wish to engage in a detailed criticism of Roberts' thesis. Suffice it to say that challenges to the underlying assumptions that research is beneficial and that the priorities of modern medicine are appropriate are not part of my thesis. At the same time, I do not wish to give the impression that knowledge is such an absolute good that its pursuit overrides all other moral concerns (cf. Midgley 1981). I believe that there should be restrictions on the use of human subjects in research, for example, and I hope to demonstrate in the following nineteen chapters that similar retrictions are appropriate in animal research.

Part I

THE BACKGROUND

CHAPTER 2

What is Biomedical Science?

In the last few years, several four-color, general science magazines have invaded the newstands. On the one side, there is the relatively august *Science 82,* published by the American Association for the Advancement of Science (AAAS), while on the other we have *Omni,* a flamboyant magazine of science fiction and sience fact, published by Bob Guccione of *Penthouse* fame. All the new science magazines have carved out a substantial niche for themselves. *Omni* claims four million readers, while *Science 82* has sales around the three-quarter million mark, and they now project their break-even point at three years from the first issue rather than the originally scheduled five.

The success of these magazines is indicative of the thirst for scientific news and analysis among the nonscientific public. The demand had been demonstrated by earlier opinion polls, but the public had to wait until Guccione and the AAAS took the plunge. The public's interest is not misplaced. Knowledge derived from scientific research, while very detailed and precise, is so wide-ranging and general in its application that no one can claim that it is unimportant. The social impact of applied research is everywhere, from the new-found sense of freedom provided by birth control pills to the information revolution being wrought by microprocessors. And yet the study of science itself, and its impact on society, is a relatively new pastime.

The question posed in the title of this chapter is not easy to answer; ideally it requires much more than a single chapter for proper treatment. However, it must be addressed here, even though

:ficially, because many of the players who argue about animal ...rch have relatively little understanding of the varied activities making up the field of biomedical science. As a result, arguments about whether or not animals are required are frequently based on inappropriate assumptions.

The term *biomedical science* refers to all those activities that play a role in finding out how living things work and interact and how best to protect humans and our dependent charges from harm. Such a broad-ranging definition covers a wide variety of skills and intellectual capabilities. The engineer who is developing a new prosthesis for human use, the doctor who has just published a paper on an interesting clinical case, the zoologist who is following the migrations of the Monarch butterfly, and the technician collecting blood from a calf fetus to turn into fetal calf serum for tissue culture research are all participating in biomedical science. As Dixon notes, close scrutiny of biomedical science reveals a wide range of intellectual activity, including "both the truly mysterious creativity of the outstanding scientific thinker, and the humdrum banality of research that differs little from the action of the child collecting car numbers" (1976, p. 22).

Most of us tend to view animal research in biomedical science as a search for a cure for cancer or some other disease, or as an exciting and widely publicized new activity such as transplanting a leg from one animal to another. This is a relatively limited view. The full panoply of the work of biomedical science as it involves animal use or research may be classified in a number of ways, among them the following: extraction of products, production of biologicals (e.g., hormones and vaccines), diagnosis of disease, biomedical education, toxicity testing of consumer goods and drugs, the search for new drugs, and basic and applied biomedical research.

Categories of Biomedical Science

Extraction of Products. Animals provide an extraordinary range of products for everyday human existence, and it is thus no surprise that animal products are also required for biomedical research and therapy. Many hormones, including insulin, are extracted from slaughterhouse material, while other products are used in research activities. For example, a number of different types of cells will not grow properly in some of the nutrient mediums that have been developed unless blood serum is added to the medium. Such serum usually comes from slaughtered calves or calf fetuses.

Production and Standardization of Biologicals. Animals are used to produce a wide range of antisera, vaccines, and antibodies which may be employed in research, diagnosis, or therapy. Smallpox vaccine is produced on the skins of calves or sheep, while diphtheria antitoxin produced in animals was one of the triumphs of animal research at the end of the 19th century that helped to turn the tide of public opinion in favor of such research (Turner 1980).

Rabbits are widely used as a source of specific antibodies for research and diagnosis. The required antigen is injected into the animal and blood samples are then taken from which the antibody sera are prepared. A rabbit may spend its lifetime in the laboratory acting as an antibody factory. A fairly recent development that permits the production of very pure samples of highly specific antibodies *in cell culture* may change all this (Yelton and Scharff 1980). Even so, these monoclonal antibodies (so-called because they are obtained from a single cloned cell) are still produced in animals because the yield of antibody is higher than in cell culture.

Diagnosis. Between 1% and 5% of all laboratory animals are used every year to diagnose diseases. In 1956, animals were used to diagnose tuberculosis, diphtheria, brucellosis, anthrax, and other diseases, as well as pregnancy (Russell and Burch 1959). Nowadays, tuberculosis can be diagnosed using *in vitro* culture techniques, and guinea pigs are no longer required (Marks 1972), while the earlier animal-pregnancy tests have given way to quicker and simpler immunological assays. However, the number of recognized and/or relevant pathogens has increased, and therefore, the demand for animal diagnosis has not declined significantly despite many advances in culture technology (Austwick 1977; Meier-Ewert 1977; Raettig 1977; Storz, Moore, and Spears 1977).

Biological Education. At least 3 million animals are used annually in the United States for secondary school and university educational purposes (Institute for Laboratory Animal Resources 1970). These range from frogs in high school biology classes to pound dogs for practice surgery in medical and veterinary curriculum. There has been much debate over the need to use live animals in educational programs in high school (cf. McGiffin and Brownley 1980). Even for colleges and professional schools, some questions have been raised about the use of animals in certain procedures. For example, in 1979, Michigan State University College of Veterinary Medicine stopped its practice of demonstrating poison symptoms by administering lethal does of unidentified poisons to dogs and sheep. They now use vido-tape recordings. (The issue of animal use in education is addressed more fully in chap. 7.)

Toxicity testing. Toxicity testing is conducted to determine whether chemicals are *safe* for general human use or to identify the *safe* limits of use for chemicals known to be hazardous (see chap. 13–17). Tests are carried out on a wide range of chemicals and biological substances (including drugs, vaccines, pesticides, food additives, industrial chemicals, cosmetics, and household products) and involve millions of animals every year. Standard toxicity tests for new drugs include procedures to detect certain specialized effects such as the induction of genetic damage, of cancer, or of deformities in the developing fetus.

The Search for New Drugs: The Shot-Gun Approach. Prontosil, the original sulfa drug, was discovered, by testing it in mice that had been inoculated with pathogenic bacteria. This discovery, followed within a few years by penicillin, sparked the beginning of the modern pharmaceutical industry. Scientists were put to work to develop screening systems that would discriminate between chemicals that are active or inactive against an infectious agent or disease syndrome. For example, animal models have been developed to screen compounds for analgesia (e.g., rat tail-flick test, tooth pulp stimulation); anticonvulsant properties (e.g., web building in spiders); antihypertensive properties (e.g., chronically catheterized monkeys); and many others (Mitruka, Rawnsley, and Vadehra 1976). At the same time, many *in vitro* models are being developed and are increasingly being used as preliminary screens in the search for active compounds (Spink 1977).

The drug industry of the Western world has, despite criticisms of its practices in other areas, been remarkably creative in discovering and developing new drug entities. The Russian pharmaceutical industry, by contrast, has not produced a single major therapeutic breakthrough. Nor have university and government laboratories worldwide been able to match the creativity that has flourished in industrial laboratories. For example, the National Cancer Institute's anticancer-agent screening program has been singularly unsuccessful, given the resources available. As Dixon notes: "Clearly the competitive edge and diversity of scientific approach maintained by commercial secrecy, are effective forces encouraging innovation" (1976, p. 125).

There are limitations to the large-scale screening approach that has proved so successful for the pharmaceutical industry. Hume (1957b) drew attention to this fact and suggested that, while some trial and error is perhaps inevitable, hard thinking and insightful research can keep it within reasonable limits. Twenty-five years later, it is clear that hard thinking is even more important as the pharmacopoeias expand and competition increases.

Basic and Applied Research. The category of basic and applied research refers to all the remaining practices that make up biomedical activity involving some animal use. It covers a very wide range of disciplines and methods and comes closest to the image of a white-coated individual who works with test tubes and animals to solve the mysteries of life and to find cures or palliatives for human and animal disease. An individual may be involved in more than "basic and applied research" alone (e.g., teaching and research, or testing and research). Nevertheless, it is usually only basic and applied research, including some drug development and research into new testing and production methods, that involves the high-quality detective work that so many of us have come to associate with "scientists."

For example, extraction of products and the production of biologicals require somebody who can follow recipes accurately and solve day-to-day problems. Sometimes, as in the development of new procedures or when major difficulties are encountered, more creative insight may be required. Diagnosis of diseases also involves a large degree of technical training and, in routine procedures at least, little creative thinking. Biomedical education requires someone who can convey principles, facts, and ideas to students. Not infrequently, the best teachers are poor research scientists, and vice versa. Animals are used solely to demonstrate points, not to generate new knowledge.

Toxicity testing is essentially an empirical exercise. For the most part, the scientist is required to follow a standard receipe, to record the effects of the test agents at different doses, and, perhaps, finally to provide some sort of interpretation. Of course, one may need a great deal of skill to comprehend and interpret observed effects, but creative science usually does not replace cook-book science until the toxicologist starts to look at mechanisms. Unfortunately, most toxicity testing is conducted for regulatory purposes where interesting scientific questions are only followed up, if at all, as byproducts of regulatory needs.

The search for new drugs can also be a process totally devoid of any theoretical underpinning. I was once told by an executive of a pharmaceutical company that they would try scrapings off the laboratory floor if they thought such a material would lead to a potential new drug. Waksman's discovery of streptomycin, for which he was awarded the 1952 Nobel prize in medicine, required little creative insight but a great deal of managerial skill as he screened one microbial culture after another for the presence of products with antibiotic properties.

In fact, not all "research" qualifies as creative, insightful activity either. Wade (1981) has documented the events leading up to the award of the Nobel Prize in medicine to Andrew Schally and Roger Guillemin for their discovery of an important pituitary hormone, thyrotropin-releasing factor. He paints a somewhat unflattering picture of both men as single-minded and very competitive scientific organizers and administrators who solved what was essentially a technical, rather than a conceptual, problem. According to Wade, intense rivalry between the two men interfered with the achievement of the overall goal but was merely an extreme expression of a common aspect of scientific research.

Another fascinating, albeit very gossipy, account of a major research discovery was Watson's (1968) book on the elucidation of the structure of DNA. Judging from the book, much of Watson's time in Cambridge, U.K., was spent trying to fit mechanical models together in such a way as to confirm Crick's calculations of the helical structure of DNA, which were based on crystallographic studies done by Wilkins, in London. For light relief, they would date *au pair* girls who had been sent over from Europe to learn English while looking after the precocious children of Cambridge academics. However, the book provides a marvelous insight into the uncertainties and frustrations of biomedical research and the odd chances or insights upon which major discoveries are often based.

The above examples provide anecdotal evidence of the range of activities that can lead to the pinnacles of scientific achievement in biology and medicine. At all levels of the biological hierarchy, whether one is studying the atomic structure of DNA or the oxygen-transport protein haemoglobin (molecular), the energy-producing pathways in cells (subcellular), the ways in which cells of the immune system are programmed to defend the mammalian body from invasion (cellular), the surgical correction of heart defects (whole organism), or the epidemiological study of the effects of cigarette smoking (social patterns), the deductive processes and thought patterns are very similar. Scientists all over the world judge research initially on the basis of its stated design and then on whether the results can be repeated or built upon to fit into a certain theoretical framework—the dogma of the day. It is the theoretical basis of research and the ease with which data can be fitted into existing constructions or, alternatively, appropriated to support a new or different theoretical construct, that together form one of the cornerstones of scientific discovery and the advance of knowledge.

Understanding the basis for the advance of science is a key to understanding how biomedical research proceeds and the place that living matter plays in that process.

The Logic of Scientific Discovery

Early on in scientific education, one comes across the notion of the *scientific method*. Usually this is outlined as the gathering of facts, developing a theory by inductive logic from those facts, deducing certain consequences of the theory, devising experiments to test the theory, and then modifying the theory in accordance with the results from these experiments. However, actual scientific research does not appear to follow such a simplistic outline. For example, the creative act of developing a theory certainly does not appear to involve the inductive logic so favored by Francis Bacon and his followers in later generations.

How many people are prone to declare that most of their ideas come to them while shaving, showering, or during some other mundane activity? Kekule, the chemist who dreamed up (literally) the structure of the benzene molecule stated afterwards that he was sitting dozing in front of the fire when he saw atoms dancing.

> My mental vision rendered more acute by repeated visions of the kind, could not distinguish larger structures of manifold conformations: long rows, sometimes more closely fitted together, all twining and twisting in snake-like motion. But look! What was that? One of the snakes had seized hold of its own tail, and the form whirled mockingly before my eyes. As if by a flash of lightning I awoke: and this time also I spent the rest of the night working out the consequences of the hypothesis (Crowther 1969, p. 179).

Faced with this sort of anecodotal evidence, which refuted the idea of careful inductive logic (although Kekule was certainly aware of all the facts since he had been mulling over the problem for some time), philosophers of science have developed a different picture of the process of scientific discovery. Medawar (1969) has provided perhaps one of the clearest descriptions of this new concept, using the tactic of setting up two opposing views of how science advances.

In the first view, which Medawar calls the romantic, science is seen as above all as an imaginative and exploratory activity. Intuition is the basis of every advancement of learning, and having ideas is the scientist's highest accomplishment. Working those ideas out is an important but lesser occupation. In this sense, the scientist is behaving very much as a poet. Such science flourishes best in complete freedom, protected from the demands of need and accountability, where funding agencies support scientists, not projects, and individuals, rather than teams.

In the second or wordly view, science is above all a critical and analytical activity. The scientist is a person who requires evidence before delivering an opinion. Under these circumstances, imagination is merely a catalyst—it can speed progress, but it cannot start projects or give them direction. In this view, science and poetry are, of course, antithetical because the usefulness of science is directly related to its success in leading to an enlargement of human knowledge of the natural world. Worldly science is best supported via projects, most of which are best carried forward by multitalented teams of scientists.

Anyone who has done research will recognize that there are elements of truth in both of these descriptions. Having ideas is very important and such activities are the domain of individuals. However, trying out ideas is a ruthlessly critical process usually best done by teamwork. Modern experimentation is, thus, essentially the critical analysis of a theory. Science today inevitably involves teamwork since the researcher across the ocean who refutes another's published findings is still part of the core group (or "team") of a particular speciality, no matter that the individuals are separated by ten thousand miles.

Some scientists are better at one activity than the other, although both processes must be present in reasonable balance. Jacques Monod, the French microbiologist, was very good with ideas but was, reportedly, a slapdash bench scientist. Thus, his "experimental" criticism of theories would not necessarily have matched his brilliance as an intellectual critic and synthesizer. Most scientists do not maintain the high quality of work and deduction described by the above model of scientific discovery (the hypothetico-deductive model). This description provides an accurate picture of only the best science.

Unfortunately, much research does not rise above pure empiricism or mere parametric tinkering.

Graduate students seeking their union ticket to the scientific profession—a Ph.D.—are well aware of the possibilities of parametric tinkering—many theses are based on little else. Data are generated by applying a tried and tested technique to another organ or a different species of animal, thus producing the "original" knowledge necessary for the successful thesis. There are, of course, many excellent and interesting theses, but I would be surprised if more than 50% (if that), of all the data generated by graduate students was published in quality journals.

It is often claimed that one cannot direct the focus of scientific research without destroying the creative insights (of the Romantic view) necessary for the advancement of knowledge. This is patently absurd. The pharmaceutical companies do not permit their employees to scamper after every red herring produced by fertile imaginations, and yet they have a successful record of innovation. On the other hand, pharmaceutical companies do not necessarily demand an *immediate* return on their research investment, their research scientists have a good deal of latitude within the overall parameters of the problem. The same is true of the manner in which society funds research. A small amount of money may be devoted to research so "pure" that no one could see any useful outcome, but most research grant applications must be justified on the basis of potential short-term (applied research) or long-term (basic research) utility.

Two other very important factors contribute to the advancement of science—luck and the availability of suitable techniques. Little can be said about luck except to repeat Pasteur's epigram: chance favors the prepared mind. Fleming's discovery of penicillin was the result of a chance observation of the inhibition of bacterial prolifenation around a fungal growth on a plate of bacterial culture. However, Fleming's mind was "prepared" because he was interested in agents that stopped or prevented bacterial growth.

The availability of suitable techniques is another matter altogether. Many problems are very difficult, if not impossible, to research meaningfully because we just do not have suitable techniques. Many important discoveries are preceded by the development of one or more techniques of suitable sensitivity and discriminative powers. The development of a successful polio vaccine was made possible by demonstrating that the virus could be grown in cell culture (Enders, Weller, and Robbins 1949). As a result, many laborious animal research projects could be replaced by a quick, sensitive, and relatively simple cell culture technique and, five years later, the first effective polio vaccine was given a field trial.

A close study of how scientists work thus reveals the following picture. Important discoveries, both in knowledge and in the development of new techniques, occur via a number of paths. Creative insights and rigorous testing are only two elements. Others include luck, blind empiricism, and a certain amount of ignorance so that the scientist does not know that what has just been observed could not have happened! As Dixon notes, the "scientific method turns out to be little or no different from the analytical processes used in many other jobs and professions—by a detective seeking a murderer for example. It amounts to no more than scrupulously applied common sense" (1976, p. 36).

Duplication and the Issue of Scientific Validity

Opponents of animals research commonly rally around the cry that there is far too much duplication and repetition of research on animals. They point to the fact that a particular researcher may have been investigating the problem of one or another particular disease for the last twenty-five years and still has not found a cure. The titles of successive research papers are often very similar, and the layperson, justifiably, becomes suspicious that the research is mere repetition designed to guarantee grants from the Federal agencies responsible for supporting such work. Scientists give credence to such suspicions when they refer, jokingly or otherwise, to the urgent need to finish a project successfully before the deadline for submission of their next grant application.

Undoubtedly some repetition does take place, but it is totally unclear how much repetition is necessary or how much research is, with the benefit of hindsight, a total waste of time. One can imagine the research effort as that of a prospector looking for diamonds; he must sift through a great deal of dirt to find even one gemstone. In rich deposits, or deposits easy to mine, the number of gems found is very high in relation to the effort expended. Thus, wherever a new theory or the development of new techniques has opened up a new research area, progress may be rapid. In other fields, the research effort may have been slowed down to the extent of merely filling in gaps in our knowledge base while awaiting a major breakthrough.

One fascinating retrospective study of the importance of particular types of research in a few specific research fields was conducted by

Comroe and Dripps (1976). They reviewed the essential bodies of knowledge that had to be developed before each of the top ten (selected by vote by a team of experts) clinical advances in cardiovascular and pulmonary medicine and surgery could reach its current state of achievement. They identified 137 essential bodies of knowledge.

For example, cardiac surgery did not really take off until almost 100 years after the first general anesthetic was put to use. What was it, therefore, that had to be known before surgeons could successfully repair cardiac defects? Comroe and Dripps argue that, first of all, the surgeon required precise, preoperative diagnosis. This required selective angiocardiography, which, in turn, was based on the earlier discovery of cardiac catheterization, which required the still earlier development of X-ray machines. The surgeon also required an artificial heart-lung apparatus to take over the function of a patient's heart and lungs, and a potent, nontoxic anticoagulant—heparin. These are just a few of the twenty-five neccesary developments before John Gibbon could, in 1954, perform open-heart surgery with some degree of confidence in the result.

The study clearly demonstrated that much research (41%) which was not clinically oriented when it was done was essential for the later development of clinical advances. A majority of the selected papers (61.7%) were devoted to the elucidation of *mechanisms* by which living organisms function, while a further 15.3% were concerned with the development of new apparatus, techniques, or procedures. Comroe and Dripps also noted that even their long list of papers "includes only a small fraction of the good, original research that helped to move us away from complete ignorance toward full knowledge" (1976, p. 108).

Nevertheless, many papers published in the modern scientific literature disappear, virtually without a trace. One of the measures of a paper's impact on a field is the number of times it is cited by other workers, the average being about twice per annum. Some important papers are cited far more often, which means that a goodly percentage of published research reports (estimated at about 50%) are not cited at all. In fact, it has been argued that the majority of published work has little or no impact on the forward march of knowledge (Cole and Cole 1972). This may well be true, but one still has a major problem of predicting which project will produce a noteworthy paper and which will not.

Some good papers are ignored because the authors are unknowns from schools with, at best, only a modest research reputation. Other papers are published and cited, even if they are not particularly good, because the authors are well known and respected scientists. Several years ago, twelve papers already published in prestigious journals were typed out in manuscript form, except that the titles, names of authors, and abstracts were altered. The authors were represented as coming from unknown institutions located in the academic backwoods of rural America. These manuscripts were then resubmitted to the journals that had published them between eighteen and thirty-two months earlier. Three of the thirty-eight editors and reviewers detected the resubmissions. Of the remaining nine manuscripts, eight were rejected, usually on the grounds of "serious methodological flaws." Peters and Ceci (1982), who carried out the study, were cautious in their interpretation of these results, but this study raises disturbing questions about the objectivity of the review process and the underlying prejudice against little-known institutions. Nevertheless, publication of data and their subsequent evaluation (possibly involving repetition of the experiment by another scientist) are an essential part of the process by which scientific knowledge is rendered *valid.* Validity is the core principle of science, and it can only be achieved by rigorous and critical analysis of new data and/or by placing new data in the context of a larger theory.

Although some experiments are repeated in order to check the validity of new data, most repetitive research is the result of accident, inadequate knowledge of what has already been published, or bad planning of the research project. In fact, even the best scientists have been known to be forgetful and repeat work unnecessarily. Merton (1973) reports that the Nobel prize winner, Otto Loewi, excitedly proved the chemical transmission of nervous impulses without realizing that he had written on the subject eighteen years earlier.

Martyn (1964) surveyed 647 scientists, 22% of whom noted that, after beginning their projects, they discovered information in the literature that they wished they had had before they started. In 8% of the cases, the research unintentionally duplicated other work. Masson (1970) noted that the 20% duplication (either in whole or in part) appeared to be a common finding and that the "failure of scientists to learn of other work in their fields in time to avoid duplication of research . . . [is] related to the literature searching habits of the scientists" (p. 193). In fact, a substantial proportion of scientists do little searching of the literature apart from covering a relatively small selection of core journals in their own speciality every month. Given this and the tremendous growth in biomedical literature over the past twenty years that makes it difficult for even conscientious researchers to keep up (Waksman 1980), the amount of accidental duplication is probably actually higher than the proportions mentioned by Martyn and Masson. It is thus clear that repetitive and/or unproductive research is a problem, but no constructive solutions have yet been developed.

Funding

Approximately $9 billion worth of biomedical research is conducted annually in the United States. The major, single source of funding is the National Institutes of Health (NIH), which supported $3.55 billion worth of research in 1981. The Alchohol, Drug Abuse and Mental Health Administration supported a further $1.05 billion, while the rest of the Federal government allocated an estimated $1.5 billion to $2 billion. Private industry accounted for a further $2 billion to $2.5 billion, while nonprofit groups (such as private foundations and universities) accounted for a further $0.4 billion to $0.6 billion.

Biomedical research is thus a major enterprise, and it is hardly surprising that various aspects have come in for heavy criticism. For example, the peer review system used by NIH to ensure that only highly qualified research is funded has been accused of fostering favoritism and conservatism. Heterodox theories and ideas, and less prestigious institutions, are regarded with suspicion while funds continue to flow to the top universities (Perry, Calloner, and Oberst 1981). For example, approximately 75% of Federal health research expeditures in medical schools is concentrated in the top forty institutions. These institutions show superior "grantsmanship" skills by both administrative staff and faculty. They are also likely to be able to put together the expensive physical plant and multidisciplinary research teams that are frequently required for today's studies on the cutting edge of biomedical research.

Part of the problem lies in the fact that some biomedical research requires such expensive and sophisticated equipment that only a few institutions have the staff and facilities to support it. In addition, peer review groups will, all other things being relatively equal, favor applications from researchers with a good reputation. As Dixon notes, a funding committee

> is looking to further the progress of science in a way which will also throw credit on the wisdom with which it has distributed the funds at

> its disposal. But such cabals are invariably packed with currently and previously successful practitioners of the branch of science concerned. They are not, therefore, likely to be receptive to heterodox proposals which offend against their own conventional wisdom (1976, p. 134).

Therefore, heterodox ideas like "alternatives" usually receive short shrift in such forums.

Conclusion

Biomedical science is therefore a very complex set of activities ranging from highly creative and important research to mundane, repetitive tasks requiring relatively limited training. Research quality also varies widely and is subject to all the foibles and failings of the human race. Given this, it would be surprising if one could *not* find something worthy of criticism. Nevertheless, we must remember that the same processes and methods used in biomedicine were also used to unlock the secrets of the atom and develop the modern microprocessor. One cannot dismiss the scientific method as useless in biology and medicine, as some critics would have us do, and yet accept it as useful in physics and chemistry. However, we should require greater accountability and care when sentient beings are the subjects of research.

CHAPTER 3

Attitudes and Assumptions

The key words people use in debating controversial issues are often part of the problem, rather than helping to resolve conflict. The terms *vivisection* and *antivivisection* are classic examples with their respective connotations of torture and irrational misanthropy. It is, therefore, hardly surprising that attempts to generate a reasoned dialogue usually founder on the rocks of earlier impassioned, abolitionist rhetoric. In fact, the term *vivisection* is derived from the Latin *vivus* (living) and *sectio* (cutting) and therefore literally means the cutting of living entities. Consequently, it should include human and animal surgery performed in clinics and hospitals but has usually been restricted to procedures, whether involving cutting or not, carried out for experimental purposes only.

In recent times, most animal welfare groups have avoided using the term *vivisection* because of its emotional undertones. Regan (1982), for example, argues that it is counterproductive to accuse one's opponents of cruelty (or sadism). He notes that cruelty is usually defined as not only causing another sentient being to suffer but also deriving pleasure from that suffering. While many laboratory animals do suffer, there is absolutely no evidence to indicate that research scientists derive any pleasure from that suffering. The problem is not one of cruelty but rather trained disinterest in, or discounting of, the question of animal suffering.

On the other side, the defenders of animal research have usually classified *all* animal welfare opponents of animal research as antivivisectionist, thereby attempting to diminish their credibility. Thus an editorial in *American Family Physician* comments that antivivisectionists these days work

> . . . very carefully, very subtly and, indeed, very logically. Unfortunately, their persistent efforts are occasionally rewarded with success. Success, in this instance, is measured by the passage of legislation, national or local, or administrative regulations that hamper the freedom of competent, qualified, humane and compassionate physicians (1975, pp. 67–68).

A decade earlier, Jones described the neoantivivisectionist as a new threat to biomedical research. "The societies of the neo-antivivisectionist should be distinguished from established, progressive (humane) societies which devote their resources principally to doing something directly for animals rather than meddling in politics of man" (1963, pp. 778–9). (The big three neoantivivisectionists were identified as the Humane Society of the United States, the National Catholic Society for Animal Welfare (now Society for Animal Rights), and the Animal Welfare Institute). In the last few years, however, more and more research scientists have come to recognize that there are differences in the policies, programs, and motivations of different animal welfare and antivivisection groups.

Therefore, both sides are guilty of confusing the issue by evoking images and emotions that may have had some validity a hundred years ago but are now largely anachronisms. Some of the errors and faults of both animal welfare and animal research protagonists are described below. Only by recognizing and facing up to our hidden assumptions can we hope to raise the quality of the debate over animal research and move toward constructive solutions.

Animal Welfare and Antivivisection Groups

Among the major shortcomings of those groups that oppose animal research have always been their lack of attention to detail and their willingness to engage in lurid rhetoric in the belief (obviously mistaken) that one needs only to show, either in print or in pictures, what happens in laboratories to turn the majority of the public against animal research. Their error is clearly demonstrated by the fact that, in the hundred years during which antivivisection groups have campaigned against animal research, animal research has grown from very modest beginnings into a multibillion dollar exercise, utilizing tens of millions of animals annually.

At the end of the nineteenth century, American opponents of research on animals were particularly delinquent in ferreting out pertinent information. They relied almost completely on materials from England and the Continent and made no effort to inform themselves of the activities of American researchers (Turner 1980, p. 93). Twenty years later, matters had only improved slightly. American antivivisectionists now knew what was happening in American laboratories but not what to do with the information. Benison (1970) notes that Dr. Walter Cannon had absolutely no difficulty in routing one opponent of animal research in 1915 hearings before the Massachusetts legislature. As Cannon wrote to his colleague, Dr. Keen, who was helping in the fight against the antivivisectionists:

> Dear Dr. Keen:
> My best thanks for your kindness in sending me the correspondence with Mrs. Henderson. She is almost too "easy." At the hearing at the State House on the dog bill, she arose and in the blandest and mildest tones informed the legislators that she had in her hands the account of an experiment performed on a dog at the Harvard Medical School by Cushing and Weed—an experiment the account of which was so horrible that she could not bear to read its details to the Committee. She said that she would only mention that the dog made 80 pants a minute, and that the experiment lasted 5½ hours. She multiplied 80 by 60 and that by 5½ and then told the Committee the total number of pants made by the dog during the entire period. The only thing that she drew the line at was the division of the product by 2 in order to determine the number of pairs of pants made by the animal. You should have seen her face when I called on Cushing to speak. Such a surprised woman you could not imagine. Cushing very clearly explained the purpose of the experiment and furthermore, stated that the animal was under thorough anesthesia throughout the experiment, and that the depth of anesthesia had to be so great as to prevent any sort of reflex motion in order that there might be proper and uncomplicated results. When I pointed out later that Mrs. Henderson had failed to state that the first words in the protocol which she mentioned, were "intratracheal anesthesia" which meant to us that the animal was receiving a constant blast of ether-laden air, she said that she understood that they meant anesthesia of the trachea but not necessarily the rest of the body! We shall have more fun with her. I am sure, as years go by (Benison 1970, p. 22).

Such simplistic criticism of animal research continued until after the Second World War. Then, in the 1950's, a reformation occurred in the humane movement, and many of the new groups who now joined in criticizing animal research also brought a more professional approach to the debate. Sympathetic scientists were either consulted or employed full-time by these new groups to ensure that their criticism was both accurate and pointed. Nevertheless, the change was slow, and it is only in the last few years that the main antivivisection societies have, under new leadership, begun to follow suit and eschew the old exaggerated rhetoric.

Misstatements and Misrepresentations. Many antivivisection arguments have suffered from a lack of solid research of the literature, displaying a simplistic understanding of animal research and its methods. There is no doubt that some campaigners find the whole topic too horrible to delve into in any detail and thus resort to sweeping generalizations. But there is no excuse for distortion or misrepresentation. For example, in May 1977, the then president of the American Antivivisection Society condemned polio vaccine and the slaughter of the 2 million monkeys that went into its development and production (Hunt 1977). He cited statistics from the New York State Office of Statistics, giving the number of reported cases of deaths from poliomyelitis, from 1912 to 1962. As he correctly pointed out, the rate of deaths per 100,000 population went from 19.2, in 1916, to 0.8, in 1917, even though there was no vaccination. In addition, he argued that the death rate remained constant, with small fluctuations, from 1917 to 1962, even though vaccination was introduced in 1953. But he did not note that, although the death rate after 1953 fluctuated, it dropped steadily to zero. The statistics from 1963 to 1976 are not given but their inclusion, plus reference to national health statistics, would have demonstrated clearly that the polio vaccine program had a major impact on both the incidence of the disease and the death rate due to polio.

It should also be noted that polio vaccines were steadily improved in the years following their introduction for therapy, in 1955. The vaccine probably did not reach peak effectiveness until the 1960's. There is no doubt that polio vaccine has eliminated all but a few cases of the disease every year. There is also no doubt that research on, and the use of, monkeys played an important role in the development of the vaccine. Nevertheless, there are vulnerable points in this triumph of modern medicine which deserve criticism. For example, the monkeys were caught and transported in circumstances that led to the unnecessary death of hundreds of thousands of animals. (See chap. 8 for further arguments on this issue.)

Another example of misrepresentation concerns the events surrounding the drug thalidomide. The animal welfare literature is full of statements that, since thalidomide was thoroughly tested on animals before being marketed, animal testing is useless. The claims appear to stem from a book by Ryder (1975, p. 43) on the use of animals in research in which he employed the thalidomide story to demonstrate the inadequacy of animal safety testing. However, the fact is that thalidomide was *not* adequately tested, and after the tragedy, drug registration authorities around the world immediately increased their animal-testing requirements. It is true that animal tests for teratogenicity (inducing fetal malformations) are not very reliable for predicting human risk, but those who test new drugs or regulate their introduction are well aware of these shortcomings (Weatherall 1982). While much animal testing can be criticized, and there are many possibilities for reducing the use of animals in safety evaluation, animal welfare protagonists should not base their arguments on the thalidomide case.

As far as can be discovered, the initial error in the animal welfare view of the thalidomide tragedy stemmed from claims by a certain Turkish scientist, Professor Aygun, that he had detected thalidomide's dangers in tissue culture experiments and had notified the German authorities. According to the story, they ignored his warning. Aygun's claims were promoted by an English antivivisectionist group and this may be how Ryder picked up the thalidomide story, leading to his arguing "that thalidomide *was* tested on animals—and as rigorously as any product was, at the time of its production," (1975, pg. 43). Five years later, in another book critical of animal research, Pratt perpetuated this error when he asserted that "tests of thalidomide on many pregnant animals had failed to produce deformities in their offspring . . ." (1980, p. 173).

The original claims by Aygun have never been substantiated, and the train of evidence that led Pratt to claim that premarket tests had been performed on pregnant animals was unsound. Such tests were not performed either by Chemie Grunenthal, the original manufacturers, or by Distillers, the British distributors, until late in 1961, when the extent of thalidomide's effects on human beings came under suspicion (The Insight Team of the *Sunday Times of London* 1979, p. 57). In fact, one of the lines of defence used by Distillers was that tests were not normally done on pregnant animals at the time of thalidomide's development because no one thought drugs might be dangerous to the developing fetus. However, this claim was false.

Ryder (1975) supports his claim that thalidomide was tested on animals without revealing any problems with a quote from Paget: "It is commonly remarked, in fact, that the toxicity tests that had been carefully carried out on thalidomide without exception had demonstrated it to be an almost uniquely safe compound" (Paget 1970, p. 4). But Paget, a well-known British toxicologist was incorrect. The Insight Team of the *Sunday Times* (1979) demonstrate quite clearly that the toxicity testing was not nearly as careful as it should have been, and that there were a number of studies showing thalidomide to be anything but "uniquely safe." They also showed that Ryder had omitted an important qualifying sentence in his quotation from Paget. Paget's qualification asserted that one did not need more tests so much as "an awareness in those concerned that situations might exist in which hazards might arise that were not covered by the extensive tests they had performed" (1970, p. 4).

By the end of 1961, the evidence against thalidomide was building up, and the Distillers' pharmacologist, George Somers (who was one of the few to emerge with credit), started a standard reproductive study on rats. He found that the drug did have noticeable effects on reproduction but did not produce fetal abnormalities. Subsequent tests on rabbits did, however, produce the characteristic thalidomide deformities (Somers 1962). Similar results were produced in monkeys, although humans appear to be more sensitive to thalidomide than are any other animals.

Ryder's book has come in for other criticism. Shuster (1978) criticized the British media and opponents of animal research for claiming that two-thirds of all animal research was nonmedical. He tracked down the source for this claim and discovered that it came from Ryder, who had stated that "less than one-third of all licensed experiments on living animals *can be seen* to be medical" (1975, p. 32). Ryder used statistics produced by the Home Office. Unfortunately, these were relatively uninformative before 1977. When the Home Office finally produced more detailed analyses, over 95% of all animal experiments were for basic biomedical research, for the development of therapeutics, or for diagnosis. Less than 1% were for the testing of cosmetics and household products.

The loose thinking that perpetuated the thalidomide error, or that can be traced from Ryder's original statement to the claim that two-thirds of all animal research in England was nonmedical, provides the justification for Cross's view:

> Few of the [antivivisection] societies feel obliged to check the factual accuracy of their charges or to consult the vast amount of scientific information freely available in the literature. The more extreme their allegations, the more apt they are to enlist the attention of the media.

> Respected newspapers have carried completely untrue "eyewitness" reports of two-headed goats and animals that were half goat, half cow. Small wonder that anxiety or even hysteria takes hold of the public (1981, p. 203).

A press release put out by United Public Relations after the NIH Bioassay Symposium (National Institutes of Health 1981b) provides a recent example of such misinformation. The press release (which reads as though it were commissioned by an animal welfare group) gives the impression that the symposium speakers were very enthusiastic about alternatives, whereas most tended to downplay the concept. For example, Arthur Guyton is quoted as having called his mathematical modeling approach a beautiful alternative to animal experimentation. In actual fact, Guyton suggested that mathematical modeling is an extremely important adjunct to animal physiological experimentation but it is not an alternative to it (1981). Similar misrepresentations are scattered throughout the press release. Neither the public nor, ultimately, the animals themselves benefit from this sort of misrepresentation.

Fortunately, matters are changing. The reliability and, therefore, credibility of much animal welfare and antivivisection literature is improving. The American Anti-Vivisection Society for example, has just produced a new edition (1982) of its Casebook of Experiments with Living Animals which, though still containing many of the key antivivisection words and phrases, is up-to-date and accurate.

The Nuremberg Legacy. There are many allusions to the Holocaust in literature condemning animal research. The deaths of laboratory animals are likened to the killing of Jews in Auschwitz. The human "research" conducted by the Nazi doctors is sometimes ascribed to the fact that researchers become totally insensitive and thus were not overly disturbed by ghastly experiments on humans or animals. There is, however, an unfortunate irony in all of this. The Third Reich came very close to banning all animal research and, before the war, animal welfare groups lauded the animal protection efforts of National Socialism. But scientists at the time had no difficulty in recognizing the cynical self-interest of the Nazis, who merely sought a semirespectable excuse for controlling the activities of their opponents. Consider the following words by Herman Goering during a broadcast on August 29, 1933:

> Compatriots! Ever since the day that I issued the proclamation against the torturing of animals by vivisection I have received a flood of

> telegrams and letters, all of which agree and expressed great relief that at last an energetic step had been taken to put a stop to this torture. The German people particularly have always shown their great love of animals and the question of animal protection was always near their hearts. . . . It is the more incomprehensible, therefore, that justice, up to now, did not agree with the spirit of the people on this point. Legal pronouncements gave to the animal owner similar rights to those which he possessed over his inanimate goods. This does not correspond to the German spirit and most decidedly it does not conform to ideas of national socialism. The owner of an animal shall not possess an absolute right over it. . . .
>
> Experiments on animals for the purpose of defining an illness in human beings, for the preparations of serums and other experimental use, need legal regulation in detail and the keen control of the state. It is a sorry sign of science that during the past two decades, amply protected by the law, materialistic scientists have wrought unbearable torture and suffering in animal experiments. . . .
>
> It may remain a matter for speculation as to how far such vivisection has helped in the last decade to achieve an advance in knowledge of the construction and functions of the human body. Today science itself holds the view that the torturing and killing of animals through vivisection can further our knowledge no longer. These experiments have been more and more discontinued by science. An absolute and permanent prohibition of vivisection is not only a necessary law to protect animals and to show sympathy with their pain, but it is also a law for humanity itself . . .
>
> I have therefore announced the immediate prohibition of vivisection and have made the practice a punishable offence in Prussia. Until such time as punishment is pronounced the culprit shall be lodged in a concentration camp (Goering 1939, p. 70–70).

Emmanuel Kant argued that cruelty to, and ill treatment of animals was morally wrong, not because of any special consideration that humans owe animals, but because cruelty to animals desensitizes the perpetrator and could, therefore, lead to cruelty to humans. The record of the Third Reich reveals that the corollary, namely, that kindness to animals leads to kindness to human beings, is not necessarily true. Hitler was unable to establish ordinary human relationships and it is possible that the nonverbal attachment and dependency of animals may have satisfied Hitler's regressed need for nurturing and comfort (cf. Rynearson 1978), thus leading to his "love" of animals and distrust of people.

Inappropriate Protection of Animals from Laboratory "Torture and Agony". The belief appears to be widespread that all animals in the laboratory suffer agony at one stage or another. British antivivisection societies have traditionally exploited this belief by pointing out, whenever the annual statistics of animal experiments are issued, that more than 80% were done without an anesthetic. The implication here is that more than 80% of the animals suffered greatly. Undoubtedly, some of the 80% suffered as a result of the induction of some toxic or pathological state, but many others suffered little more than the stresses of handling and confinement.

For example, a Dutch survey reported in the *International Journal for the Study of Animal Problems* (1981a) notes that only 10.7% of 1980 animal experiments in Holland were performed under anesthesia, but that a further 37.8% involved no appreciable discomfort. The fact that slightly more than 50% of the animals ran the risk of appreciable discomfort is, of course, a matter for legitimate concern. Unfortunately, there are instances where individuals who try to protect animals from this fate end up by subjecting them to equal suffering, or worse.

Early in 1982, the president of the Maryland Anti-Vivisection Society, William A. Snyder, was charged with animal abuse by the authorities. Apparently, Snyder was keeping more than 200 dogs on a one-acre enclosure outside Baltimore to prevent the use of the animals in medical research. Although Snyder denied the charges of animal abuse, the local animal control officer noted that the enclosure was rat-infested and that the dogs were very run down. Many were reported to have such bad mange that they were virtually hairless. The animals also fought constantly, and some were reported to have missing limbs and eyes. The authorities were eventually forced to take action by those living near the enclosure, who complained of the stench. Snyder may have acted out of the desire to prevent suffering but his method backfired. None of the animals in the enclosure could have been described as leading a healthy and happy existence.

The Roots of Opposition to Animal Research. Research on animals touches a very raw nerve in some people. For example, I was told by one opponent of animal research that she had been unable to sleep properly or relax since she had first learned what was being done to animals in American laboratories. What is it about animal research that produces such strong reactions? Intensive farming methods, whereby animals are essentially protein factories, is of concern to animal welfare groups, but the issue does not evoke nearly as much passion. While those who protest against some or all animal research are very diverse and their motives reflect this variety, one can speculate about the forces underlying opposition to animal research.

Michael W. Fox (personal communication, 1982) has suggested that some of the raging against animal research may result from the unconscious identification of the protestor with the helplessness of the research animal. In the modern world, individuals can find the indifference and unresponsiveness of the establishment to their own fears and concerns very frustrating. In some instances, the individual could easily identify his or her helplessness and fear with those of the research animal, which is, after all, helpless to prevent the scientist from carrying out the experiment. The fact that the experiment may be painless and involve little or no suffering is no consolation; the victim is still helpless. Richard Adams' novel, *The Plague Dogs,* about two dogs who escape from a laboratory and defy their would-be captors has been widely praised by opponents of animal research (Adams 1978). Its appeal, as well as the popularity of others of this genre (e.g., Kotzwinkle 1976), probably grows from the dogs' ability to avoid their fate.

In recent years, younger and more militant groups have taken opposition to the establishment to new lengths (*Nature* 1981). Research establishments have been raided, animals released, and equipment destroyed. Demonstrations and angry pickets are now commonplace in England, and there are signs that such protests are picking up steam in the United States. One newcomer to the animal welfare movement has now produced a handbook for animal activists (Morgan 1980). The publication is a standard activists' manual adapted for the animal issue. It contains a wide range of information on organizing, communication, direct action, and resources, including such items as a recommendation to wear two sets of underwear and socks on a mass demonstration since this can help one keep clean if one is in jail for any length of time. There is little doubt that Morgan's activism is a direct challenge to the establishment. He and others could act as a focus for frustrated and disaffected individuals who are tired of the slow change effected through dialogue, conciliation, and compromise.

Many newcomers to the animal cause have been attracted by the notion of concern for other species and the idea that their exploitation is analogous to racism or sexism. For example, one black person once told me that, after reading Singer's *Animal Liberation,* (1975), he suddenly realized the anology between racism and speciesism. After all, he said, slavery had, at one stage, been justified because blacks were perceived as subhuman (Mason 1981) and therefore not entitled to moral consideration. Racism and sexism have been rejected by society (although this unfortunately does not mean that these prejudices have dissappeared), and the Young Turks of the animal welfare movement are now demanding an end to "speciesism" (Ryder 1975, p. 11). This trend is part of the general revival of interest in the moral status of animals, which is discussed in chapter 18.

It is also clear that there are elements of anti-intellectualism and antiscience among a few opponents of animals research. Members of antivivisection groups are often very sympathetic to antivaccination campaigns as well as the philosophies of fringe medical groups and mystics. Such sympathies do not, of course, prove that a person is antiscience, but mystical revelation is not a comfortable bedfellow with deductive logic and experimental analysis.

One of the strongest elements leading to opposition to animal research centers on the issue of pain and suffering. Many of those working in animal welfare see the pain and suffering of animals as the evil that must be eliminated. Alternatives that can reduce animal use are important, but so is the reduction or abolition of pain. According to Turner (1980, p. 97), animal research revolted those who were campaigning for improved animal welfare because it was conducted mainly by men from the healing profession who were looked up to as cultivated and compassionate individuals. Despite this reputation, many doctors either defended animal research or carried it out themselves. This paradox was rejected by the public in no uncertain terms. In modern biomedical research, scientists are required to use anesthetics and painkillers, but there are many instances where their use is not practical. The subsequent animal suffering is a constant aggravation to animal welfare groups (cf. Pratt 1980).

The above concerns and motives do not cover the gamut of reasons why people find themselves opposing some or all animal research. Some individuals are Luddites and fear progress, and others do not understand how a human being could deliberately cause an animal to suffer. Some seek a cause, while others fight research that is wasteful and frivolous, in their judgement, at least. This variety partly explains why animal welfare groups have, until recently, had so much difficulty in cooperating and collaborating. The most recent example of this internecine warfare has been an attack on the Humane Society of the United States (HSUS) by United Action for Animals and Friends of Animals for alleged collaboration with the enemy. The fact that the HSUS had a veterinary school dean on its board of directors and had other associations with biomedical scientists was sufficient evidence, according to UAA and FOA, that the HSUS had undermined a bill on alternatives which had been introduced into the 97th Congress. In fact, the bill was ambiguous and poorly worded and called for a radical and immediate reallocation of 30% to 50% of Federal animal research funds to alternatives. Thus, when the relevant congressional subcommittee came to consider the issue, it decided that the *only politically viable* course of action was to write its own bill. This decision was not specifically influenced by any of the animal welfare groups, and the HSUS, for one, lobbied constantly to have the subcommittee bill strengthened, despite the attacks by UAA and FOA, who relied largely on the tactic of guilt by association, a tactic that had been used effectively thirty years earlier by Senator Joseph McCarthy.

Biomedical Researchers

On the other side, biomedical researchers carry their own complement of assumptions into debate. It is common for animal welfare advocates to be labeled as antivivisectionists—and thus implied to be irrational—in the biomedical literature (Jones 1963; American Family Physician 1975). But, if one defines antivivisectionism as a general wish to see an end to animal suffering in biomedical research, then surely everybody is antivivisectionist. Medawar, who won the 1961 Nobel Prize for medicine, gave implicit expression to this idea when he said that "nothing but research on animals will provide us with the knowledge that will make it possible for us, one day, to dispense with the use of them altogether" (1972, p. 86). Of course, even if everybody would admit that they share the same goals, researchers and animal welfare advocates have proposed very different timetables and strategies to achieve these goals. The difference in timetable is the real source of the current conflict.

Spokespersons for research also vary in their approach and attitudes but have, historically, been much more united among themselves with better access to the power brokers of the day. This does not necessarily mean, however, that they are always right, and there are certainly signs that many have misunderstood the changes that have taken place in the last decade (cf. Lindsey 1980). Also, antivivisection groups have no monopoloy on inaccurate claims or distorted rhetoric. (Antivivisection rhetoric has, however, traditionally been less subtle and more offensive.) Some of the arguments scientists use against their animal welfare opponents are either inconsistent or just plain wrong.

Objectivity versus Emotion. A reasonably common complaint from scientists is that animal welfare groups use emotionally evocative words and images, whereas they (as scientists) are constrained to objective fact and dispassionate reporting. Thus the concentration on dogs, cats, monkeys, and rabbits by animal welfare groups is decried because it is an appeal to public sentiment (in contrast to the image evoked by rats and mice). However, public emotion and sympathy has also been harnessed by biomedical interests to promote their own causes.

The fight against polio included many emotional appeals to the public for donations, as well as one or two questionable scientific decisions to keep the campaign fires burning (Wilson 1963). When India proclaimed its ban on rhesus monkey exports (Wade 1978a), the biomedical research authorities fought back with pictures of children in leg braces, crippled by polio, implying that a shortage of rhesus monkeys would threaten further live-saving advances. In the 1981 Los Angeles City Council hearings on the release of pound animals, one of the witnesses for the medical research side was a woman with multiple sclerosis, thus providing emotionally compelling evidence of our need for further research, especially animal research.

I do not wish to give the impression that appeals to human emotion are necessarily bad, but biomedical groups must recognize that they also use emotional appeals to public sentiment when promoting their own interests. For example, Jukes appeals to emotion, not reason, in the following passage from an editorial critical of animal welfare attacks on research and, in particular, of the attack against Dr. Taub and his treatment of experimental monkeys (described later).

> Support of the animal welfare movement may be expected from Science magazine, which published highly colored accounts of the monkey episode on October 2 and 9, 1981. The accounts were based on hearsay and contained extensive quotations by Michael Fox, a picturesque animal rights advocate who allegedly patrols the streets of Washington with a pet wolf. The article in the Washington Post was better balanced and more moderate (1982, p. 4).

Jukes's criticism of *Science* appears to be based more on his own prejudices than on a reasoned analysis. The testimony of individuals interviewed by *Science* was more than "hearsay." They had first-hand experience of the conditions in Taub's laboratory, which is more than can be said for Jukes' comments about Michael Fox.

Self-Criticism and Self-Regulation. One of the common defenses used by biomedical groups against animal welfare attacks is that they already regulate their own activities and make sure that abuses cannot occur. However, the record of the response of various professional organizations and institutions to criticism about animal welfare issues from within their own ranks is not good. Dr. Robert Gesell, a longtime member of the American Physiological Society (APS) horrified those attending a 1952 business meeting by alleging that there was much inhumane use of animals in biological and medical research (Visscher 1979). But their horror was directed, not at the idea that there might actually be some truth to Gesell's allegations, but at his temerity for bringing up the issue.

Nevertheless, there were good grounds for Gesell's criticism, and most scientists are prepared to agree that standards of animal care and use have improved considerably over those of the 1950s and 1960s. But this does not mean that there are not still grounds for self-criticism or improved self-regulation. For example, several years ago, two papers exemplifying a very questionable technique for inducing traumatic injury were published in the *American Journal of Physiology* (Altura 1976; Kaplan and Saba 1976). This technique involves tumbling lightly anesthetized animals in a Noble-Collip drum (which has internal shelves projecting out from the surface) to produce injury and trauma. The device has drawn criticism from both within and without the biomedical research community. Recently, a distinguished pharmacologist and well-known defender of animal research has added his voice to the others criticizing experiments involving the Noble-Collip drum (Paton 1979).

As an added quirk, the *American Journal of Physiology* contains instructions to authors on the issue of animal research that include this statement: "Consideration should be given to the appropriateness of experimental procedures, species of animals used, and number of animals required." It is arguable that this policy should have precluded the publication of any paper using the Noble-Collip drum.

Another more recent example of the stifling of self-criticism dealing with animal research comes from a Texas military research establishment. Donald Barnes, who used to be a psychologist at the School of Aerospace Medicine in San Antonio, was dismissed after he started questioning the necessity and humanity of certain experiments on rhesus monkeys. Barnes had been involved in this work for many years (from 1966 to 1978) and gradually came to question the need for the studies, involving irradiated monkeys and their performance on a flight simulation platform. In 1978, he became more vocal in his criticism, and he was dismissed early in 1979. Barnes claims that he lost his job because he raised the issue of animal welfare. Authorities at the school denied this, claiming that he had not fulfilled some tasks assigned to him. Barnes claimed that the tasks were impossible to complete in the assigned time and took his case to a grievance committee in the Air Force hierarchy. They ordered the School of Aerospace Medicine to reinstate Barnes, thereby vindicating his claims.

In England, Harold Hewitt, a cancer researcher at a Cancer Research Campaign laboratory, criticized the effectiveness of the British Cruelty to Animals Act and supported his laboratory technician's criticisms of some of the animal research methods used at the laboratory. This criticism was aired publicly, but anonymously. Subsequently, the head of the laboratory challenged Hewitt, who admitted that he was the anonymous critic. Hewitt was immediately asked to resign his senior appointment, and his laboratory technician, Angela Walder, was dismissed on trumped-up charges, which were successfully challenged by the technicians' union. Walder, however, was forced to resign.

The director of the laboratory did not stop there. He also solicited from other scientists around the world several letters criticizing Hewitt and commissioned an investigation of Hewitt's work and professional approach. These actions are hardly those of someone who welcomes constructive criticism. It is also not uncommon to see a strong reaction of such criticism in the scientific literature. For example, when one psychologist questioned the ethics of some experimental psychology on animals (Bowd 1980a), he drew an extraordinary reaction from Sudak:

> Bowd's (February, 1980) Comment should be seen for what it is: part of the current highly successful antivivisectionist campaign whose efforts are greatly impeding animal research in psychology. The Comment is thinly disguised with a distorted sense of ethics and morality. Its sole purpose is to aggravate the *guilt and self-doubt* of scientists who are already experiencing severe threats to their careers, livelihood and reputation as a result of budgetary cuts and adverse public opinion. By printing Bowd's Comment, the APA [American Psychological Association] does great disservice to its members in research and academia" (1981, p. 312 [emphasis added]).

Two rejoinders to the above diatribe come immediately to mind. First, as a professional body with strong links to academic research, the APA would do its members a greater disservice by not printing Bowd's Comment. Second, it is ironic that Sudak should have brought up the notions of guilt and self-doubt. Antivivisection rhetoric is full of questions asking how animal researchers can live with themselves, but this is one of the few occasions when a researcher has alluded in print to any feeling of guilt associated with animal research.

These examples are not given to indicate that all scientists are defensive about animal research or criticism of it. Pain researchers, for instance, have responded in a constructive and concerned manner to questions from their peers about the ethical problems raised by their work. However, too few organizations and individuals have been willing to engage in a free and detailed exchange of ideas about the moral issues surrounding animal research. Fortunately, that is changing, but voicing concern about the welfare of research animals is still not encouraged in many biomedical laboratories.

Animals Quickly Replaced with Alternatives. The biomedical establishment often argues that, wherever possible, animal methods are replaced without external prompting because, if an alternative is available, it is cheaper and simpler and gives less equivocal answers. There certainly are pressures within science to encourage scientists to move to simpler nonanimal techniques but, equally, there are pressures that encourage them to stay with tried and tested methods. A scientist who is familiar with the quirks and short-comings of a particular method (using animals, let us say) of assessing a biological response, is not likely to welcome a new nonanimal technique unless it has very obvious advantages.

There is also the question of reproducibility. If a technique has been in use for some time, its margins of error and limitations are understood. This will not be true of a new technique that will take time to develop and validate. This is one of the reasons why toxicology stays with the old tried and tested methods. With the exception of the long-term carcinogen tests, which are very expensive and time-consuming for relatively small return in reproducible data, there is little incentive to try to develop new methods that use fewer animals or none at all. Therefore, animal welfare campaigns have attempted to "encourage" regulators and toxicologists to reassess the methods they use (see chaps. 14 and 15).

Biomedical Research Is Already Closely Regulated. Biomedical researchers commonly argue that they are already closely regulated when they use animals. In the United States, nothing could be further from the truth. Rosenfeld quotes a scientist from California, neurobiologist John Allman, as follows:

> People don't realize that we are already extensively reviewed. In my work I must follow the ethical codes laid down by the National Institutes of Health and the American Physiological Society, among others. And we might have a surprise visit at any time from the U.S. Department of Agriculture's inspectors. It's the USDA field veterinarians who do the enforcing. Believe me, these inspections are anything but routine, and these fellows have a great deal of power. Because their reports can adversely affect federal funding, their recommendations are, in reality, orders.
>
> More than that, we are all required to keep detailed reports on all our animal experiments. And if pain or surgery is involved, we must tell them what anesthetics we used and in what dosages, what post-operative pain relievers and care were given, and so on. These reports are filed annually with the USDA, and they keep tabs on what goes on all over the country (Rosenfeld 1981, pp. 18, 22).

Unfortunately, the animal welfare movement does not believe such statements. This is not to say that there are not good USDA inspectors who enforce the Animal Welfare Act—there are. However, they are not as common as they should be. Furthermore, the sanctions against facilities that do not comply are limited. The animal care veterinarian at the University of California, Berkeley, had been complaining for several years about the inadequacies of Berkeley animal facilities and violations of the Animal Welfare Act within these facilities. Despite his complaints, and the support of the USDA and local animal welfare groups, nothing was done to change the situation—until the problem was highlighted by the media.

In addition, the Animal Welfare Act specifically excludes any comment on, or regulation of, how animals are *used*, with the exception of the need for pain relief where possible. But, even on the question of pain, the USDA has never defined painful research and has enforced this provision inadequately. It is perfectly clear from various examples presented later in this book and from the critique by Solomon and Lovenheim (1982) that the Animal Welfare Act is a paper tiger, that the ethical guidelines promoted by the NIH do not prevent abuses, and that the USDA reporting and inspection system is defective.

Misdirection. In my discussions with scientists over alternatives and humane research, I have occasionally been met with the defense that everything is satisfactory and under control in industrial (or university) laboratories, it is in the universities (or commercial laboratories) where the real abuses occur. I first heard this from scientists in a British pharmaceutical firm who were claiming to be very concerned themselves while pointing the finger at universities. For a contrary view, I quote below from a letter to the *Baltimore Sun* (November 9, 1981) by Dr. Robert Fiscella in the wake of the prosecution of Dr. Taub for cruelty to his laboratory monkeys.

> Considering Dr. Taub's undisputed research contributions and the relatively small number of animals being sacrificed in alleviating human suffering, we must question the perspective, priorities, and motivations of the individuals responsible for this harassment, as well as of the government agencies which seem to be more responsive to mindless dramatics than unpleasant realities. We should keep in mind that the pharmaceutic and cosmetic industries torture, maim, and sacrifice thousands of animals daily for what are economic rather than scientific reasons. . . . As a naive medical student, I witnessed the forced feeding, blood-letting, killing, and dissection of hundreds of dogs in order that a major drug company could back up minor changes in its television advertisements for aspirin.

There is, of course, no reason why there should be complete agreement on "necessary and justifiable" animal research among biomedical scientists, but the attack by Fiscella on commercial "torture" was unusual, coming as it did from a scientist. Such an attack merely provides support for the animal welfare movement, which is concerned about all use of laboratory animals, whether it occurs in nonprofit or industrial laboratories.

The Public Attitude

The animal welfare and biomedical protagonists are fighting for the support of the public because public opinion is the final arbiter in most democratic societies. On the whole, it appears that the public prefers not to know too much about biomedical research or enquire too deeply into its practices. I remember one woman who flatly refused to accept that cosmetics were tested on animals. Even among active animal welfare supporters, it is almost a truism that many do not want to see pictures of animals undergoing experimentation.

Despite the general desire for blissful ignorance, there are signs that the public is becoming increasingly concerned about animal research. While researchers argue that antivivisectionism is an aggressive new anti-intellectual force that seeks to stifle freedom of inquiry (Taub 1982), the public support of science is slowly eroding (Walsh 1982). In addition, there is more explicit concern over the fate of laboratory animals (cf. Braithwaite and Braithwaite, 1982; chap. 4). As a result, the pendulum appears to be moving in a direction that favors animal welfare. Whether this trend can be reversed by animal researchers will depend on whether they are prepared to be innovative and constructive. The old platitudes and the arrogant cliche that doctor knows best are no longer sufficient in the face of a more sophisticated approach by the animal welfare movement.

CHAPTER 4

Historical Notes on Animal Research and Antivivisection

Animal Research: Ancient Times to 1800

From the time that human beings first began to cut up dead animals for storage as food, a curiosity must have developed as to the structure and function of different body organs. The first recorded use of live animals for research appears to be the study of body humors by Erasistratus, in Alexandria, in the third century B.C. (Straight 1962). However, a century earlier, Aristotle was a keen student of the natural world, and his observations laid the foundations for comparative anatomy and embryology. Nevertheless, it was Galen of Pergamum, in the second century A.D., who put animal research on the map, not only for his contemporaries but also for the next fifteen centuries.

Galen recognized that the arteries contained blood and not merely air. He stressed the value of anatomy and was the founder of experimental physiology. Since dissection of the human body was illegal in Rome at the time, he based his knowledge on observations made on apes and pigs. After the fall of Rome, learning was no longer held in high esteem and experiment was definitely discouraged, until the thirteenth century heralded the beginnings of the Renaissance and the revival of Aristotle's science and philosophy.

The Renaissance was more than a revival of interest in Greek and Roman culture. It brought a desire for discovery and for new ideas. Andreas Vesalius (1514–64), at Padua, challenged some of Galen's findings and created the first modern anatomy. He also experimented on animals, as did many of his contemporaries (Schiller 1967). Francis Bacon (1561–1626) argued the value of animal experimentation in his *De Augmentis Scientiarum* (The Advancement of Learning) in which he stated:

> Wherefore that utility may be considered as well as humanity, the anatomy of the living subject is not to be relinquished altogether . . . since it may be well discharged by the dissection of beast alive, which, not withstanding the dissimilitude of their parts to human, may with the help of a little judgment, sufficiently satisfy this inquiry (French 1978, p. 76).

While the seventeenth and eighteenth centuries saw the growth of the scientific revolution, led by such as William Harvey (1578–1657), René Descartes (1596–1650), Anthony van Leeuwenhoek (1632–1723) and Lazzaro Spallanzani (1729–99), it was not until the early part of the 19th century that organized, systematic animal research really began and widespread opposition to it developed. However, in Britain at least, early experimenters had already started to voice humanitarian concerns. According to one analysis (Shugg 1968), Boyle, Hook, Lower, and other Fellows of the Royal Society indicated a real concern for animal suffering as well as a desire to advance medicine and surgery. On the Continent, European scientists expressed no similar level of concern. Certainly, Descartes saw no moral problem in animal research.

According to Descartes, animals were no more than machines and were, therefore, incapable of thinking or feeling: "The greatest of all the prejudices we have retained from our infancy is that of believing that the beasts think" (Oeuvres, X, p. 204). Whatever the reasons behind Descartes' extraordinary attempts to exclude animals from the universe of feeling and suffering beings, various authors have argued that his ideas paved the way for vivisection, especially as practiced by the French experimentalists, François Magendie (1783–1855) and Claude Bernard (1813–78). The research on living animals conducted by both these men had a major impact on the vivisection controversy, not to mention the development of medical knowledge.

On the other hand, European scientists and thinkers were not oblivious to animal suffering (see chap. 18). Louis Pasteur (1822–95), the focus of much antivivisection criticism, was far from the hardened and cruel investigator he is sometimes said to have been. The following passage is an interesting illustration of Pasteur's attitude.

"Ordinarily an experiment once conceived and talked over was put under way without delay," says Dr. Roux. "This one, on which we are counting so much, was not begun immediately. Pasteur, who had been obliged to sacrifice so many animals in the course of his beneficient studies, felt a veritable repugnance toward vivisection. He was present without too much squeamishness at simple operations, such as the subcutaneous inoculation, and yet, if the animal cried a little, Pasteur immediately felt pity and lavished on the victim consolation and encouragement which would have been comical if it had not been touching. The thought that the skull of a dog was to be perforated was disagreeable to him; he desired intensely that the experiment should be made, but he dreaded to see it undertaken. I performed it one day in his absence; the next day, when I told him that the intracranial inoculation presented no difficulty, he was moved with pity for the dog: 'Poor beast! His brain is without doubt wounded. He must be paralyzed.' Without replying, I went below to look for the animal and had him brought into the laboratory. Pasteur did not love dogs, but when he saw this one full of life, ferreting curiously about everywhere, he showed the greatest satisfaction and straightway lavished upon him the kindest words. He felt an infinite liking for this dog which had so well endured trepanning, and thus had put to flight for the future all his scruples against it" (Duclaux 1920, pp. 296–7).

Scientific Medicine in Europe

The progression of animal research from a relatively surreptitious activity to the forefront of medical advance ran into surprisingly strong opposition not only from the public, but also from certain sectors of the medical profession (Stevenson 1955; Turner 1980). The battle between Magendie and Bell exemplifies one of the sources of this tension—namely, professional competition (Gallistel 1981).

In 1811, Charles Bell concluded that the ventral nerve roots from the spinal chord were responsible for orchestrating voluntary behavior while the dorsal roots were responsible for involuntary behavior. Bell's conclusions were steered in this direction as a result of a theory of nervous system function which he had developed on the basis of his anatomical studies. In 1822, Magendie published a paper reporting contradictory findings that the dorsal roots carried sensory signals (e.g., input from the limbs) while the ventral roots carried motor signals. His conclusions were based on experiments in puppies, in which the ventral and dorsal roots of the peripheral nerves come together *outside* the spinal column, unlike adult animals in which the roots fuse before exiting from the spine. This permitted him to sever the ventral and dorsal roots selectively, something that was impossible in animals where the spine had to be broken open (the lack of anesthesia to quiet the animal meant that it was all but impossible to break open the spine without damaging the spinal cord).

After Magendie published his paper, Bell and his students began an aggressive campaign to claim priority for Magendie's discovery and, according to Gallistel, were largely successful. In the course of the campaign, Bell repeatedly reproached Magendie for the cruelty of the experiments, claiming that they were unnecessary and counterproductive and that the correct conclusion could be reached by anatomical observation alone. Paradoxically, he also claimed that he had performed the experiments in 1811, and that Magendie had been inspired to "replicate" them by one of Bell's pupils.

In Britain, Marshall Hall (1790–1857), Magendie's contemporary, was subject to both antivivisection and medical opposition. According to Manuel (1981), many of Hall's papers were rejected by the Physiological Committee of the Royal Society because most of the members of the committee were anatomists who developed their theories of function from the spatial arrangement of organs and were anxious to preserve the supremacy of their own subject on medical education. Turner is also of this opinion. In discussing the rise of experimental medicine, he notes that:

> This new laboratory doctor (medical experimenter) often disturbed other physicians as much as laymen. Occasionally uneasiness burst into open hostility. Most doctors understood clinical investigation and comparative anatomy but, if trained before the 1880's, knew little of the new scientific medicine and its experimental methods. Not surprisingly, they often resented it, not least because of the contemptuously superior bearing that medical scientists too often seemed to adopt toward their less up to date colleagues. Old-fashioned doctors carped at what they considered endless multiplication of petty specialities and viewed the new scientific spirit with "grave doubts and keen apprehension." Science threatened their standing with the public and within the profession. . . . Not by mere chance was Henry J. Bigelow, who led the opponents of President Eliot's remodelling of Harvard Medical School along scientific lines, also a tart critic of vivisection (1980, p. 98).

Hall persevered with his work, in spite of the feelings against his animal experimentation (and against his Francophile sentiments) from within his own profession. But the following passage shows that he was concerned about the suffering of the animals:

> Unhappily for the physiologist, the subjects of the principal department of his science, that of animal physiology, are sentient beings; and every experiment, every new or unusual situation of such being, is necessarily attended by pain or suffering of a bodily or mental kind (1831, p. 7).

Hall felt that animal research should be regulated by specific laws. Without these laws, he believed that physiologists would not escape the imputation of cruelty. He therefore proposed five principles of animal research.

First, experiments should never be done if the necessary information could be gained by observation. Second, no experiment should be performed without a clearly defined and attainable objective. (The use of the word "attainable" is noteworthy since much confusing data has been and is produced by using techniques that are inadequate for the task at hand.) Third, one should avoid unwarranted repetition of experiments, especially when such experiments have been performed by reputable scientists. Fourth, any justifiable experiment should be carried out with the least possible infliction of suffering. Finally, to avoid needless repetition, every physiological experiment should be witnessed. In many ways, Hall displayed remarkable sensitivity to the issues of animal suffering considering the environment in which he worked. Certainly, many scientists later in the century could not lay claim to the same concern.

Magendie died in 1855, but his pupil Claude Bernard not only took up the mantle but also established experimental medicine once and for all. His classic work, *Introduction a l'étude de la médicine expérimentale,* described the techniques and laid out the philosophical rationale for experimental science. In particular, he preached the importance of controlling extraneous factors and studying the response of a single isolated variable.

As French (1978) notes, great benefits for clinical medicine had been promised by propagandists for the experimental approach, but significant support for experimental medicine within the *medical profession* was not seen until the second half of the 19th century. This was a period of spectacular medical advances. Ether anesthesia was first used in 1846 at the Massachusetts General Hospital. Lister's arguments in favor of surgical antisepsis in the 1860's revolutionized the attitude of surgeons. Pasteur laid the foundations for bacteriology,

and Koch discovered the tubercle bacillus (1882) and the Vibrio of cholera (1883). Many other disease-causing organisms were identified before the century ended and, by 1900, the benefits of animal research had begun to tip the balance of *public opinion* in favor of the research scientist (Turner 1980).

In 100 years, experimental research had emerged from dingy laboratories to restructure medical practice and to increase the therapeutic capability and reputation of the medical profession. There were, however, many obstacles to be overcome, notably the opposition of antivivisection organizations (French 1975) and another segment of the medical profession who argued that improved sanitation and better public health would answer as well, if not better than animal research (Stevenson 1955).

According to Stevenson, it is not entirely accidental that the Public Health Act should have been passed in 1875, the same year that a Royal Commission on Vivisection was appointed. To many medical men who found the research of Magendie and Bernard repugnant, the creed that one could improve health merely by cleaning up the water supply and improving the disposal of waste appeared a heaven-sent alternative to medical advance through vivisection. For example, Sir Benjamin Ward Richardson (1822–96) was a leading champion of public health and also a major advocate of avoiding all but a few, exceptional animal experiments. Richardson was no mere obscurantist languishing anonymously outside the medical establishment. He was a distinguished physician, a Fellow of the Royal Society, and very well regarded by his peers. George Wilson (1848–1921) was another pioneer in public health who shared Richardson's sentiments and who actually sat on the Second Royal Commission on Vivisection, in 1906.

Despite the general resentment of many physicians of the new scientific methods, when the profession was threatened by the antivivisection movement, most doctors resolutely defended both the profession and animal research (Turner, 1980). Thus, Richard Owen, the greatest British anatomist of his age, and T. H. Huxley were themselves both temperamentally incapable of doing animal experiments, but they did not hesitate to defend the need for animal research. Owen, in particular, was one of the most energetic opponents of antivivisection campaigns, despite his personal antipathy to animal experimentation.

Antivivisection Opposition

The roots of the antivivisection movement may be found in Britain, the birthplace of anticruelty crusades of all kinds. However, this is not to say that animal research was not opposed in continental Europe as well. Claude Bernard was the focus of much antivivisection sentiment in France and suffered the special fate of having his wife and daughters become passionate antivivisectionists. Bernard married the daughter of a wealthy man in order to have the funds to support his research. The alternative would have been entering medical practice and giving up his research career. However, his wife did not approve and eventually joined the ranks of the antivivisectionists, taking their two daughters with her into the crusade.

Bernard was thus not insensitive to criticism of animal research, and he defended the practice in his writings. However, it is interesting to note that he refused to experiment on monkeys because of their resemblances to human beings (Schiller 1967). Schiller also notes that Bernard's prestige was such that he was not attacked directly; the attacks were instead directed at Magendie and were led by Chauffard, Professor at the Faculty of Medicine and Dubois d'Amiens, Secretary of the Academy of Medicine.

The most powerful antivivisection organizations were definitely those based in England. Their development was influenced by the Utilitarian philosophers, Jeremy Bentham being one of the most quoted by animal welfare organizations. The passage that particularly caught their imagination dealt with the issues of rationality and language and is found in his *Introduction to the Principles of Morals and Legislation* published in 1789.

> . . . a full grown horse or dog is beyond comparison a more rational, as well as a more conversable animal, than an infant of a day, of a week or even a month old. But suppose the cause were otherwise, what would it avail? The question is not, can they *reason?* Nor, can they *talk?* but can they suffer? (Bentham 1962, pp. 142–43).

This concern about suffering was, according to Turner (1980), a feature of the Victorian mind that proved fertile ground for the development of the various anticruelty and animal welfare movements in Britain. Stevenson (1956) also speculates that the antivivisection trend was strongly influenced by religious beliefs, especially Methodism, which held that animals would share immortality. While the concern for pain and suffering in Victorian England, backed by arguments for the immortality of animals, may have been of major importance in explaining the strength of the British antivivisection and animal welfare movements, there were other factors. The influence of Darwin's Descent of Man, for example, served to break down the assumption that humans and animals were different in kind. The antivivisection movement was also, as described earlier, considerably strengthened by the opposition to animal experiments from an influential segment of the medical profession led by the sanitarians, or public health advocates (Stevenson 1955).

The outcome of the British struggle between experimentalists and antivivisectionists (see French [1975] for an excellent account) was the passage of the Cruelty to Animals Act, in 1876. This bill regulated painful research but did not abolish it and was thus strongly opposed by the antivivisection groups who, when they failed to enlist sufficient Parliamentary support to effect additional legislative changes, altered their tactics to focus on a long-term public education campaign. They managed to force the issue to a Second Royal Commission on Vivisection, in 1906, but the advent of the First World War and the many successes of experimental medicine, some spectacular, led to a steady decline in their influence in Britain.

In the second half of the 19th century, vivisection was rarer in the United States than in Britain but, as Turner (1980) notes, "vivisection touched raw nerves on both sides of the Atlantic." Henry Bergh, who was a passionate antivivisectionist as well as the founder of the American Society for the Prevention of Cruelty to Animals (ASPCA), battled during the 1870's to ban vivisection through legislation in New York State but was foiled by the state medical society. There were other clashes, in Boston and Philadelphia, and, in 1883, the American Anti-Vivisection Society was founded in Philadelphia. However, much of the argument on both sides was based on experiences in England, and the American antivivisection movement relied so heavily on English examples that, during hearings on a restrictive bill in 1896 in the District of Columbia, they were badly embarrassed by their lack of knowledge of local practices. (The District was a major center for experimental medicine at the time.)

American research laboratories had steadily grown in number through the 1880's and 1890's, and the United States had become a major center of Scientific Medicine. The growth of animal experimentation alarmed the antivivisectionists, but it also concerned more influential bodies such as the Department of Mercy of the Women's Christian Temperance Union, the American SPCA, the Massachusetts SPCA, and the American Humane Association (Turner,

1980). In 1896, Representative McMillan, of Michigan, introduced a bill in the U.S. Congress to regulate vivisection in the District of Columbia. It was endorsed by six Supreme Court justices, by leading Washington clergymen, by eminent academics, and by a long list of practicing physicians. As in Britain, some physicians and medical educators felt threatened by the new scientific medicine.

The bill was denounced by the National Academy of Sciences, the American Medical Association, and a large number of other medical and scientific bodies. Faced with such pressure, the bill died in the full House of Representatives. Turner notes that the development of diphtheria antitoxin in 1894, which slashed the mortality rate of diphtheria sufferers from 40% to 10%, had a major impact on the public's perception of possible benefits from animal research. In 1894, McMillan's bill might have had a chance; by 1896, it was doomed; and, by 1898, McMillan himself had deserted the cause.

The influence of experimental medicine was growing and that of the antivivisectionists was declining. Even the forces favoring regulation appeared to be backing away from the issue in the early part of this century. In 1908, Henry Bergh, treasurer of the ASPCA and nephew of the founder, wrote:

> As a member of the committee on vivisection of the American Society for the Prevention of Cruelty to Animals, I have found every disposition on the part of representative men of the [medical] profession to more than meet us halfway in any intelligent and honest effort to properly restrict the practice [of operations on living subjects], . . . Let humanitarians, therefore, not attempt to scoff at such learned opinions and substitute therefor their own uninformed sentimentalism; but with the medical profession and ourselves unite in an earnest and well-meant effort to bring about such changes as may not interfere with the legitimate and necessary workings of science (McCrea 1910, p. 273).

Rodman (1977) suggests that the humane movement became respectable and relatively ineffectual in the twentieth century. Having achieved some of its objectives, such as state anticruelty laws and humane education reforms, it settled down to police local leash laws and the running of local shelters. The vivisection issue was allowed to drift into the background as many societies accepted a compromise with medical research. In 1914, delegates to the American Humane Association convention assured an observer for medical research interests that they wished to "leave vivisection alone" (Turner 1980, p. 118).

Nevertheless, the antivivisection groups were still active. Schultz (1968) describes the formation of many new societies at the beginning of the twentieth century and reports active antivivisection lobbying in the northeast. Therefore, in 1908, the American Medical Association decided to establish a lobbying and propaganda group, called the Committee for the Protection of Medical Research (Benison, 1970).

Between the two world wars, the reputation and prestige of the medical research scientist continued to grow. Antivivisection groups at the time were not known for their calm presentation of the facts, and there is little indication that their material had much impact. In California, the powerful Hearst press group backed state legislation sponsored by antivivisection groups. Even with such support, however, "Antivivisection Initiative No. 7" was defeated by a 2 to 1 referendum vote in 1920 (Whipple 1921). The medical profession remained very concerned, nonetheless, and, in 1946, Ivy noted with alarm that one measure was "*barely* defeated by a 2 to 1 vote" (emphasis added).

The Hearst press continued to support antivivisection causes and in 1935 moved beyond the confines of California. In the same year, the American College of Surgeons published a booklet giving the views of thirty-four leading medical researchers, including Banting, Cannon, Carrel, McCoy, and Rous, on the benefits of animal research (American College of Surgeons 1935). The medical profession was well organized and had powerful friends in both Federal and state legislatures. Antivivisection rhetoric may have been vocal, but their resources were spread thin across the states and their credibility suffered from association with such unorthodox medical theories as the repudiation of the germ theory of disease and opposition to vaccination and antisera.

The Research Bonanza: 1945–75

After the Second World War, the humane movement (as opposed to the antivivisection societies) was jarred out of its apathy to the animal research question by the research community. As Rodman (1977) notes, the sudden increase in funds available for medical research and the passage of a number of pound *seizure* laws (requiring release of unclaimed dogs and cats to medical research institutions) broke the uneasy truce, which had existed for forty years, between the humane movement and animal researchers.

New funds for medical research were funneled through Federal government institutions. Before the war, support of science was not regarded as a responsibility of the Federal government, although Congress had appropriated funds for medical research as early as 1878. In 1887, the Laboratory of Hygiene was established within the Marine Hospital Service, and this eventually evolved into the National Institute of Health in 1930, and the National Institutes of Health in 1948 (Frederickson 1978).

In 1938, the NIH budget was an insignificant part of national expenditure on medical research but, for the first time, the Federal government made extramural grants-in-aid, totaling $91,000. The passage of the Public Health Service Act, in 1944, provided the legislative basis for the subsequent growth in research funding, from $0.7 million in 1945, to $98 million in 1956, to $930 million in 1963. After 1963, the growth rate slowed although passage of legislation in 1971, 1972, and 1974 brought new funds to research on cancer, cardiovascular diseases, digestive diseases, and aging.

As might be expected, the rapid growth in funds for biomedical research also led to a much increased demand for research animals. A survey by the International Committee on Laboratory Animals (1959) reported that 17 million rodents and rabbits were used annually in research in the United States. By 1965, the total demand was estimated to have grown to 60 million. (W.B. Saunders and Co. 1966). The growth in demand was not restricted to rodents; the infusion of research funds and the growth in the training of biomedical scientists and health care professionals also increased the laboratory demand for dogs and cats.

The National Society for Medical Research (NSMR), founded in 1945 by Drs. Carlson, Ivy, and Wakerlin, devoted considerable time and effort to the passage of animal procurement laws (Stevens 1978). In 1948, a bill was passed in Minnesota requiring release of unclaimed animals from municipal pounds as well as state-assisted humane societies. In 1949, Wisconsin passed an even more sweeping law requiring any stray animal to be released on request to a scientific institution. A similar bill was then defeated in Illinois, and subsequent animal procurement laws passed in New York, South Dakota, Oklahoma, Massachusetts, Connecticut, Utah, Ohio, and Iowa did not attempt to go so far.

The passage of these procurement laws indicates that the medical community had considerable support at the time. A battle between medical researchers and antivivisectionists in Los Angeles in 1949 provides solid evidence for this (*Journal of American Medical Association* 1951). In the spring of 1949, antivivisectionists started a campaign to induce the Los Angeles City Council to pass an ordinance prohibiting the use of pound dogs in research. At a public hearing on April 19, the antivivisectionist plea was thrown out, but the medical community decided that they needed to protect their supply of dogs and they persuaded the city council to pass an ordinance permitting animals from the city pound to be used in research.

As might be expected, this spurred the antivivisection groups, who were successful in obtaining a temporary restraining injunction and sufficient signatures to call for a referendum. After vigorous campaigns by both sides, the animal procurement ordinance was left intact, the citizens of Los Angeles voting 357,393 to 261,699 to permit unclaimed dogs and cats to be used in research. Other votes, in Baltimore and Illinois, confirmed the public's support for medical research by even larger margins. Thus, public support was, if anything, even greater in 1950 than in 1920.

Virtually all the established humane societies in the country centered their work around the provision of shelters for homeless or lost dogs and cats. Forced surrender of these animals threatened the humane movement's basic structure, namely, a suffering-free sanctuary for animals. In 1953 (*Journal of American Medical Association*), the Royal Society for the Prevention of Cruelty to Animals (RSPCA) noted:

> The mere fact that a dog has become a stray means that he has suffered; and to change the law here, as has been done in the United States, would be a step of the most retrograde kind. Furthermore, the Society could not break faith with the public who hand their dogs, cats and other pets to us in order that we may give them a painless end (1953, p. 1039).

Thus, animal welfare groups felt that animal procurement from shelters had to be fought, and the American Humane Association (AHA), a national association of local societies, took up the cudgels.

Dr. Robert Sellars, president of AHA at the time, decided that they should attempt to reason with the NSMR. A meeting was organized on the understanding that neither side would publicize it but, for whatever reason, the NSMR immediately sent out an announcement about the meeting, which so inflamed antivivisection groups that the AHA was forced to discard any further idea of rational negotiation (Stevens 1978). The AHA reacted by avoiding further confrontation with medical research protagonists. This, in turn, led to the establishment of two new groups to raise the issue of using animals in research, the Animal Welfare Institute, in 1951, and the Humane Society of the United States, in 1954. The early

1950's thus mark the beginning of the reformation in the humane movement and renewed efforts to protest animal research.

It is interesting to contrast the attitudes of researchers at that time with more recent pronouncements. In 1951, Dr. H. Barcroft and three others from the British Research Defence Society (Barcroft et al. 1951) castigated several of their colleagues for daring to criticize work on shock by Gregerson and Root and by Noble and Collip. Barcroft and his colleagues suggested that these critics would do better to combat cruelty "where ignorance and indifference propagate it, instead of joining in the antivivisectionist witch hunt" (p. 1380). Twenty-eight years later, Professor Sir William Paton, a recent chairman of the Research Defence Society, wrote that he was very glad that work involving the Noble-Collip drum would not be allowed in England since he did not judge the benefits worth the suffering (Paton 1979).

In the decade of the fifties, anyone who dared to criticize animal research was regarded as an unwitting antivivisectionist, no matter how justified such criticism might have been. However, according to Animal Welfare Institute records, there was much to criticize.

> From the time in 1953 when a Health Department Inspector took AWI representatives through Cornell Medical School explaining how excellent the care for the animals was while passing by a dog whose incision had opened allowing his internal organs to fall onto the floor of the cage, to the time in 1960 when the AWI was called to inspect the animal quarters at St. Vincent's Hospital where filth and gross infestation of ticks, roaches, and other insects were found, to the time in 1963 when the AWI was called by a secretary in New York University Dental School about epizootics which were running through the animal colonies due to the fact that wild rodents were fouling the cages and cleaning was put off for so long that there was scarcely a clear spot to set foot in the dog runway, abuses continued (Stevens 1978, p. 53).

On the other hand, animal welfare organizations suffered from a lack of hard data and real political clout, and it was not until the 1960's that Federal legislation dealing with some aspects of animal care and procurement became a reality. It should also be noted that, in the sixties, the prospects for Federal (centralized) legislation became much more favorable (Morrison 1981).

The Laboratory Animal Welfare Act, 1966

Between 1960 and 1966, when the Laboratory Animal Welfare Act was finally signed into law, numerous bills were introduced into both the Senate and the House of Representatives (see Stevens [1978] for an excellent outline). At first, many of the bills introduced were based on the British Cruelty to Animals Act. However, the American research community has generally eyed the British Act with great suspicion. For example, according to Dennis:

> The vast majority of advances in surgery since 1876 have come from the United States and other free countries, not from England. These include open-heart surgery, surgery of the arterial system in major measure, development of pacemakers, methods of closed intestinal anastomosis, studies leading to the understanding of the fundamental problems of intestinal obstruction, replacement of hopelessly damaged heart valves, kidney transplants, and many others. This must not be construed as to denigrate British scientists, but rather to stress that the restraints imposed upon them have blocked their progress in humane endeavors, for they have excelled in other directions, such as in the development of penicillin, or as in the development of the Brock procedure, in which the need for large animals was less specific (1966, p. 831).

Dennis also described the experiences of several scientists who fled Britain because of the restrictions under which they were obliged to conduct their medical research.

On the other side, there are many British scientists more than willing to praise their Act. Dr. Lawrence Abel, who was vice president of the Royal College of Surgeons in London, made the following comments during Congressional hearings, in 1965:

> We do not commit the atrocities which are reported from time to time in some other countries. We do not allow the extravagant cruelty committed by some investigators of stress and shock. We have proved that the desired results can be obtained by less inhumane methods. We are convinced that the freedom of all and sundry to use animals indiscriminately would not improve the value of research (Stevens 1978, p. 55).

Nobel Laureate, Sir Peter Medawar is another who has repeatedly affirmed the value of the British Act and he has had the support of many of his peers (Hume 1962). However, it is certainly true that the British requirement for licensing of individual researchers and the monitoring of their activities by the Inspectorate would necessitate a much larger regulatory effort in the United States because of the vastly greater biomedical research effort.

In the midst of all this legislative activity in the U.S.A., the British government appointed a committee to examine the whole question of animal research and its proper regulation (named the Littlewood Committee after its chairman, Sir Sydney Littlewood). The general tenor of its findings may be gauged by paragraph 543 of the report:

> Animal experiment is a complex and highly specialised subject. It is also a moral and social problem of the first magnitude and one that does not exclusively concern the expert (1965, par. 543).

This well-reasoned and reasonable report encouraged those who were seeking to introduce Federal legislation, but its published findings alarmed researchers, who categorized it as a "source of arguments favoring regulation of experimentation and as a source of ideas for proposing paralyzing legislation" (Dennis 1966, p. 829). However, the enactment of American legislation depended less on reasoned argument than on two idiosyncratic events that caught the public and, hence, Congress's eye (Stevens 1978).

Pepper, a pet Dalmatian owned by the Lakavage family, was missing. The family searched for Pepper without success, until Mr. Lakavage saw a news photograph of a group of animals that had been temporarily unloaded from an overcrowded animal dealer's truck. One of the dogs look very like Pepper. Further inquiry indicated that the dog had been taken to Mr. Neresian, a big New York State dog dealer, but Neresian refused entry to the family. An appeal to Congressman Resnick, the representative from the congressional district in which Neresian was located, was also unsuccessful; the dog dealer refused Resnick's pleadings on behalf of the family. This arrogant attitude angered Resnick, and he decided to introduce a bill to regulate the trade in dogs. This was done on July 9, 1965, and a similar bill was introduced into the Senate by Magnuson and Clark. Pepper was never positively identified, since the trail eventually ended at a laboratory incinerator.

The second event was a 1966 photo-article in *Life Magazine* (Feb. 4, 1966) exposing the shocking abuse of dogs at the hands of animal dealers, many of whom sold to laboratories. *Life* was inundated with mail and so was Congress. The Resnick bill, requiring that dealers and laboratories be licensed, gathered additional momentum. In the face of such support, its opponents modified their opposition to the bill by attempting to have laboratories exempted instead. However, they failed, and the Laboratory Animal Welfare Act, after many battles typical of Capitol Hill, was signed into law on August 24, 1966. Subsequent amendments, in 1970 and 1976, broadened the scope of the Act, including the insertion of a qualified requirement to use pain-relieving drugs and changing the name to the Animal Welfare Act.

In retrospect, the Animal Welfare Act has generally been regarded as beneficial to animal research interests (Lindsey 1980). Laboratory personnel who take care of animals have been able to use the act in their requests for more money to upgrade their facilities. However, animal welfare advocates are dissatisfied because it does not prescribe how animals may be used. Scientists can still do precisely what they wish to animals in the name of research although, in an increasing number of institutions, the animal care veterinarian has sufficient authority to prevent careless or gratuitous abuse.

The Present Scene

Since the most recent amendment to the Animal Welfare Act, in 1976, public pressure has been building for further regulation of laboratory animal care as well as for regulation of actual animal research. The medical research community has responded with concern and the formation of another major lobbying organization. In 1979, Dr. J. Russell Lindsey, Chairman of the University of Alabama Department of Comparative Medicine, criticized the National Society for Medical Research because they "consistently maintained a defensive posture while claiming that all practices of animal use and care within the biomedical community have been lily-white." In addition, he continued, they have followed "the erroneous concept that all who speak out for the humane interests of animals are arch enemies of medical progress" (1980, p. 230). NSMR did not change fast enought, and the Association for Biomedical Research was formed to provide a focus for reasoned concern.

The research community has reason to be concerned since the animal welfare (or animal rights) movement has certainly become more effective and efficient in the past five years, for a number of reasons. First, at least some of the groups show a greater willingness to work together. For twenty-five years, internecine squabbles and jealousy between groups, or within a single organization, have diminished the effectiveness of the animal welfare lobby. There are still organizations who refuse to work with others but, in general, there is a greater sense of co-operation.

Second, the growing debate among academic philosophers on the moral status of animals (Singer 1975; Regan and Singer 1976; Rollin

1981) has injected the animal welfare movement with new vitality, a sense of purpose, and confidence (cf. Wade 1976).

Third, the animal welfare movement has benefited from the development of a more radical and militant animal rights movement. These new recruits, who advocate the establishment of certain rights for animals, whether legal or moral, are far more willing to take to the streets or engage in civil disobedience in order to highlight the plight of the animals. In England, animal breeders and laboratories are raided regularly and the homes and cars of research scientists daubed with red paint. In the United States, such activity has, until recently, been limited to a few isolated cases, but the activists have brought new energy and political skills to the attack on animal research.

Fourth, more scientists have been willing to stand up and criticize some aspects of animal research. Some have even taken jobs with animal welfare organizations and helped to develop a constructive dialogue between animal research organizations and the animal welfare movement. Of course, few scientists with research experience are willing to espouse or support an abolitionist viewpoint, but few animal welfare groups call for an immediate stop to all animal research and even some of those that do are prepared to work on gradual reforms, given the realities of the modern world.

Finally, science is losing public support and there is less willingness to accept reassuring statements from scientists that all is well. A recent survey by the National Science Foundation indicates that there are now more people who believe that scientific discoveries make our lives change too fast and break down people's ideas of right and wrong (Walsh 1982). Most of those surveyed still believe that science makes our lives more comfortable and that the benefits outweigh the harmful results, but support for the latter contention is declining at about 1% annually. An uncontrolled survey of its readers by *Glamour* (December 1981, p. 59) gave startling results (table 4.1). Of course one must be very cautious in interpreting results from returns on a magazine's reader survey. However, the recent repeal of a number of animal procurement bills and ordinances that were passed in the early 1950's indicates a definite shift in public attitudes concerning animal research.

Another element that has come to the forefront in recent years is the concept of "alternatives to laboratory animals." This appears to provide an obvious answer to conflict between the need to develop biomedical knowledge and the wish to eliminate animal research. However, our knowledge is still far too limited and imperfect to

TABLE 4.1
GLAMOUR MAGAZINE READER SURVEY

	Question	Percentage Yes	Percentage No
1.	Should we continue to conduct tests on animals to aid medical research?	37	63
2.	Should we continue to conduct tests on animals to aid in the development of safe cosmetics?	16	84
3.	Would you be willing to use a drug knowing it might not be as safe as it otherwise might be if animals had been used in testing?	59	41
4.	Would you be willing to wait an additional five years for a breakthrough drug that would save human lives in order to prevent testing on animals?	66	34

SOURCE: Adapted from *Glamour* magazine December 1981, p. 59.

replace animal research altogether with studies using cell cultures and computer modeling. If we knew enough to build a computer model of a mouse, we would probably not need to build the model in the first place. However, the concept of alternatives does provide hope for those who are prepared to work for a reduction in animal use.

The concept has its roots in a book by Russell and Burch (1959) on *The Principles of Humane Experimental Technique,* which enunciated the three R's—reduction, replacement and refinement. That is, one should work toward a refinement of techniques to reduce potential animal suffering, toward a reduction in the number of animals needed and, where possible, toward a total replacement of animals for specific purposes. The key is that the idea of "alternatives" offers a pro-science notion of gradual reform and is therefore not inimical to biomedical research. (The general concept is explored in greater detail in chap. 19, but the term is used throughout the book.) In fact, scientists have shown a cautious interest in the concept (National Academy of Sciences 1977; Pratt 1976; Rowan and Stratmann, 1980; Smyth, 1978).

The subject of animal rights is also being considered by scientists. At the 1978 annual meeting of the American Association of Laboratory Animal Science, one of the researchers, speaking on nonhuman primate availability, directed his audience to pay attention to the topic of animal rights since it would increasingly impinge on their activities. In April 1979, the College of Medicine in Cincinnati held a meeting on animal rights, alternatives to laboratory animals, and related ideas. (The Cincinnati group holds a laboratory animal science meeting every year; it is always well attended because they have a reputation for selecting topical subjects). In 1980, animal rights was the focus of several scientific meetings, including one organized by the Association for the Study of Animal Behavior (U.K.) and another by the American Psychological Association. An analysis of some of the issues and a code of ethics, resulting form a closed conference in France, have appeared in the *Journal of Medicine Primatology* (vol. 9: 103–106, 1980).

Scientific journals in general are beginning to carry more articles on the topic of animal research and animal rights (e.g., *New England Journal of Medicine* 302:115, 1980). The Federation of American Scientists (FAS) (1977) published a newsletter devoted to a report that castigated scientists for taking so little interest in animal welfare issues. The FAS report led to the formation of the Scientists' Center for Animal Welfare. This organization and the Institute for the Study of Animal Problems (established by the Humane Society of the United States in 1975) together provide a nucleus of technical expertise as well as a platform for debate by concerned scientists.

Despite the growing scientific interest in, and attention to, the issues of animal research, alternatives, and animal rights, groups promoting animal welfare and animal rights are steadily increasing the pressure. The following examples are indications of the growing political effectiveness and broader base of the revitalized humane movement. (Until the mid-seventies, the effective animal welfare groups on Capitol Hill could be counted on the fingers of one hand; the leader was Christine Stevens of the Animal Welfare Institute.)

In the spring of 1976, the American Museum of Natural History became the focus of a vocal demonstration against cat sex experiments conducted by two of their research scientists (Wade 1976). During the course of the campaign, the museum was picketed and the public were asked not to enter, letters were written to the museum's members, donors, and trustees and, according to the director, it was clear that the institution's reputation was being damaged. Eventually the museum stopped the cat research. Lester

Aronson, the scientist in charge of the project, retired and the affair blew over.

The chief architect of the campaign was a New York English teacher, Henry Spira. Spira is no stranger to demonstrations and campaigns; he is one of several people who have moved on to the animal rights cause from the civil rights and peace movements. As a result of his earlier experience, the campaign was carefully planned and the target carefully chosen. The study, because it involved sex research on cats, was bound to arouse strong public reaction, and the American Museum of Natural History was vulnerable to such public pressure. Finally, the campaign to fight this single issue managed to draw in a broad coalition of humane and antivivisectionist groups with widely differing views.

Spira employed a similar device in his plan to defeat the New York State animal procurement law, the Metcalf-Hatch Act. For a number of years, the Society for Animal Rights, as well as some New York groups, had been campaigning to repeal this bill. They had been successful in getting the repeal measure through the State Assembly but not through the Senate. Spira, using the good will he had built up through the museum campaign, and his position as an unaffiliated individual, put together another single-issue coalition to coordinate the activities of all the groups. In 1979, the repeal bill was passed by the New York State legislature and was signed into law by Governor Carey.

Then, at the beginning of 1980, Spira embarked on his most ambitious project yet, an attack on the Draize rabbit-eye irritancy test. This test is routinely employed to check for the irritancy of cosmetics, household products, and other chemicals. Despite published shortcomings (Weil and Scala 1971), little effort had been made to modify it or to seek alternatives. Spira put together a national coalition of more than 400 humane organizations to campaign for change, focusing on the cosmetic industry. Two years later, several Federal agencies had modified their test requirements to make the test more humane, and the cosmetic industry has allocated approximately $2 million for research seeking possible alternatives.

In the area of new legislation, four laboratory animal bills were introduced into the 96th Congress (1979/80)—one (H.R. 6847) seeking to amend the Animal Welfare Act and three on the topic of alternatives. Most of the activity centered on the Research Modernization Act (H.R. 4805), which mandated the establishment of a National Center for Alternatives Research and reallocation of 30% to 50% of animal research funds to the development of alternatives.

Members of Congress received thousands of letters (some individuals received more than 600) pressing for passage of H.R. 4805.

All the bills were reintroduced into the 97th Congress and public pressure for action continued. Finally, the Subcommittee on Science, Research, and Technology held hearings in October, 1981, to answer the concerns of congressional constituents who had inundated Congress with mail. The prime mover in all of this was a New York antivivisection group, United Action for Animals, that had written the Research Modernization Act.

Although the public was clamoring for action on the Research Modernization Act (specifically reallocation of 30% to 50% of animal research funds to alternatives), biomedical organizations began to mobilize against it (Broad 1980). By the time of the hearings, most major biomedical societies had come out against it. Even the Society for Mathematical Biology, which might have been expected to have a vested interest in computer model alternatives, opposed the Research Modernization Act. Faced with such united opposition from the biomedical lobby, the subcommittee decided to avoid direct confrontation and merely held hearings on the issue of animal research and alternatives, rather than on any specific bill.

As the subcommittee was developing its outline for hearings, their orderly progress was torpedoed by another event that demonstrated the development of the opposition's tactics. On September 11, 1981, police officers seized seventeen monkeys from the Institute for Behavioral Research in Washington, and charged Dr. Edward Taub, the institute's director, with cruelty to animals. The case had been developed by Alex Pacheco, a student and animal rights activist, who had been taken on by Taub as a summer volunteer. Pacheco had taken numerous photographs of filthy, encrusted cages, monkeys with bloody stumps where fingers had been and dirty rooms. He had also taken five experts through the facilities after working hours and these individuals then signed affidavits attesting to the general filth and lack of veterinary care.

Taub was found guilty of providing inadequate veterinary care for six of the monkeys, on November 23. (This was reduced to one count of animal cruelty on appeal.) In the meantime, the case had attracted national attention. The first day of the subcommittee hearings focused primarily on how the NIH, which had funded the laboratory, and the U.S. Department of Agriculture, which inspected it, could have overlooked such conditions. At the hearings, Dr. William Raub of NIH admitted that the system had failed, but USDA witnesses declined any detailed comment.

The hearings did not lead to any legislation, but Dr. Taub's trial and conviction alarmed his colleagues and served dramatic notice on members of Congress that things are not all they could be in the nation's laboratories.

CHAPTER 5

Laboratory Animal Ecology: The Numbers Puzzle

Today, vast numbers of warm-blooded animals are used every year in biomedical laboratories, and any thorough analysis of the issue of animal research and its regulation must address the questions of how many and what type of animals are used, and for what purpose. Unfortunately, such data are usually scanty; even estimates for total laboratory animal use differ widely from one source to another.

The best statistics come from England, where records of animal use have been kept since 1876. These give some idea of the growth of biomedical research in this century (fig. 5–1). For the first twenty years, the number of animal experiments (roughly equivalent to actual number of animals used since each animal used is counted as one experiment) grew relatively slowly, from about 10,000 per annum to an average of 80,000 per annum. Between 1920 and 1945, the growth rate increased, and then, after the Second World War, the rate increased still further as more money was pumped into biomedical research and drug production. The major increases prior to the end of the Second World War probably stemmed from greater demands for standardization of biological therapeutics (e.g., insulin, digitalis, vaccines, and sera) and for diagnosis. After 1945, the major growth areas have been drug discovery and development, cancer research, and immunology. It is probable that similar growth patterns occurred in other Western nations, including the U.S.A.

In the late 1950's, the International Committee on Laboratory Animals (1959; 1962) conducted an international survey of laboratory

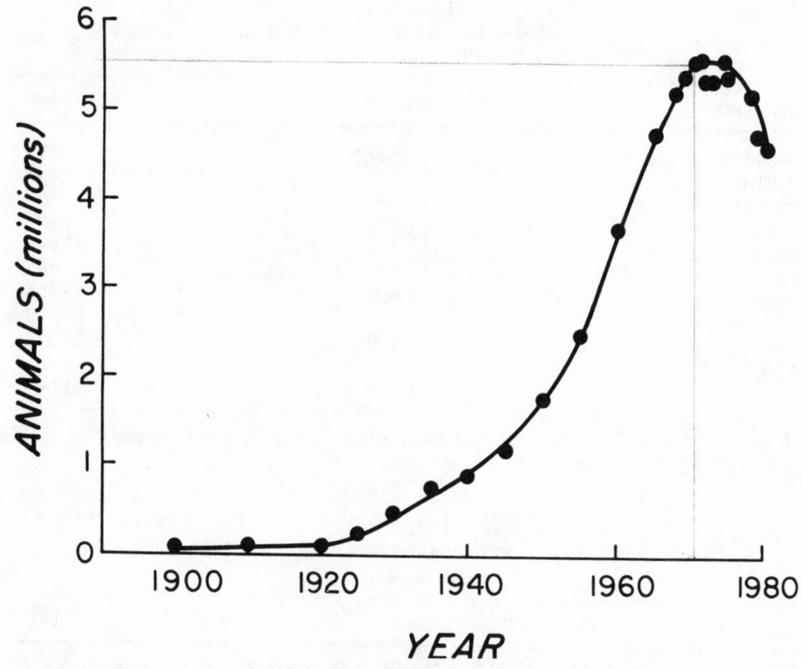

Fig. 5.1. Growth of animal experiments in England. Compiled from Home Office statistics, 1920–82.

animal use. It identified the United States (18 million), the United Kingdom (2.5 million), Japan (1.6 million), West Germany (1.4 million), and France (1.25 million) as the major users. Czechoslovakia, the Netherlands, Poland, and Switzerland all used between 500,000 and one million animals a year. Adding the totals for all the countries produced a grand total of 30 million, although this is probably a low estimate of world-wide use because returns from some countries (e.g., West Germany) were incomplete, and there were no figures from a number of other countries, such as Canada and Russia.

Another survey-cum-literature search by Tajima (1975) indicated that laboratory animal use had doubled in most countries by 1971 and, in some cases, had increased more than two-fold (table 5.1). Thus, Japan's use of laboratory animals increased from 1.6 million in 1956, to 13.2 million in 1970. Use in the United States had increased from 18 million in 1957, to at least 51 million in 1970. Estimates of total world use ranged from approximately 100 million to as many as 225 million.

TABLE 5.1
ANNUAL LABORATORY ANIMAL USE
(In Thousands)

COUNTRY	1956–59	1969–71
Australia	400	802
Austria	120	805
Finland	140	165
France	1,250	4,420
India	270	1,066
Israel	350	545
Japan	1,600	13,155
Norway	21	93
Sweden	170	875
U.K.	2,500	5,735
U.S.A.	18,000	51,000

SOURCE: Adapted from International Committee on Laboratory Animals 1959, 1962; Tajima 1975; Adamiker 1977.

TABLE 5.2
ILAR SURVEYS OF LABORATORY ANIMAL USE: 1965–1971
(In Thousands)

ANIMALS	1965	1966	1967	1968	1969	1970	1971
Mice	24,222	27,925	27,014	36,749	35,625	25,687	30,282
Rats	9,941	7,940	9,204	10,267	12,322	9,870	10,204
Hamsters	891	838	1,097	804	848	870	938
Guinea pigs	347	660	848	987	889	738	646
Other rodents	10	76	147	68	56	80	56
Rabbits	247	363	639	614	576	495	443
Dogs	93	415	371	409	367	183	193
Cats	33	143	137	171	156	57	76
Primates	63	63	70	85	68	54	57
Birds	903	1,812	3,655	1,287	1,675	880	1,600
Total	36,750	40,835	43,182	41,441	52,582	38,914	44,495
% Return of Questionnaires	39.5	60.6	50.3	63.0	69.7	49.2	61.1

SOURCE: Adapted from Institute for Laboratory Animal Resources 1966–69, 1970–71.

In the United States, annual surveys of laboratory animal use were carried out from 1965 to 1971 by the Institute for Laboratory Animal Resources (ILAR) (table 5.2). The surveys' response rates varied from 40% to 70% and produced a wide variation in totals. These surveys indicate the problem of attempting to gauge the total demand for laboratory animals from the mere distribution of questionnaires to users and the tallying of responses. Over the seven-year period of the ILAR surveys, the total use of birds recorded fluctuates erratically. As regards mice, the use of 26.7 million is reported for 1968, while the next year this figure increases dramatically to 35.6 million. No similar increase is seen in other species. However, the figures reported for 1969 are probably as accurate as any, since the questionnaire response was almost 70% (the highest return for the seven years).

After 1971, the regular ILAR surveys were discontinued and the only regular records for animal use are those compiled by the United States Department of Agriculture's Animal and Plant Health Inspection Service (APHIS). Unfortunately, the APHIS figures suffer from a number of shortcomings. For example, mice and rats are not included, yet they account for more than 80% of all laboratory animals used. Also, those filling out the APHIS annual reports are not given clear guidelines as to what is required. This does not help in attempting to determine how accurate the APHIS totals (averaging 1.8 million dogs, cats, primates, hamsters, guinea pigs, and rabbits per annum) might be (Animal and Plant Health Inspection Service 1972–80).

Current Animal Demand, U.S.A.

The current level of laboratory animal use is far from clear since there are many conflicting reports, and estimates range from about 70 million (my best guess) to 20 million (Institute for Laboratory Animal Resources 1980). The ILAR survey was a follow-up on a similar study in 1968 (Institute for Laboratory Animal Resources 1970) and was intended as a guide to trends in the laboratory animal field. The results, in table 5.3, show a 40% decline in animal use. On the other hand, the study reports that animals are held in the laboratory far longer.

It is not clear why the ILAR survey should produce figures so much lower than other estimates, but one clue comes from the identification of the proportionate value of the research covered by the survey returns, namely, $2.2 billion. This is only about 25% of the total annual expenditures for biomedical research programs in the United States. Multiplying the ILAR 1978 survey figures by four gives a total of 80 million animals. If one disregards the ILAR surveys, one can employ the following evidence to generate a figure for laboratory animal use in the U.S.A.

TABLE 5.3
LABORATORY ANIMALS ACQUIRED BY
NONPROFIT, COMMERCIAL, MILITARY, DHEW, AND
OTHER FEDERAL ORGANIZATIONS (FY 1968 AND FY 1978)

	Number of Animals	
Species	FY 1968	FY 1978
Mice	22,772,300	13,413,800
Rats	6,131,000	4,358,800
Hamsters	785,900	368,900
Guinea pigs	613,300	426,700
Rabbits	504,500	439,900
Dogs	262,000	183,100
Cats	99,300	54,900
Ungulates	106,200	144,400
Nonhuman primates	57,700	30,300
	31,332,200	19,420,800

SOURCE: Adapted from Institute for Laboratory Animal Resources 1970; 1980.

TABLE 5.4
SAUNDERS SURVEY ESTIMATES OF U.S. LABORATORY ANIMAL USE
(In Millions)

	1965	1970 (projections)
Mice	36.84	54.56
Rats	15.66	25.32
Guinea pigs	2.52	4.07
Hamsters	3.30	5.34
Rabbits	1.56	2.52
Exotics	0.12	0.19
Total	60.00	97.00

SOURCE: Adapted from W. B. Saunders and Company Market Survey 1966.

• At the end of 1965, W.B. Saunders and Company (1966), a group of economic consultants, conducted a market survey of the current and projected demand for small laboratory animals in the U.S.A. Their figures were based (a) on NIH use and the determination of NIH use as a percentage of the total demand and (b) on extrapolation from the sales figures from a known sample of laboratory animal breeders. The difference between the two totals was less than 2%; their final totals are given in table 5.4.

Conversations with laboratory animal breeders indicate that the laboratory animal market did indeed increase from 1965 to 1970 (though the size of the increase is in dispute) and then steadied in the 1970's when users began to increase their demand for higher quality animals. Assuming the Saunders survey was reasonably correct and that the breeders have provided an accurate picture of the laboratory animal market since 1965, an estimate of 70 million animals used annually in the 1980's is not unreasonable.

• In 1971, the Veterinary Extension Service at Rutgers University estimated laboratory animal use in 1971 at 63.5 million—rodents (45 million) and frogs (15 million) making up the bulk of the total (Santamarina 1976). The basis of the Rutgers estimate is not clear, but it has been widely quoted. Once again, if laboratory animal demand remained relatively static in the 1970's, a current estimate of 70 million animals used per annum would not be far wrong.

• In 1976, Dr. F. Homberger estimated that 35 million mice, 6 million rats and 1 million hamsters were used annually by the pharmaceutical industry alone, in the United States. The pharmaceutical industry accounts for only about 20% of biomedical research expenditure, although they probably use proportionately more animals than other laboratories. The National Cancer Institute (NCI) reported, in hearings before a congressional appropriations committee on their 1980 budget, that they supported research which utilized approximately 6.5 million rodents every year (U.S. Congress 1979). The NCI budget of $950 million is approximately one-ninth the national expenditure on biomedical research. Therefore, a direct extrapolation produces an estimate of 57 million rodents used in 1979. A study by Foster D. Snell Inc. for the Manufacturing Chemist's Association (1975) on the impact of the proposed Toxic Substances Control Act reported that, according to interviews with industry sources, approximately 35 million mice and 40 milion rats are produced every year in the U.S.A.

• Probably the best source of information on laboratory animal demand is the major commercial breeder. However, for various reasons, representatives of such companies are not particularly forthcoming on precise numbers. Recently, however, several publications have directly or indirectly provided an insight into the output of the Charles River Breeding Laboratories. Charles River is by far the biggest commercial breeder in the United States. One indirect estimate, that 50 million mice are used world-wide, is contained in the preface of a book edited by three laboratory animal experts, including the president of Charles River (Foster, Small, and Fox 1981). One direct estimate is attributed to Gilbert Slater, sales manager of Charles River, in an article in *MD Magazine* (October, 1981). He noted that Charles River produces more than 20 million animals annually and that they have 20% of the U.S. market. However, Charles River's output is not limited to the U.S.A.

Probably the best information on Charles River's production is found in a stock market analysis (Brown & Sons 1981). The report notes that Charles River produces 22 million animals annually, more than 5 million of which are produced overseas. This would indicate that domestic (i.e., U.S.) output is approximately 16 million animals. The report also indicates that Charles River holds 20% of the total domestic market (see table 5.5). Thus, extrapolation would indicate that about 70 million rodents are produced each year for the American market. This would not include rabbits, dogs, cats, frogs, and birds. The first three of these species probably account for about 1 million animals while the last two account for 5 to 10 million animals annually. My estimate breaks down as shown in table 5.6.

How the Animals Are Used

Assuming that 70 million animals are used every year, who uses them and for what purpose? The 1968 ILAR survey (Institute for Laboratory Animal Resources 1970) reported that 39% of the animals were used by commercial laboratories, 29% by government laboratories, and 32% by other noncommercial laboratories.

TABLE 5.5
CHARLES RIVER'S SHARE OF DOMESTIC AND INTERNATIONAL MARKETS, 1980

Domestic	Sales (millions)	% of Market
Charles River	$ 25	20
Harlan-Sprague-Dawley	7	6
Jackson Laboratories	4	3
Simonsen	3	3
Others	81	68
Total	120	100
International		
Charles River	10	5
Charles River, Japan	5	2
Others	95	45
China and Russia	100	48
Total	210	100

SOURCE: Adapted from Alex Brown and Sons 1981.

TABLE 5.6
ESTIMATED LABORATORY ANIMAL USE

Mice	45 million	63.1%
Rats	15 million	21.0
Hamsters	1 million	1.4
Guinea pigs	1 million	1.4
Rabbits	750,000	1.1
Dogs	250,000	0.4
Cats	100,000	0.1
Primates	25,000	0.04
Ungulates	200,000	0.3
Birds	5 million	7.0
Frogs	3 million	4.2
Total	71.325 million	100.0%

SOURCE: Compiled from available data, excluding ILAR Survey.

TABLE 5.7
LABORATORY ANIMAL USE

	Percentage	Number (in millions)
Teaching programs	8	5.7
Research programs	40	28.5
Toxicology programs	20	14.3
Drug development programs	26	18.5
Other programs	6	4.3

The commercial laboratories would use animals mainly for the purpose of drug discovery and development, and for toxicology testing. If the British statistics are any guide, approximately 35% of all commercial laboratory animal use would be for toxicity testing and 55% for the development of therapeutic substances.

In the ILAR survey (1970), it was reported that the noncommercial (not government) laboratories used 25.7% of their laboratory animals for teaching purposes, 68.2% for biomedical research, and 4.2% for diagnosis. The breakdown of animal use in government laboratories was not given but is likely to include substantial basic research, some diagnosis, some toxicity testing, and some drug development. With a number of fairly broad assumptions, one could allocate laboratory animal use in the United States as shown in table 5.7.

It is sometimes assumed that all animals used in laboratories suffer dreadfully. Considering the scale of the enterprise, it is undoubtedly true that some animals suffer, but it is surely also true that some do not (e.g., an animal kept in a good facility, used under anesthesia, and not allowed to recover). Once again, the best figures are those from the United Kingdom. Table 5.8 outlines the animals used under anesthesia or no anesthesia.

At the same time, the British statistics identify the number of animals used in procedures that are likely to be (or are definitely) noxious to the animals. These procedures do not include animals used in toxicological feeding experiments or in the study of infectious diseases. For the three years from 1978 to 1980, the figures are 457,000, 416,000 and 401,000, respectively (Home Office 1981). These figures represent about 9% of overall use. Toxicology testing accounted for another 900,000 to 1 million experiments in these three years.

In the Netherlands, figures on animal research for 1980 indicate that 37.8% of their animal experiments would have involved no appreciable discomfort. A further 10.7% were performed under anesthesia (compared to 18% in the U.K.) and 51.5% of all experiments involved risk of some or appreciable discomfort (International Journal for the Study of Animal Problems 1981a). These figures cannot, of course, be applied directly to the United States, but they do provide some indication of the manner in which animals are used in research and testing. It would not be unreasonable to assume from them that approximately one-third to one-half of the animals used in the U.S run the risk of some, or appreciable, discomfort and pain over and above the stress imposed by caging and handling. Certainly, the animals used in toxicology testing (with the exception of the control groups) and many of those used in drug discovery and development are likely to suffer some discomfort at the very least. Finally, there is a great deal of interest in toxicology testing at the present time, and the United Kingdom statistics provide some breakdown of how animals are used in this process (table 5.9).

The acute test category would include animals used for determination of LD50's, eye irritancy, skin irritancy, and the like. Carcinogenicity testing falls into the chronic test category. A Home Office

TABLE 5.8
ANIMAL USE UNDER ANESTHESIA
(In Thousands)

Year	No Anesthesia	Anesthesia	% Anesthesia	Total
1978	4,276	959	18.3	5,195
1979	3,874	846	18.2	4,720
1980	3,731	849	18.5	4,580

SOURCE: Adapted from Home Office 1981.

TABLE 5.9
TOXICITY TESTS IN THE UNITED KINGDOM—1977
(No. of Experiments[a])

	Diagnosis	Select. medical or vet. prod.[b]	Legislative requirement	Other	Total	(%)
Acute tests	39,784	77,956	311,410	165,487	559,917	(55.8)
Subacute or chronic tests	706	37,761	113,074	47,933	199,474	(19.9)
Teratology tests	814	1,996	19,358	6,482	28,650	(2.9)
Distribution, metabolism, etc.	9,646	73,193	25,819	52,101	160,759	(16.0)
More than one of the above	1,415	4,043	34,660	14,237	54,355	(5.4)
Total	52,365	194,949	504,321	286,240	1,003,155[c]	

SOURCE: Adapted from Home Office 1978.
[a] Each animal used is counted as one experiment.
[b] This category refers to animals used in the development of new medical and veterinary products, such as drugs and vaccines.
[c] Represents 18.6% of the total experiments recorded for 1977.

(1979, p. 9) report indicates that approximately 230,000 of the 560,000 animals used in acute toxicity tests were used to determine LD50's on mice, rats, fish, and birds. Thus the majority of animals are used in short-term acute tests and to satisfy legislative testing requirements. The pattern is probably similar in the U.S.A.

Conclusion

Our lack of detailed knowledge on the use of laboratory animals is both unsatisfactory from a policy point of view and indicative of a general lack of interest in the impact of biomedical programs on animals. (Interestingly, we have an even vaguer idea of how many human research subjects are used.) We should attempt to improve the quality of the information and at least identify the approximate number of animals (of different species) used in education, research, testing, and diagnosis. This would seem to be the least that should be done in the U.S. when Europe (the U.K., the Netherlands, and other countries) are beginning to generate more detailed data on laboratory animal use.

CHAPTER 6

Pain and Suffering in Laboratory Animals

J. Turner (1980) notes that "all animal suffering distressed animal lovers. But nowhere did it stand out more starkly and dreadfully than in the laboratory" (p. 86). He argues that the infliction of pain on laboratory animals evoked much more horror than animal suffering arising from the thoughtlessness of an ignorant drover. This was because the laboratory animal's agony resulted from "the deliberate calculation of a rational scientist."

In 1875, the physiologist Emmanuel Klein became the personification of this particular brand of rational heartlessness when he calmly admitted that he only used anesthetics for his own convenience and had "no regard at all" for the suffering of his experimental animals. Even Thomas Huxley, who supported the need for animal research, was disgusted by Klein's lack of concern, although Dennis (1966) argues that Klein was misunderstood and that he was referring only to frogs, since he used anesthetics for dogs and cats. Physiologists hastened to repudiate Klein but it was too late; he had provided the classic example of what antivivisectionists feared in animal research, and his apparent callousness was an important factor in the passage of the British Cruelty to Animals Act, in 1876.

Unfortunately for biomedical research, there has been enough evidence of apparent insensitivity to animal suffering by medical researchers to keep the spectre of the cold, rational scientist deliberately inflicting agony on an animal very much alive in the minds of many antivivisectionists and animal welfare workers. For example, another Klein, in referring to the use of monkeys in polio vaccine testing, recently commented that "any qualms at the 'inhumanity' of injecting viruses into the spinal cords of these 'cute' creatures, who look so much like little people, is soon dispelled by their many annoying attributes" (1972, p. 52).

Some researchers seem intent on dispelling the notion that animals feel pain as humans do and develop terms that appear to be little more than an attempt to disguise the fact that the animals are in pain. For example, it is not unusual to read of "nociceptive" (pain-producing) or "escape-provoking" stimuli.

Recently, Dr. D. Rioch has argued to an NIH review team that one cannot apply "human expectations of pain to animal surgery because pain is primarily a matter of societal conditioning to which animals are not subject" (National Institute of Health 1981). Dr. Rioch's view is clearly unacceptable. Animals are used in pain research and the search for analgesics, and they show obvious signs of pain under certain circumstances. There is also a tendency to downplay the pain-sensing mechanisms of cold-blooded animals and other "lower" animals.

Recently, the National Advisory Eye Council (NAEC), prompted by concerns over the use of frogs, fish, and other cold-blooded creatures, approved a statement of policy calling on researchers supported by the National Eye Institute to adopt "effective and uniform procedures . . . to minimize pain in these (cold-blooded) animals" (Carter 1979, p. 1363). This initiative was prompted by Professor Kenneth Brown of the University of California School of Medicine, in San Francisco. He argued that, although it may be impossible to prove conclusively that cold-blooded vertebrates feel pain, the argument advanced that they do not is "so strained that one wonders whether it would be advanced at all except in self-justification." He then noted that he knew of one well-known investigtor who, having removed one eye from a live fish, would replace it in its tank to await an experimental need for the second eye. According to Brown, "The investigator even joked about this in a group of experimenters in a social situation, which seems to indicate the generality with which such practices are accepted" (Carter, 1979, p. 1363).

Studies in human beings clearly demonstrate that pain perception (not the same as sensation) is governed by subjective phenomena. There are people who can sit through an appointment with the dentist without any local anesthetic, whereas others even feel (perceive) pain after a couple of healthy jolts of novocaine. Thus, pain is a multifactorial phenomenon, consisting on the one hand of physiological responses to the stimulation of certain nervous pathways and, on the other, of the central integration and appreciation of these events, including a subjective psychological component. It is interesting to note that human beings who have undergone frontal lobotomies still sense pain, and although their pain-detection thresholds are little changed by the operation, their tolerance for pain is much higher (cf. Vierck 1976).

In 1965, the Brambell Committee in the United Kingdom produced a report on the welfare of farm animals which includes an eloquent and concise passage on the problems raised when attempting to define pain.

> Nobody can experience the feelings of another individual, however well that person may be known to them. They can be evaluated only by analogy with one's own feelings, from what that person tells us and from one's own observation of his looks, behaviour and health. The evaluation of the feelings of an animal similarly must rest on cries, expression, reactions, behaviour, health and productivity of the animal. The better we know a person the more fully we can appreciate his feelings; we cannot estimate those of a stranger as well as we can those of a friend and we are still less able to appreciate those of a person of alien race and culture. We are correspondingly even less competent to appreciate those of an animal, which cannot communicate verbally and whose expression, reactions and behaviour we are much less able to interpret. Nevertheless, our understanding of their feelings is not different in kind, but rather in degree, from that which we form of a fellow human being.
>
> Animals show unmistakable signs of suffering from pain, exhaustion, fright, frustration, and so forth and the better we are acquainted with them the more readily we can detect these signs. Judgment of the severity of their suffering must be subjective. There are sound anatomical and physiological grounds for accepting that domestic mammals and birds experience the same kinds of sensations as we do (1965, p. 9).

In fact, an animal may not show any real signs of pain. Human beings learn from infancy that expressions or cries signifying distress will bring help and attention. However, Baker et al. (1949) notes that animals that show signs of distress in the wild are likely to attract attention from predators rather than assistance from their fellows. Thus, an animal may simply remain quiet when in pain rather than showing obvious signs of distress. Yoxall notes that "it is surprising . . . how much a dog's 'quality of life' . . . may be improved by the administration of a simple analgesic if the dog is suffering from a tumour which, although painless on palpation, may be causing considerable chronic pain" (1978, p. 423). Thus, an animal may react to a sharp pain with a clearly recognizable behavioral response, such as a yelp or sudden movement. But chronic pain does not necessarily produce clear behavioral signs of suffering, and the veterinary clinician must rely on relatively subtle behavioral cues.

There is a simple behavioral model that can be used to indicate pain in laboratory animals. A stimulus is said to be painful if it is consistently terminated or escaped by the subject. Vierck (1976) notes that animals begin to escape stimulation at about the same stimulus intensity that human subjects begin to report pain sensations. While this tends to confirm similar systems of pain sensation in both animals and man, these pain-detection thresholds are unaffected by analgesic drugs or therapies. However, pain *tolerance* thresholds are very sensitive to analgesic drugs. It is clear that the topic is complex, and the problem will take much research to unravel.

The Physiology of Pain in Animals

Research into the detailed structures of the peripheral nervous system has shown that there are specific receptors responsible for the perception of pain in humans. These have been called nociceptors, but they are very difficult to distinguish from other unspecialized thermo- or mechanoreceptors. Similar receptors and similar nerve fibers have been found in other vertebrates, including mammals and fish. Yet, because no clear morphological differences have been recognized which distinguish ordinary heat or touch receptors from true nociceptors, it remains impossible to decide by anatomical or microscopic investigation alone whether an animal can feel pain.

Functionally, the chief defining characteristic of nociceptors as a class is an insentivity to mild or low-intensity thermal or mechanical stimulation. In fact, they respond (with a discharge of nervous impulses passing along the axon) only to levels of thermal or mechanical stimulation that are actually or potentially damaging to tissue.

There is also a difference between the detection of painful stimuli and the interpretation of those stimuli as being painful. Breazile and Kitchell (1964) note that one can transect the bundle of nerve fibers in human beings that are instrumental in transmitting nerve impulses subserving pain perception. This results in an inability to perceive pain from a noxious stimulus applied below the lesion. However, the pain reflexes may still be intact and such an individual will withdraw his foot from a hot object even though there is no conscious pain perception. In animals, the nerve fibers subserving pain are far more diffuse and cannot be cut without producing a large lesion in the central nervous system. As a result, Breazile and Kitchell (1969) caution that it should not be assumed that postsurgical responses in animals are not associated with pain perception simply because in a similar situation man does not perceive pain.

Direct, percutaneous recordings in conscious human subjects have demonstrated that pain sensations are correlated with activity in small myelinated (A delta) and unmyelinated (C) nerve fibers. In fact, some research workers have claimed that activation of "A delta" fibers is associated with 'first,' fast, sharp, localized pain, and activation of "C" fibers is associated with 'second,' slow, burning or aching, poorly localized pain (Liebeskind and Paul 1977). Research on anesthetized animals indicates that these same fibers are activated exclusively (or most potently) by stimuli of noxious intensity. These small-caliber fibers with "free" nerve endings appear to be present in all vertebrates.

A number of chemicals have been implicated in pain sensation and perception. If cells around the peripheral nerve endings are damaged or stressed, they appear to release a substance that causes the nerve to discharge. Research indicates that this substance may be a peptide, called *bradykinin.* Other substances such as histamine and the prostaglandins may also play a role. When bradykinin is injected into humans it produces pain sensations that can be strong enough to over-ride the effects of a local anesthetic. Bradykinin is not only present in the "free" ends of the peripheral small-caliber nerves, it is also present in those parts of the dorsal horn of the spinal cord that respond when nociceptors are stimulated.

From the dorsal horn, the pain message passes up the spinal cord to the thalamus. At this stage, another peptide molecule, known as substance P, appears to be involved. Both bradykinin and substance P might offer opportunities for relatively simple pharmacological tests for pain sensation. Substance P occurs in all mammals, birds, and frogs so far investigated and also in fish (Royal Society for the Prevention of Cruelty for Animals 1980, p. 9). Finally, a discussion of substances involved in pain sensation and perception would be incomplete without mentioning the recent discovery of endogenous opiates (Hughes 1975).

These endogenous opiates are peptides (of twenty to thirty residues), which are now generally known as endorphins. The active portion of these peptides, the part that actually binds to the brain cell receptor (to which morphine also binds), is a pentapeptide (enkephalin). These substances have been shown to produce analgesia and nerve endings containing enkephalin appear to be closely associated with those containing substance P. It has also been postulated that the endogenous opiates act by blocking release of substance P (Jessell and Iversen 1977). To date, endorphins have been found in all classes of vertebrates, as well as in other phyla. In 1979, Swedish researchers reported finding endorphins in the nerves of earthworms (Alumets et al. 1979). However, there is no simple relationship between endorphins and pain relief, and the more research that is done, the more complicated does the picture become (Murphy, 1982).

It is now generally accepted that the physiological mechanisms of pain sensation in animals and man are very similar. Unfortunately, these mechanisms are still not well understood, and there is certainly room for disagreement on the issue of pain *perception* where psychological factors appear to play a more prominent role.

One other point should be included in any discussion about pain. Pain is not inherently bad—it is, in fact, a very important defense mechanism. Sharp, acute pain indicates that the subject is in some danger and must take immediate evasive action if it is to escape injury. Dull pain probably functions to ensure that the affected part is rested, thereby preventing further damage and promoting healing. There are, for example, some humans who feel no pain who have to be extraordinarily careful to avoid injury, such as chewing their tongue while eating. However, intractable, chronic pain such as that suffered by cancer victims, appears to have little adaptive value.

Pain Research: Ethical Issues

The knowledge that has, so far, been generated on pain physiology has been derived from experiments on animals and human beings. General anesthesia is usually used in studies involving surgical intervention, but it is not suitable for many studies on nerve physiology because it depresses the nervous system. Therefore, one must seek other approaches, one of which involves the use of live, conscious animals.

As Professor Wall notes in the opening editorial for the journal, *Pain:* "In editing a journal on the subject of pain, we shall face a particular problem of science and ethics. To what extent may scientific studies be allowed to produce or prolong suffering in man or animals?" (1975, p. 1). He commented that no rigid code could be developed to cover all eventualities, but that the journal would refuse sh any report where the animal was unable to indicate or e onset of suffering. "The torturing of prisoners, whether human or animal, degrades man and teaches nothing."

However, Sternbach (1976) objected to some elements of the policy as stated by Wall. He argues thus: First, there are degrees of pain, and the range from threshold to tolerance limits may be wide. One should be able to employ experimental pain stimuli that fall into the slight to moderate range and not inflict unbearable suffering on the animal. Second, there are distinct differences between acute and chronic pain, and the many studies of acute pain have been of little value in attempting to treat chronic pain. Third, since the differences between acute and chronic pain mechanisms are unknown, we need an animal model to test some of the hypotheses. Fourth, cruelty, in the sense of inflicting severe pain, is clearly unnecessary when attempting to study chronic pain. For example, household pets with painful limbs that took weeks to mend continued their normal range of activities, indicating that the pain was not incapacitating (excessive?).

Sternbach therefore proposed that any model of chronic pain should use pain stimuli that are well below the tolerance limits as judged by the animal's ability to continue its usual range of activities and behaviors. Wall (1976) responded that his intentions were primarily to forbid the publication of work where painful stimuli are given to unanesthetized animals paralyzed with curarelike drugs. Such experiments, he noted, "are blind cruelty and bad science." He also accepted that there may be a need to study the differences between acute and chronic pain in animals, but suggested that before attempting to duplicate the human chronic pain syndrome in animals, we should search veterinary clinics to see if sick animals suffer a mood change and a changed reaction to drugs and to injury, as in human chronic pain cases.

Professor W. Kerr, at a recent conference organized by the Scientists Center for Animal Welfare in November, 1981, in Washington, also had very strong reservations about the use of local anesthetics and paralyzing agents in studying neurophysiology. As he described it, it is not unusual in neuroscience laboratories for animal surgery to be performed under general anesthesia, for local anesthetics to be applied around the wound edges and at the pressure points of the stereotaxic apparatus, and then to blow off the general anesthetic while administering a paralytic agent to keep the animal immobile.

In his personal opinion, this sort of procedure is highly questionable since one does not know if the local anesthetic is working.

This does not mean that all pain research causes extreme suffering. One common procedure is the rat tail flick test in which a beam of light is focused on the tail of a rat. When the spot becomes too hot, the rat is free to flick its tail out of the way. Another procedure involves attaching a shock device to the foot of an animal. The animal receives a reward for enduring the shock but is free to terminate the shock at any time by pressing a lever. Both these techniques could be modified for application to humans and Professor Kerr suggested that this should be a general criterion for pain research.

Unfortunately, too much research on animals is conducted without considering some of the above points. For example, Duffy et al. (1976) studied vision in kittens using a protocol that included skull surgery using only local anesthetics and paralytic agents. Campbell and Masterson (1969) write at length on their work on the "psychophysics of punishment." In their quest for thoroughness, they proceeded methodically to examine, for both AC and DC current, detection, aversion, tetanization, and death thresholds in animals. One could perhaps justify modest studies to determine detection and aversion thresholds, but the data presented by Campbell and Masterson indicate a fascination with the results that could only be described as parametric tinkering, resulting in intense suffering for the animals concerned.

The Committee for Research and Ethical Issues of the International Association for the Study of Pain has published guidelines for investigators planning research on pain (*Pain* 1981). These include review of the proposed study by both peers and ethologists, testing the pain stimulus on themselves first whenever possible, and an assessment of the animal's deviation from normal behavior as a measure of the extent of the pain. Parameters such as the EEG, feeding and drinking behaviors, body weight, and social interactions could all be used as part of the measure. Widespread adoption of these rules would certainly provide considerable relief for animals used in pain research and other procedures involving aversive or noxious stimuli. In addition, we need to grade the various research procedures so that individual scientists will have a clearer idea of what is judged to be painful. The Swedish authorities have done this and their grades (table 6.1) provide a good idea of what might be considered noxious (Ross 1978).

TABLE 6.1
RESEARCH TECHNIQUES, PAIN AND DISTRESS

Categories	Examples
1. No pain or only minimal and momentary pain	Injections,* blood samples, tube-feeding,* diet experiments,* breeding studies, behavioral studies without aversive conditioning, routine procedures from small animal vet. practice
2. Animals painlessly killed or anesthetized animals not allowed to recover	Blood pressure studies, organ and tissue removal, studies on organ survival, perfusion experiments
3. Surgery on anesthetized animals with recovery but where postoperative pain will be minimal	Biopsies, transfusion or vascular studies, cannulation, castration, pituitary removal in rodents using standard techniques, some CNS lesions
4. As above but with considerable postoperative pain	Major surgical operations, burn studies, graft studies
5. Experiments planned on unanesthetized animals expected to become seriously ill from the treatment or to suffer considerable pain or distress	Toxicity testing, radiation, transplants of tumors or infections, stress, shock or burn studies, behavior experiments involving aversive conditioning
6. Experiments on unanesthetized animals (or only local anesthesia) where the animal is curarized or paralyzed	Some physiological or pharmacological studies on CNS

SOURCE: Adapted from Ross 1978.

* These procedures may produce pathological states (e.g., injection of pathogens, feeding of toxic chemicals) and, if so, would have to be graded differently.

Animal Suffering and Distress

If pain in animals is difficult to determine conclusively and unequivocally, how much harder is it likely to be to determine when an animal is suffering. The Littlewood Committee (1965) report on animal experimentation concluded that pain was too narrow a term when discussing laboratory animal use and suggested that "suffering" should be used. This would include pain, discomfort (indicated, e.g., by such signs as torpor or poor condition), and stress (i.e., a condition of tension or anxiety). The Brambell Committee (1965) report lists fear, pain, frustration, and exhaustion as examples of suffering, although this is by no means a complete catalogue of states involving possible suffering. There may, in fact, be states of suffering that other animals experience but that are unknown and unimaginable to humans.

Many of these states include the idea of an emotional response. However, some researchers question whether vertebrates experience the same depth of emotion and hence suffer in the same way as humans do. Vierck (1976) mentions the example of human beings with prefrontal lobotomies, who have pain sensations but do not appear to be disturbed by them. Brain (1963) suggested that laboratory animals, with their smaller (or virtually nonexistent) cerebral lobes, will be similarly unconcerned and therefore will not suffer. (However, it may be that animals have a more primitive nerve system subserving emotion than do human beings.)

Yet other scientists contend that animals do not suffer "anxiety" in the same way that human beings do. For example, the U.S. Department of Agriculture (1979) has issued a regulation stating that "the word 'anxiety' is a psychiatric term that is only applicable to humans." The following statement reflects similar attitudes.

> The effects of the benzodiazepines [antianxiety drugs] in the relief of anxiety can readily be demonstrated in experimental animals. In conflict punishment procedures, benzodiazepines greatly reduce the suppressive effects of punishment. However, anxiety in rat and man can hardly be equated (Goodman and Gilman 1975, p. 190).

On the other hand, brain receptors for benzodiazepines have been found in mammals, reptiles, birds, amphibians and bony fish, but not in cartilaginous fish or invertebrates (Nielsen, Braestrup, and Squires 1978). This suggests that most vertebrates are capable of experiencing a form of anxiety which is physiologically similar to that seen in humans—at least it appears to be mediated via similar receptors in the brain. Perhaps the notion of an "anxious" and hence suffering rat is not as ridiculous as some contend.

Research on the benzodiazepine receptors is proceeding apace (Kolata 1982a). The drug industry is obviously very interested because a clearer picture of the mechanism of action of the benzodiazepines could lead, not only to better antianxiety drugs, but also to better sedatives, muscle relaxants, and anticonvulsants. One of the interesting results of the recent research is the discovery that some ß-carbolines produce opposite effects to those of the benzodiazepines and may even promote anxiety. Four human volunteers injected with one ß-carboline reported feeling great anxiety, and one person became so anxious that he had to be physically restrained and given a benzodiazepine, which reversed the symptoms in less than a minute. This same product was reported as appearing to increase anxiety in animals. Over the course of the next few years, we should learn a lot more about anxiety and its treatment in humans. It is to be hoped that some thought will also be given to whether the animals used as models also experience strong anxiety.

Vierck (1976) comments on the difficulties of assessing the quality of the arousal-emotional systems in laboratory animals, noting that a number of researchers have suggested that the relatively primitive spinoreticulothalamic system plays an important role in mediation of emotional feeling and expression (in human beings, the frontal lobes appear to be more important in emotional response). He further notes that punishing a pet, or the application of intensely noxious stimuli, elicits "in subhuman mammals emotional reactions that appear comparable to those of human beings." Furthermore, studies have demonstrated clear relationships between the intensity of noxious stimulation and the intensity of associated behaviors. Of course, this does not help us to decide the cut-off point when an animal passes into a suffering state.

Dawkins (1980) has written an excellent scientific monograph on the question of animal suffering in which she notes that the search for measures of suffering leads one to a variety of concepts, including stress. It has been suggested that stress and suffering are directly correlated, but Hans Selye (1973), the father of stress research, argues that stress is not something to be avoided and, in fact, cannot be avoided. Eustress (too little stress) may be as "bad" for the animal as excessive stress and, in both cases, the animal should be considered to be suffering.

A variety of physiological and behavioral responses have been linked to the concept of stress. For example, the short-term stress response in animals (producing a state of fight-or-flight readiness) is associated with changes in heart rate and in catecholamine levels in the blood stream. In situations of chronic stress, the animal's adaptation process includes an increase in the blood levels of adrenocorticotrophic hormone and cortisone. However, once again, we have the problem of determining how large a change in these physiological parameters can be tolerated before the animal can be said to be suffering. A similar problem exists in using behavior as a measure of suffering since abnormal behavior may merely represent an increase or decrease of certain types of behavior, and who is to say when such an abnormality correlates with suffering?

There are no definitive indicators, or combinations of indicators, that can identify whether an animal is suffering in the intermediate stages between robust health and *joie de vivre* on the one side, and obvious organic pain and fear and psychopathology on the other. This does not mean that "suffering" should be ignored. More research is required on the topic and, in the meantime, we should at least recognize that many laboratory animals are capable of experiencing at least some emotional states and that, as a result, we must attempt to distinguish between well-being and suffering and perhaps establish some parameters to help us make the decision. The Swedish system which grades research into various categories according to the likely pain is an example of how such parameters might be established.

The Alleviation of Pain and Suffering

The oldest law dealing specifically with research on animals—the British 1876 Cruelty to Animals Act—resulted from a compromise between research scientists and animal welfare advocates. The compromise focused on the issue of painful research—animals could be used in research, provided such research was unlikely to cause pain. If pain was likely, then the animal should be anesthetized to preclude pain. Unfortunately for the animals, this prohibition on painful research was far from complete since exemptions were permitted. Large numbers of animals have been used over the past 106 years in projects that have caused some pain and suffering.

Currently, there are attempts in the U.S. to regulate painful research for the first time. Across the Atlantic, the Council of Europe is drafting a convention on animals used in research and is having a difficult time arriving at a consensus on the issue of a "pain" clause. Representatives of the British government and animal welfare advocates want to forbid "severe and enduring pain" (Cherfas 1982). Most of the other representatives at the meeting, including the British Department of Health and Social Security, want to allow exemptions to the above "no pain" rule so that toxicity testing, for example, is permitted by law and not just by accepted practice.

The generally accepted methods for preventing or alleviating pain and suffering in laboratory animals include the use of a wide variety of anesthetic and analgesic agents. However, it is not always clear that a particular agent is producing pain relief or unconsciousness. Drewett and Kani (1981) describe a controversy in the scientific literature on the issue of appropriate anesthesia.

Nitrous oxide and oxygen were used as an anesthetic and combined with a paralyzing agent for a long series of vision experiments on cats (e.g., Eggers and Blakemore 1978). However, it has been demonstrated that nitrous oxide is not itself a general anesthetic in cats (Russell 1973), although it was subsequently claimed that satisfactory anesthesia is produced as long as the anesthesia is first induced with barbiturates (Blakemore et al., 1974). This claim has also been disputed. Richards and Webb (1975) have found that nitrous oxide only maintained anesthesia for about two hours, and then only if the initial dose of barbituate was large. By contrast, neurophysiology research investigations can continue for periods of time extending into days.

Animal welfare advocates also argue that animals should be given postoperative pain-killers and analgesics when necessary. On the other hand, veterinarians have argued that postoperative pain is an important element in the healing process. Yoxall (1978) notes that "pain is a natural protection response" and it is important "to minimize treatment of pain in circumstances in which, by its presence, pain is reducing the likelihood of further damage occurring." Yoxall is, however, a strong advocate of the use of analgesics in other situations, but his suggestions leave much room for individual interpretation. Much more work needs to be done to clarify the appropriate circumstances and conditions for anesthesia and analgesia in laboratory animals.

Pain and Suffering: Its Effects on Research Data

Hillman, a physiologist who has researched the problems of resuscitation in animals, has stated:

> There is hardly a single organ or biochemical system in the body which is unaffected by stress. . . . The changes in some of the parameters cited may be up to 300% of the normal values at rest. This would obviously invalidate painful experiments claiming to examine any changes less than those already known to be due to stress itself. It is almost certainly the main reason for the wide variation reported among animals upon whom painful experiments have been done (1970).

Many researchers agree with Hillman, but when it actually comes down to attempting to control for stress and pain, their enthusiasm dwindles, judging by the lack of attention paid to these and other subtle environmental factors. For example, at a 1979 seminar on stress held by the American Association for Laboratory Animal Science, W. Isaac of the University of Georgia, was very critical of the fact that there was little or no data on the "optimal" conditions for caring for or using rodents in the research laboratory. "We have not been concerned with behavioral variables," he said, "even though we give them a great deal of lip service and write regulations dealing with behavioral variables."

In the laboratory itself, a warning was sounded, by a group of German scientists, for those who use *in vivo* metabolite levels to study regulatory mechanisms (Faupel et al. 1972). In an elegant study, the metabolite levels of rat liver were measured, using the standard "freeze-clamping" technique in which tissue is frozen to −193°C. virtually instantaneously by clamping between aluminum plates that are precooled in liquid nitrogen. However, with this technique, there is either an appreciable delay (greater than 10 seconds) in removing tissue from the killed animal, or the animal is anesthetized so that the tissue can be frozen *in situ* before the animal is killed. The possible effects of delay, killing methods, or anesthesia are usually ignored because of the problem of control.

Faupel and his colleagues, using a simple double guillotine and unstressed rats, showed that anesthetics, stress, and violent killing techniques caused substantial variation in the levels of certain critical metabolites, such as adenosine monophosphate. By doing so, they called into question a great deal of earlier work and sounded a warning for anyone not taking these factors into account. Yet their study either is perceived to be an interesting curiosity or is ignored. The extra care that would be required is more than most researchers are willing to entertain, and they would probably argue that such extra control is not a requisite for the success of their particular research.

Another study on the response of rats to the stress of handling (moving the cages about) reports that a wide variety of metabolic and endocrinological parameters were affected (Gartner et al. 1980). The authors note that "experimental or sampling procedures must be performed within 11 seconds of first touching the animals' cage." This is important for studies looking at most of the endocrine characteristics and for all plasma values that are linked with circulatory change, capillary permeability, energy and mineral metabolism, and acid-base balance. If the experimenter is unable to perform the procedures quickly enough, "he must explain in detail how the stress due to manipulation influences the characteristics being studied."

If the above studies clearly demonstrate the negative effects of stress, the following example indicates what can be achieved through positive contact. Five groups of male rabbits were subjected either to normal laboratory animal care (2 groups) or to a regime of petting, handling, and individual attention (3 groups) while on a 2% cholesterol diet (Nerem, Levesque, and Cornhill 1980). The animals were killed after five or six weeks and the aortas examined. The petted animals had 60% less atherosclerosis than the other groups. As the authors note, "Clearly, more must be learned about the effects of social environment in animal studies of disease. If nothing else, our results suggest that, in specifying the protocol for an animal study, careful consideration should be given to sociopsychological factors" (pp. 1475–76).

Another fascinating review of the effects of stress on subtle experimental variables has appeared recently (Riley 1981). The stress-related release of corticosteroids has an adverse affect on important elements of the organism's immunological apparatus. Riley reports that usual laboratory animal housing produces a variety of stress responses that elevate circulating corticosteroid levels in the plasma. Therefore, any study of stress-related increases in the incidence of disease must be conducted using special low-stress housing and careful control of a variety of other factors, such as population density, male-female proximity, and handling stress.

As Riley warns, there is a clear need for

> both quiescent protective animal facilities and the use of appropriate animal handling techniques in biological studies, especially if optimal immunocompetence and normal physiology are of relevance. . . . Because of . . . largely unappreciated and uncontrolled elements, the question arises as to how much of the present and past work with small animals may be severely flawed. In any event, the information now available calls for a reassessment of the current standards for laboratory animal housing and for techniques related to animal experimentation (p. 1109).

Conclusion

While there are still many scientists who condemn—as did the behaviorist John Watson—empathy and anthropomorphism, it is apparent that the tide has changed. Donald Griffin (1976) challenged orthodoxy with his book on animal awareness only a few years ago, raising a storm of controversy from those who wished to defend scientific dogma against intrusions of "sentimentality." The heated argument over ape "language" has also breached the dike of scientific "objectivity" on the issue of animal consciousness. Even though the concept of human uniqueness has been defended from the claims of "talking" apes by a demand to demonstrate yet higher communication abilities before an ape can be shown to have acquired "true" linguistic abilities, animal consciousness and feeling have reappeared as acceptable topics for scientific investigation.

At the 1981 Dahlem Conference in Berlin, about fifty scientists and philosophers gathered together to discuss *Animal Mind—Human Mind* (Griffin 1982). Griffin noted that we really know remarkably little about animal minds, in part because "scientists have so long ruled out *a priori* the possibility that mental experiences could occur in animals." By the end of the conference, there was general agreement that it is appropriate to discuss animal minds and to attempt to investigate, in a scientific context, what type of mind is possessed by different animals. The conferees discussed definitions of consciousness and the problems of language but always came back to the problem of sapience versus sentience. Just because an animal possesses a certain degree of intelligence or ability to learn is not a clear indication that it *feels* something. As Solomon (1982) notes, the question of whether an animal is suffering in a particular situation is the dominant question in animal welfare and animal rights debates.

> Animal psychologists once dismissed out of hand the idea that animal minds, animal consciousness and animal experience might be part of science. Now, that idea has become their basic premise, the starting point for much of their work. The question now is one of degree. The old—and, it is to be hoped, moribund—question about the validity of ascribing consciousness to creatures other than ourselves can be replaced with hundreds of more precise experimental questions about the sensitivity, intelligence, and experience of animals. With this recognition of continuity from species to species can also emerge a renewed appreciation of differences. We need not ask whether animals have intelligence, or language, or emotions, but rather what intelligence, what kind of language and which emotions. However, the answers to such questions will not come easily. If they come at all, it will be only after more observation, experimentation, and conceptual clarification than the past few decades of science, or centuries of story-telling, have required of us. (Solomon 1982, p. 47).

These issues are all central to the question of animal suffering and perception of pain. In laboratory animal science, there is little information on such issues. Unfortunately, there is also little interest in these research questions among those who fund research in laboratory animal science. Apart from the fact that merely raising the question of animal mind, emotion, and feeling sometimes threatens those whose research is now protected from ethical probing by underlying Cartesian assumptions, these issues are considered unimportant compared to the need to protect research animals from disease. Perhaps disease control should be the primary task of laboratory animal scientists, but it is also clear that other, less tangible events can have a marked effect on research data. We must expand our horizons and deal with the ethical and research questions stemming from the revived notion that animals, including laboratory animals, have feelings.

Part II

THE ISSUES

CHAPTER 7

The Use of Animals in Education: A Failure to Deal with Contradictory Values

It is most improbable that any reader will disagree with the premise that education of the population is essential to maintain our technology and culture and that this applies to the science of biology as much as to any other profession or skill. Most school children encounter animals very early in their education. Indeed, humane education, namely, teaching children to be kind and not cruel to animals, was and still is a major program area in grade school, and twenty-two states require some sort of formal program for humane education. Such programs are usually aimed at children from the ages of 7 to 12. After this, it is assumed that the "kindness" message is ingrained and that the adult behavior will reflect this early educational experience.

Unfortunately, the continuing need for humane societies, animal welfare campaigns, and anticruelty statutes indicates that humane education programs are not enough. We know that the message is not reaching a sufficient number of children, and it may also be imperfect or poorly delivered. Other factors may also be operating. For example, perhaps the "kindness" message is inadequate to deal with the contradictions that occur later in life, or maybe the values taught in grade school cannot be sufficiently ingrained. As a result, they are lost as other value systems are brought to the fore in later education.

The high school biology student provides an example of some of the later contradictions. The student is taught to perceive the animal as a model of living processes, and the usual approach fosters an attitude of distancing oneself from the object of study and not allowing feelings or sensitivities to interfere with the collection of data. Unfortunately, many students take this process too far and come to perceive any manipulation of, or interference with, an experimental animal as "scientific." The corollary is that the demonstration of an ethical concern for the animal is perceived as sentimental and "unscientific." Thus, students tend to become preoccupied with the mechanical elements of animal experimentation and do not develop the self-critical and intuitive qualities that form the basis of top-quality research.

Rollin (1981) stresses the negative aspects of this process and talks of the training, rather than the education, of scientists in universities. But "training" actually starts in the high school biology class.

> Beginning at the undergraduate level, the student is put through a series of courses that emphasize techniques, manipulation of data, and manual dexterity, rather than thought and understanding. The tests given are typically short answer, true or false, or multiple choice, geared to the regurgitation of discrete bits of information. No emphasis is typically placed upon conceptual understanding or upon ability to synthesize. . . .
>
> But it is on the level of graduate education that one can really see the pernicious nature of science education assert itself. One can do virtually nothing but wash test tubes or become a lab technician with only a bachelor's degree in science, so typically, students who genuinely wish to pursue a scientific career must proceed to a master's and doctoral level. Perhaps, one would expect, it is here that science as thinking is inculcated into the student. This, unfortunately, is not the case—in fact, the situation is even worse than on the undergradute level. On the undergraduate level, the option at least sometimes exists for students to take classes in a wide variety of fields, to take humanities and social science classes, to enter into learning experiences that are reflective upon the nature and activities of science. Often, the option does not exist even here as the major requirements are so stringent and restrictive. On the graduate level, anything outside the immediate area of apprenticeship is viewed as frivolity and is frowned upon (Rollin 1981, p. 108).

Rollin continues by arguing that graduate education is nonconceptual and that only science technology is drummed into the aspiring researcher. On graduating, the scientist can then take his or her place in normal scientific activity, defined by Kuhn (1970) as puzzle solving.

In the professional schools, the student is being trained to conform to predictable (professional) behavior with a dependable set of skills. This is not bad per se, but problems appear when the cult of objectivity leads to the disregard or devaluing of normal sensibilities.

Rollin (1981) recounts the following anecdote which indicates how attitudes which are inculcated in the science classroom may affect the later treatment of and regard for animals.

> How does all this relate to the treatment of animals? In very direct and dramatic ways, which are easily illustrated anecdotally. One of my good friends, an experimental psychologist, recounted to me a telling incident. As a young graduate student, he was running an experiment with rats. The experiment was over, and he was faced with the problem of what to do with the animals. He approached his advisor, who replied, "Sacrifice them." "How?" asked my friend, assuming that the professor would produce a hypodermic needle and barbiturates. "Like this," replied the instructor bashing the head of the rat on the side of the workbench, breaking its neck. (While this is not in fact a cruel way to kill a rat if done correctly, since cervical dislocation causes instant death, it is not easy to learn and is highly offensive to the uninitated.) My friend, a kind man, was horrified and said so. The professor fixed him in a cold gaze and said, "What's the matter, Smith, are you soft? Maybe you're not cut out to be a psychologist!" (1981, p. 109–10).

In such a manner, the sense of moral concern that embryonic scientists and doctors start out with may be devalued as squeamishness and sentimentality that has no place in the laboratory. Of course, such sentiment is most certainly permitted outside the laboratory, and many scientists will point to their collection of pets as proof that they are animal lovers and, thus, imply that they are incapable of the insensitivity toward other beings of which they are accused. Whether one is an animal lover is beside the point. The important issue is, does one *respect* the interests of laboratory animals and are these interests accorded any real consideration before the animals are "sacrificed" to the religion of objective and impartial science?

Aspiring biologists and biomedical professionals are given little or no help by the educational system as to how one might deal with the contradictions of being required to be kind to animals on the one hand, and the need, for example, to inject an experimental animal with malignant tumor cells on the other. No one can categorize most biomedical research on animals as being kind. Equally, it is usually incorrect (and unfair) to call it cruel. The practice, thus, falls into the grey area between kindness and cruelty, and we need to provide students with a thorough framework within which they can address the complex moral issues surrounding the use of animals in research and testing. Current biomedical education not only does not do this, it actually discourages the raising of these moral issues.

The High School Experience

High school biology teachers and animal welfare groups and advocates have not enjoyed the best of relations over the past two decades. The main points of friction have centered around two different but related activities—the use of live animals in classroom exercises and the use of animals in science fair projects. Criticism of classroom use of live animals by animal welfare groups has not been particularly vocal and tends to be confined to isolated protests about a particular practice in a single high school. On the other hand, there has been a sustained and relatively effective campaign against the use of living animals in projects for science fairs.

Prior to 1960, live animals were used on a limited basis in school biology classes. However, some form of dissection was practiced, generally limited to the frog and fish as vertebrate representatives (Emmons 1980). Then, new curriculums were developed (e.g., Biological Sciences Curriculum Study—BSCS) and implemented. The BSCS curriculums in particular emphasized the study of biology rather than necrology (Mayer 1973), and suddenly living vertebrates were in heavy demand for biology classes.

Use of animals in biology classes. In 1969, approximately 9 million wild-caught frogs were shipped by U.S. suppliers to educational institutions. Just under half of them were preserved preparations, the remainder being alive (Gibbs, Nace and Emmons 1971). However, the wild populations declined rapidly, and by 1972 supplies had dropped by 90% (Emmons 1980). The BSCS curriculums have changed since they were first developed and there is perhaps less overt emphasis on pure technique. But Mayer (1980), the director of BSCS, still affirms the need to study living animals. He notes that of one thousand students entering fifth grade, only 732 will graduate from high school, only 220 will graduate from college, and only 40 of these will obtain science degrees. Thus, high school biology may be one of the few opportunities to train citizens to be biologically literate. For this, live animals are, from his perspective, absolutely necessary.

A recent survey conducted by BSCS (Mayer 1982) as part of a project to assess whether there was a perceived need for materials on issues in human-animal interactions indicated that the use of live animals is not particularly great—41% of teachers reported that no time was spent on the study of live animals, while only 26% reported spending more than five hours per semester on live animal study. By contrast, 65% reported that more than five hours per semester were spent with preserved animals.

The attitudes section of the survey was particularly interesting. Table 7.1 demonstrates the differences between students and teachers in their response to a selection of the questions (the original categories "Completely Agree" and "Moderately Agree" are combined in the table for the sake of simplicity and clarity). It is clear that students were more likely to be concerned about individual animals than populations and and that a surprisingly large proportion express opposition to animal research. By contrast, students were more likely to view rats as appropriate experimental animals requiring no humane consideration. These and other questions indicated that the students' attitudes are not arising out of any coherent ethical framework. The vast majority of both teachers and students felt that a discussion of values and attitudes in science classes was important.

These results indicate relatively strong but idiosyncratic student support for humane issues. A similar study in Israel, produced the same type of results (Tamir and Hamo 1980). It is not clear what happens to those students who oppose animal research. Either they move on to pursue careers that do not involve animal experimentation, or their views are changed and/or sublimated by their biomedical training. The Tamir and Hamo study indicates a significant shift toward a utilitarian attitude between seventh and ninth grades. This supports the idea that students should be exposed to some formal educational exercises involving an examination of their values and attitudes (see also Kieffer 1979; 1980).

Before moving on to discuss the use of animals for science fair projects, I would like to touch on the dissection question. Whether dissections should be performed is not much of an issue in the United States but, in Britain, animal welfare opposition to the practice is relatively vocal. For example, a recent issue of the *Liberator* (the official publication of the British Union for the Abolition of Vivisection) praised the courage of two Yorkshire schoolgirls who refused to dissect rats in their biology class. The case received national publicity, the school authorities noted that the students' views should be respected, and the National Union of Teachers also supported

TABLE 7.1
ATTITUDES OF STUDENTS AND TEACHERS TO HUMAN-ANIMAL INTERACTIONS

Statement	% Agreeing	
	Teacher	Student
1. All mammalian animals should have rights.	61	76
2. There is nothing wrong with killing unwanted pets if it is done painlessly.	55	23
3. It is morally acceptable to keep and slaughter livestock for humans to eat.	93	67
4. It is wrong to experiment on mammals because they have not given us permission to do so.	5	32
5. I am in favor of medical research involving the sacrifice of many nonhuman animals because of the benefits to human health.	79	40
6. Rats are good experimental animals because they are pests and do not require humane treatment.	12	48
7. National ecosystems should be protected from destruction by humans, even if it results in less food for people.	73	42
8. If I could contribute to only one of two organizations that help animals, I would choose the one that worked to prevent cruelty to individual animals rather than the one that worked to preserve populations of endangered species.	22	51

SOURCE: Adapted from Mayer 1982.

their action. It is thus not surprising that the question of dissection is receiving serious consideration from the authorities.

Those in Britain who are responsible for the educational curriculums still require some dissecting skills, but there is a growing acceptance of the view that dissection training has relatively limited educational value. For example, Kelly notes that "the use of dead specimens helps to develop some skills of observation and dissection. It possibly helps understanding of morphology and anatomy and provides some insights into functions. But it is debatable as to whether it does much more" (1980, p. 53). It can also have detrimental effects. In this country, Krause (1980) recounts an anecdote from his daughter's education. She was so upset by the killing and dissection of a live fish that she turned vegetarian and avoided any further classes involving animal experimentation (she ended up with a degree in botany and horticulture). Tamir and Hamo (1980) suggest that students should not be forced to peform dissections or other experiments and that dissections should be postponed to the higher grade levels since students, especially girls, in the seventh grade are particularly sensitive about harming animals.

Use of animals in individual science projects. In 1942, Westinghouse began sponsoring a Science Talent Search designed to find outstanding science students and encourage them to seek careers in science. Their record speaks for itself; up to 1980, four Nobel Prize winners had previously been national winners of the competition. Eight years later, another competition, the International Science and Engineering Fair, was started, under the administrative aegis of Science Service Inc., in Washington, D.C. Both competitions have undoubtedly provided encouragement and incentive to budding scientists, but sometimes at great cost in animal suffering.

By 1969, "sanctified torture" (Hillaby 1969) was a widespread result of student attempts to produce a project that would carry off the grand prize (together with its cash awards and travel perquisites) in both local and national competitions. Hillaby noted that goldfish were bathed in detergents, 15-year-old students carried out splenectomies, and heart transplants were performed by gowned and masked students in front of television cameras in Columbus, Ohio. In this last example, ice was used in place of a more conventional anesthetic, but it melted under the hot studio lights. The would-be cardiac surgeons were thus forced to restrain their squirming charges by hand. Horrifying as these reports may be, one particular study must take the award for elaborate butchery.

The Mississippi State 1968 award winner used 25 squirrel monkeys to demonstrate "neuro-electrotelestimulation and electric form reactions" (sic). Four relics of the student's attempts, including one dying animal with suppurating holes in its head, were photographed and displayed at that year's International Science and Engineering Fair (ISEF) in Detroit. The monkey displayed at the fair died of a variety of ills. A necropsy disclosed large areas of sloughed and necrotic skin and demonstrated that the electrodes had not passsed through the holes in the skull into the brain. The only change instituted by the ISEF organizers after this particular horror was a prohibition of the display of live, warm-blooded animals at the competition.

In 1969, the Westinghouse Science Talent Search gained the attention of the *New York Times* in an editorial, "Prizes for Torture": "Many adult organizations thoughtlessly encourage high school students to perform these atrocious 'experiments'. Science fairs at the local, state and national level often award prizes to students whose only real achievement has been the deliberate or inadvertent torture of animals" (May 10, 1969). One of the award winners performed skin grafts on 1,000 mice, while another bisected the brains of 25 mice in his home, resulting in the death of most of the animals.

However, the project that gained most notoriety was displayed by an eighteen-year-old high school student from Virginia. Five house sparrows were blinded by removing the eyeballs, using a technique she had learned at the University of Texas. After the eyeless birds recovered from the anesthetic, they were placed in a Y-shaped box with food in one arm and an electric shocking device in the other. However, the birds were extremely reluctant to move. Food was withheld to increase the incentive. After six days, the student's conclusion was that "birds are likely to die when starved to 70% of their bodyweight" (Animal Welfare Institute 1969). Bob Gronie of the *Chicago Tribune* commented "The Westinghouse Electric Corporation may consder the blinding of five house sparrows for use in experiments by a teen-age high school girl worthy of an award in its Science Talent Search contest, I consider it outrageous and a horror" (Animal Welfare Institute 1969). Westinghouse crumpled under the public outrage, and the following year no projects were allowed that caused pain or suffering to vertebrate animals.

However, the ISEF did not change its policies and, under the sponsorship of General Motors, it continued to accept projects involving animal surgery and animal suffering. Over the next ten years, there was a running battle between those who contended that the science fairs were inhumane (Fox and Ward 1977; Orlans 1972a; 1972b) and those who felt that students had to be encouraged and motivated to pursue scientific careers by hands on experience in detailed projects with the possibility of winning a substantial prize (Grafton 1977). The ISEF rules changed slowly but have been overtaken by standards that have been set by the National Science Teachers Association (1980), which prohibit the use of vertebrate animals in experimental procedures that result in pain or discomfort to the animal. Surgery, the use of pathogenic organisms, toxic substances, ionizing radiation, aversive stimuli, and deficient diets are specifically prohibited.

ISEF has responded with alarm to this code and argued that it "would seriously limit what responsible teachers and students could do in and out of the classroom" (International Science and Engineering Fair 1980). The basic argument used by ISEF in justifying their rules—which include the need for adult supervision, proper animal care, and the restriction of projects involving surgery to research and clinical laboratories—is as follows. Bright students must be motivated, via encouragement to undertake extracurricular projects, to pursue careers in the life and health sciences. It is further argued that excessive restrictions on the students will, in some way, undermine their motivation.

However, the experience of science fair organizers in Canada indicates that establishing a requirement for appropriate adult supervision is not the answer, since animal abuse continues (Rowsell 1980). The Canadians put a great deal of effort into the effective application of their guidelines but, in 1975, decided that they could not eliminate human error and thus prohibited all projects involving animal pain or discomfort. Projects involving observations of normal animals in a free living state were still permitted. Since the new regulations were adopted, the number of biological exhibits has increased and their scientific quality has improved, according to Rowsell. The adverse publicity accompanying the science fairs has also been eliminated. With the benefit of hindsight, Rowsell recognizes that their early guidelines sounded excellent on paper but were, in practice, unenforceable and impractical.

A report on the 1982 ISEF in Houston (Scientists Center for Animal Welfare 1982) indicates that there are still plenty of grounds for objection by animal welfare groups. One project followed a line of study that crops up in every (both local and national) science fair. The animals were fed junk food (cookies, lollipops, chewing gum, and french fries) and photographs of them in poor condition were displayed. In another, pregnant rats were forced to drink a toxic solution, resulting in lethargic and sick offspring. The student's stated intent was to repeat the study with a different toxic agent. In other projects, ascorbic acid was injected into the abdominal cavity of small mammals, nude mice were irradiated (producing skin lesions and extensive necrosis) in a proposed laetrile trial, and skin burns were produced in rats, using creosote. NASA has also come in for criticism recently for permitting a student to send an arthritis research project on rats up into space (Holden 1982a). These sorts of projects are not a necessary part of encouraging bright students to pursue a career in the life and health sciences. Other societies are able to encourage bright new entrants to follow such careers without resorting to tacit approval of the Dr. Kildare syndrome where a white coat and a scalpel effects an immediate transformation of a student with rudimentary skills into a scientist. Mayer comments that "students are naturally attracted to frontier kinds of research, usually the more bizarre the better, and they attempt sophisticated experimentation with crude apparatus, little comprehension of what is to be done or how to do it, in a largely unsupervised milieu" (1980, p. 15).

Perhaps the last word should be left to Sir Peter Medawar, who was approached by an American high school student for advice on an immunology project.

> "I was once shocked to receive a letter from an American schoolgirl asking me how to inoculate mouse embryos to induce a state of immunological tolerance so that by doing likewise she might win a prize in her school science fair. I accordingly wrote her a long, grave, and doubtless boring letter explaining why I did not think schoolchildren should do experiments on animals. My letter was exhibited and won her the coveted prize" (Medawar 1981, pp. 1308–1309).

University Education

Undergraduate biology teaching in America is only a relatively small step away from the high school use of animals, and many of the arguments and caveats that apply to the high school situation are also relevant to undergraduate courses. However, very little attention has focused on this aspect of animal use in education. Russell notes that "one can question the need to kill animals in undergraduate teaching situations" and that undergraduate experiments often inflict unnecessary suffering on animals and have "a hardening and desensitizing effect" (1978, p. vi).

Tennov (1980) has demonstrated that freshmen are, according to their own comments, less willing to carry out research involving painful electric shock than are seniors. However of the students who stated that they would refuse to participate (less than 10%), many qualified their refusal by stating that they did not disapprove of painful research on animals but they, themselves, would find it difficult to participate.

These results indicated that students may well become desensitized as they proceed through the educational process, and that they believe there is cultural disapproval of any expression of concern for the animal subject. It must be recognized, though, that the type of study carried out by Tennov is only an opinion poll. Few, if any, of those who said they would refuse to participate would actually do so when confronted with the real situation. Protest from students concerning humane issues takes a great deal of courage in the absence of explicit leads from lecturers.

Unfortunately, students rarely receive more than general platitudes (recognized as such by the student body) from university teachers. Those teachers who do raise the issues explicitly in the classroom can find themselves out of work when the time comes to renew their contract. One lecturer at Illinois Wesleyan, a Dr. John McArdle, included instruction on the concept of alternatives in his classes. His students then raised the issue with other life science teachers. This went on for a few years, accompanied by rumbles of disapproval from members of the biology department. His contract was then not renewed and the biology students were exposed to less controversial topics with less student-teacher confrontation. According to McArdle, he lost his job because he was raising ethical questions about animal research in the classroom (*Cincinnati Enquirer* Jan. 28, 1983).

Textbooks are another means by which the general desensitization process can proceed. In animal behavior studies, books that give much space to the ethical issues, such as the publication by Silverman (1978), are rare. Far more common are such texts as those by Hart (1976) and Bures, Buresova, and Huston (1976), which set out to provide experimental exercises for students. Drewett and Kani are scathing in their criticism of these works:

> It is hard to know quite how to comment on books that recommend experiments as cruel as these for the routine stuff of student practical classes. Many aspects of our use of animals are open to debate; what is proposed here is so obviously wrong that one would have hoped that simply to draw attention to the contents of these books would be enough to ensure that they were condemned. Yet clearly it cannot be so. For

> publishers must know the content of the books they publish, send the drafts out to referees, have them evaluated and approved before proceeding with publication. Can it really be that no voices were raised against them? And if so, is this because we are so bemused by the jargon of techniques and procedures that we can no longer even see what is being proposed; or is it because a substantial body of psychologists really does believe that there is nothing to object to here? It is hard to understand how publishers of the standing of Elsevier could disgrace themselves by promoting a book like this (1981, p. 194).

One experiment selected by Drewett and Kani for special comment involved swimming rats to exhaustion while varying water temperature, using low doses of anesthetics or taping weights to the animals' tails. In another, shock-induced aggression exercises are suggested, using shocks of up to 2mAmps, lasting up to 5 seconds at a rate of up to 50 shocks per minute. Yet another experiment suggested a study of rats paralyzed with gallamine triethiodide in order to examine the effects of conditioning on heart rate.

Bures, Buresova, and Huston (1977) argued that these and the many other painful studies outlined in their book are used in 90% of the studies dealing with physiological psychology and that a "student not familiar with them could have hardly learnt anything at all." They are particularly outraged at Drewett (1977), comparing them to seventeenth century Cartesian physiologists, and state that "such accusations would be naive when made by a layman but are deliberately offensive when pronounced by a fellow researcher and teacher" (p. 872).

Nonetheless, Drewett's criticisms are valid. The type of procedures suggested in these books for student learning exercises are inappropriate for undergraduate courses. Many people who study psychology do not continue on to conduct animal research. This group needs only to learn about the state-of-the-art concepts and the general manner in which these have been derived. A detailed training in the techniques used in an animal research laboratory, especially when such techniques involve (the potential for) a great deal of animal suffering and pain, should be put off until the student decides to pursue a research career. Then the relevant techniques can be taught, under close supervision, in the research laboratory. Undergraduate practical classes are, in any case, rarely of much use in graduate research, since most research projects require extensive on-the-job training.

The situation in the professional schools is a little different; doctors and veterinarians must learn the techniques of their profession before being let loose on their unsuspecting clients. In America, medical and veterinary students have traditionally been given their first surgery exposure on dogs obtained from a pound or animal shelter. In some institutions, the animal is subjected to several different surgical procedures during the course. At others, the animal is not allowed to recover from anesthesia after the particular technique has been completed. Some institutions argue that postoperative survival and care is a very important element in the educational process and therefore oppose any attempts to restrict student practical classes to nonsurvival surgery only. Nevertheless, in planning multiple surgery courses, it must at least be recognized that edema and tissue reaction from the previous surgery usually last at least two weeks (Wood et al. 1980).

Debate over the use of dogs in practice surgery usually turns at some point to the situation in Britain, where the use of live animals solely to develop manual skill is forbidden. This does not necessarily mean that medical and veterinary students do not improve their techniques by using live animals, but such activities must have some other purpose. In a recent review of the British legislation covering animal research, the consensus that has evolved is that some use of anesthetized animals in nonrecovery surgery practice should be permitted (Select Committee 1980). The Royal College of Physicians and Surgeons of Glasgow, for example, calls for a relaxation of restrictions on the use of anesthetized animals for teaching students physiology (Select Committee 1980, vol. 2, p. 323). The British Veterinary Association opposes the notion of allowing undergraduates in the biological sciences to undertake surgery on anesthetized animals but recognizes the need for some, closely regulated practice surgery for students training to be health professionals.

By contrast, the National Antivivisection Society is opposed to lifting the prohibition on the use of animals for attaining manual skill, arguing that British-trained surgeons are not held to be inferior to those trained in countries that permit surgery practice on dogs (Select Committee 1980, vol. 2, p. 319).

One interesting aside to this issue: the Royal College of Surgeons of Edinburgh argued that there is a real need for practice on animals in the case of certain microsurgical techniques (Select Committee 1980, vol. 2, p. 324). It is true that the trainee could learn only a limited amount "at the shoulder" of the expert in such instances. However, McGregor (1980) has noted that the human placenta offers a satisfactory, economical, and readily available source of tissue for microsurgical training. Nevertheless, he also notes that use of rat, rabbit, or dog can be extremely valuable in mimicking the *in vivo* situation, but that U.K. restrictions prevent the use of such animals to all intents and purposes.

There is some valid use of animals in the training of health professionals, but this does not imply that medical and veterinary educators should be given carte blanche to introduce animal studies into every practical exercise. The habit of administering clinically important poisons to some unfortunate stray dogs in front of a class of veterinary students to demonstrate the symptoms has, fortunately, been stopped in American veterinary schools. Even so, there are still some who feel that live poisoning demonstrations are necessary in veterinary education. When the College of Veterinary Medicine at Michigan State University stopped the practice in 1979, Dr. Frank Welsch, co-ordinator of the course, stated that the action "compromises our education" (*Detroit Free Press,* Feb. 19, 1979).

One can also question the educational value of some of the exercises. It is true that hands-on experience provides a quality of experience that cannot be duplicated by video tapes or lectures, but this does not mean that a single thoracotomy will turn a student into a surgeon. Too often, educational exercises are instituted in a vague belief that this or that will be "a good thing," but the actual educational objectives are rarely stated explicitly.

For example, Wood et al. (1980) describes a course of animal surgery developed as an adjunct to training in obstetrics and gynecology. They evaluated the program and decided that multiple survival surgery provided the best learning experience and reduced the number of animals required. The authors note that the program realized the following goals:

1. Residents were exposed to major surgical procedures related to gynecology and expanded their knowledge of abdominal and pelvic anatomy
2. Residents benefited from exposure to a biomedical research facility
3. Practice on various animal models increased their understanding of basic research literature using such models
4. Work with the animals stimulated the residents to ask clinical questions

These appear to be rather modest goals considering the time invested in the practical training. Another program using dogs, this time for cardiopulmonary resuscitation training for nurses (Miller et al. 1980), was severely censured by peers. Keith and Donoff (1981) commented that there was no indication of what, if any, benefits the dog exercise had over any of the other training techniques already in use.

A somewhat more bizarre episode of using dogs in training courses involves a company that manufactures surgical staplers (The Sunday Advocate, November 8, 1981). Every year, the United States Surgical Company used approximately 900 dogs to train sales representatives in the proper use of their staple gun—a tool that is rapidly replacing conventional stitching of wounds or operation cuts. The representatives are chosen primarily for their sales ability and thus may have little or no medical knowledge. Before being sent out on the road, they must pass through a six-week training course. The company is now the focus for animal welfare protest in Connecticut. Their position has not been improved by allegations of animal abuse in the newspaper expose or the fact that one of the dealers who supplied them with dogs has been convicted of animal cruelty and of receiving stolen animals.

Conclusion

The use of animals in biomedical research and training is the subject of contentious and passionate debate. Students of the life and health sciences should not be shielded from this fact, nor should they be lulled into accepting the status quo by platitudes regarding humane care and consideration. Veterinary training, in particular, should include a substantial introduction to ethical issues relating to animals.

In *The Ethical Animal,* Waddington (1960) asserts that the human ability to alter the environment has significant social and psychological implications. Biological evolution is no longer the imperative that it once was, either for human beings or for the animals we use to provide food, comfort, entertainment and knowledge. The shift toward social and psychological evolution should result in a greater awareness of our supposed role as responsible stewards and our ethical obligations to the rest of the biosphere. The greater our intervention, or our power to effect change, the more aware we should be of our ethical obligations.

Unfortunately, many people perceive ethics to be little more than a statement of personal opinion. There is no doubt that a person's ethical arguments often produce an answer that is remarkably close to the individual's own *weltanschaung.* But this does not mean that one cannot educate professionals, beginning with the high school science student, to develop skills that promote sound analysis and effective decision making in social and public policy.

CHAPTER 8

Primate Research: Monkey Puzzle or Creative Science

Any human activity measured in the billions of dollars is going to be associated with a substantial bureaucracy. Scientific research is no exception. In the physical sciences, the only immediate losers as a result of red tape and bureaucratic infighting are the human competitors. In biomedical research, however, the animals used as models or as research and testing tools may also suffer. Primate research in the United States, especially as organized in the Primate Center program, provides a number of examples of "monkey business" and of the impact of a science bureaucracy on the lives and fates of research animals. However, let us first examine the background to research using primates and to their present care and use.

Development of Primate use in the Laboratory

Monkeys and apes, or nonhuman primates as they are commonly called, have a long history as laboratory animals. Galen based his anatomical knowledge on ape and pig dissection, and others have followed in his footsteps, although Claude Bernard refused to experiment on monkeys because of their resemblance to human beings (Schiller 1967). Few of the early studies using primates were particularly systematic; thus, Professor David Ferrier, who conducted an extensive study of the brain using living monkeys, in 1873, is credited with establishing the monkey as an experimental animal (Ross 1963).

After the First World War, primate research began to take hold. In Britain, Leyton and Sherrington (1917) published a paper reporting data from 22 chimpanzees, 3 gorillas and 3 orangutans. In the 1920's, Voronov was transplanting monkey testes to man in rejuvenation cures in Europe. In Russia, Sukhumi was being established as a primate research center; ultimately it became the example on which the American Primate Center program was based. In the U.S.A., Hartmann (1932) conducted extensive research on rhesus monkeys, while Yerkes was establishing a chimpanzee research colony in Florida. However, it was not until after the Second World War that the nonhuman primate was elevated to its current status as a research animal.

The main event leading to the expansion of primate research was the development of the polio vaccine in the 1950's. Enormous numbers of rhesus monkeys were exported from India for poliomyelitis vaccine development (table 8.1).

Inevitably, research scientists with other interests started to explore the opportunities presented by this influx of primates into the Western world. The demands of the vaccine program peaked in the late fifties; by 1978, it was estimated that of the 14,015 rhesus monkeys required for biomedical programs in the United States, less than half were destined for vaccine testing or other testing programs (National Primate Plan 1980)

Primates are used in a wide variety of research projects. According to the Institute for Laboratory Animal Resources (1975), the majority are used in pharmacology and toxicology (25%), neurophysiology

TABLE 8.1
IMPORT OF PRIMATES INTO THE U.S.A.
RHESUS MONKEY IMPORTS AND USE

	Total Primate Imports	Total Imports	Rhesus Imports and Use	
			Medical Research	Pharmaceutical
1952	32,000			
1956		128,634	16,079	111,555
1958	223,000			
1960	221,000	107,819	13,040	97,776
1962	162,000	53,978		
1964	115,000	47,905	5,328	42,577
1968	126,857	30,933		
1973	69,528	25,413		
1975	40,814	15,339		
1978	29,578	348		

SOURCE: Adapted from Conway 1965; LeCornu and Rowan 1979; and Greenhouse 1980.

(16%), vaccine production and testing (12%), infectious disease research (10%), and cancer research (9%). Reproductive physiology, behavior, experimental surgery, physiology, dental research, and other disease studies make up the bulk of the remainder.

A few years ago, the Interagency Primate Steering Committee (IPSC) published a National Primate Plan (1980), which estimated the annual research and testing demand for nonhuman primates (table 8.2). Between the time that these estimates were first made (the same table appeared in the 1977 draft of the final document) and their eventual publication in 1980, the import situation had changed dramatically. India had banned all export of rhesus monkeys in 1978, followed a year later by Bangladesh, which effectively cut off any further supplies of wild-caught rhesus. Nevertheless, the IPSC, in a classic example of bureaucracy in (slow motion) action, did not modify their projections of primate use at all.

Most users began to switch to cynomolgus macaques. For example, Malaysia had exported approximately 10,000 cynomolgus annually

TABLE 8.2
U.S. ESTIMATED NATIONAL REQUIREMENTS FOR NONHUMAN PRIMATES IN BIOMEDICAL HEALTH PROGRAMS—1977

Species	Required by Law or Reg.	Production of Biologicals	Testing	Research	Total
Rhesus macaque	5,300	200	1,160	7,355	14,015
Cynomolgus macaque	900		100	5,005	6,005
Other macaque				995	995
Gibbon				100	100
Squirrel monkey		300	1,100	3,045	4,445
Owl monkey			250	1,215	1,465
Saguinus species			800	1,390	2,190
Common marmoset				170	170
African green monkey	750	500	15	810	2,075
Baboon				1,282	1,282
Chimpanzee			40	140	180
Other				990	990
Total	6,950	1,000	3,465	22,497	33,912

SOURCE: National Primate Plan 1980.

from 1975 to 1977, but in late 1978 and early 1979, export increased to an annual rate of approximately 15,000 monkeys. Malaysia then also instituted a partial ban and in 1980 exported (to bona fide biomedical users) 3,194 cynomolgus (Nordin 1981).

As a result of these actions, American domestic breeding programs were increased. By 1980, over 7,000 primates, mainly rhesus, were being produced annually throughout the United States (Soave 1981) (table 8.3).

In the meantime, the rhesus has lost favor as a research primate and the cynomolgus has taken over. The Primate Clearinghouse lists (an organization for advertising available research animals or animals for sale) carry many notices of available rhesus monkeys, as investigators either switch to other species or give up primate research altogether. Paradoxically, there is now such a surplus of home-bred rhesus that government representatives are seeking buyers for their contract-bred animals.

Nonhuman primates are "essential" for relatively few research programs. A special study group of the Committee on Medical Research (EEC) drew up a partial list (table 8.4) of the need for primates in various areas. Even then, the "essential" need for macaques for toxicology and teratology can be disputed. Dayan has noted that "in research and development of drugs for man and evaluation of their safety, it is striking how limited has been the contribution of experiments in nonhuman primates" (1978, pp. 691–2). He does admit that only a primate is suitable for some needs (e.g., hepatitis testing and testing of antihuman lymphocyte globulin), but

TABLE 8.3
U.S. BREEDING OF NONHUMAN PRIMATES—1980

	Primate Centers	Contracts	Other	Total
Rhesus	1,284	3,500	900	5,689
Other macaques	635	150	100	885
Baboons	33	100	200	333
Chimpanzees	15	2	—	17
Owl monkeys	14	—	51	65
Squirrel monkeys	128	75	130	333
Marmosets	63	—	135	198
Others	136	—	—	136
Total				7,656

SOURCE: Adapted from Soave 1981.

believes that there are very few areas in pharmacology and toxicology for which primates are essential.

Housing. Although primates account for the use of only 20,000 to 30,000 laboratory animals a year, their phylogenetic closeness to human beings demands a special status. This means that primates should be accorded extra consideration. A psychologist who does some work with primates has commented:

> Some years ago I made a discovery which brought home to me dramatically the fact that even for an experimental psychologist, *a cage* is a bad place in which to keep a monkey (Humphrey 1976, p. 241).

He found that a rhesus monkey, from whom the visual cortex had been removed five years earlier, rapidly recovered almost perfect spatial vision after only a week of being taken for walks in the fields. During the previous five years, the monkey had been in a cage and showed no indication of recovering any three-dimensional vision. Humphrey concluded that the limits on the monkey's recovery had resulted directly from its impoverished living conditions.

Primates are generally housed in laboratories under conditions that are not just impoverished, there is almost no environmental enrichment. There have been a few initiatives to change this, but far too many primates spend their lives (a chimpanzee can live for fifty years in captivity) in barren cages that provide little more than room to turn around and stretch. Relatively simple changes can make a world of difference. Housing the animals on woodchip litter rather than bars or bare floors has been shown to reduce aggression by a factor of five (Chamove and Anderson 1979).

McGrew (1981) comments that the vast majority of nonhuman primates in captivity live in pathogenic conditions. In both laboratories and zoos, the mental and physiological health of captive monkeys are liable to suffer. This is especially regrettable since many of the conditions are the result of ignorance and could be remedied or ameliorated with relative ease.

The Indian Ban. The orderly and relatively uneventful course of primate research was rudely interrupted in April of 1978, when the Indian government banned any further export of rhesus monkeys. The Interagency Primate Steering Committee had forecast an annual American need for 14,000 rhesus monkeys out of a total demand for nonhuman primates of 33,912. (National Primate Plan [1980];

TABLE 8.4
NEED FOR PRIMATES FOR BIOMEDICAL RESEARCH AND TESTING
A PARTIAL LIST

Species	Essential	Highly Desirable
Chimpanzees	Hepatitis B Hepatitis "non A—non B"	Hepatitis A Human cancer virology Certain cardiovascular diseases Antifertility Production of antiserums to human tissue and cancer antigens
Macaques: rhesus and cynomolgus	Production and testing of vaccines (mainly poliomyelitis) Toxicology and teratology	Reproductive physiology and antifertility Endocrinology Diagnostic virology (kidney cell cultures) Immunology and transplantation
New World monkeys: mainly marmosets	Hepatitis A Hepatitis "non A—non B" DNA and RNA tumor viruses Hematopoetic chimerism Malaria studies (owl monkeys)	Teratology, reproductive physiology and antifertility Cardiovascular diseases Pharmacology and toxicology Immunology and transplantation Slow virus diseases Odontology and ophthalmology Nutrition
Baboons		Reproductive physiology Human cancer virology

SOURCE: Adapted from Committee on Medical Research 1978.

the discussion draft with the same figures was issued in 1977). Since India was then the only supplier of rhesus monkeys, the sudden elimination of 40% of the country's primate supply, resulted in some rapid and frantic reordering of priorities. The circumstances leading up to the ban and subsequent efforts to reopen the rhesus trade make for an interesting story.

In 1955, India had banned the export of rhesus monkeys because of the appalling mortality rate in their capture and transport and the general concern expressed by animal protection groups. However, because this was at the beginning of the polio vaccine era, scientists all over the world protested the ban. As a result, India reopened the trade on the understanding that the monkeys were to be used humanely, that they were to be used only in medical research and vaccine production, and that the U.S. Surgeon General would sign a certificate of need for each order of rhesus monkeys. Wade (1978a) notes that the agreement also contained a statement that the monkeys "will not be used in atomic blast experiments or for space research." The Division of Research Resources at NIH was responsible for reviewing requests but, by 1977, the original elements of the agreement appeared to have faded into the bureaucratic background.

> The bubble burst in May, 1977 when Anthony Tucker of the Manchester Guardian (UK) wrote a story about the U.S. Navy "irradiating and burning monkeys to death" to determine how long combat personnel can function after massive neutron radiation. This research was conducted on rhesus monkeys by the Armed Forces Radiobiology Research Institute (AFRRI) in Washington and, according to Defense Nuclear Agency director R. R. Munroe, these experiments on rhesus monkeys were "vital to our national security" (Wade 1978a, pp. 280–81).

The question of whether AFRRI was in compliance with the Indian agreement was never explicitly resolved. The U.S. Department of State advised their Embassy in India that the reports that rhesus were "being used for purposes other than for medical research . . . are not factual" (1977). AFRRI argued that they were not using the animals in atomic blast experiments. The animals were exposed to radiation, which only *simulated* the effects of atomic blasts (Wade 1978a). Some individuals also tried to represent the research as primarily medical (studies of radiation sickness), but reports filed with the Smithsonian Science Information Exchange (Numbers ZQP–90247–1 and ZQP–9024B–1) specifically noted that these studies were performed to model the behavioral response or performance capability of combat personnel. India never gave explicit reasons for terminating the export of rhesus monkeys, but there is little doubt that U.S. compliance with the 1955 agreement was, at best, questionable and many believe that the radiation experiments were an important development prompting the Indian action.

After India announced its intention to ban the export of rhesus monkeys, the United States began to look for ways around the embargo or to seek to change the Indian position. One approach was an attempt to influence the Indians via a World Health Assembly Resolution, in May, 1978, which would highlight the serious consequences for world medicine of a continuing rhesus export ban. Support for a draft resolution was initially good, but it faded away when one or two African countries threatened to accuse the United States of using monkeys in neutron bomb testing.

Meanwhile, the United States was exploring the possibility of obtaining rhesus monkeys from Nepal, Burma, and Bangladesh. Bangladesh appeared to be a particular target. In March of 1977, Mol Enterprises of Oregon had reportedly been awarded an exclusive permit to export rhesus monkeys. In 1978, a telegram from the U.S. Embassy in New Delhi to the State Department noted:

> America is making frantic efforts to get as many rhesus monkeys as it can from various sources. It had recently entered into an agreement with Bangladesh for supply of these animals. Bangladesh does not have enough of these monkeys to meet American requirements. But, it is reported that large number of these monkeys are being smuggled out of India to Bangladesh (U.S. Department of State 1978).

In May 1978, Abdul Hamid, Chief Conservator of Forests in Bangladesh, confirmed that, in his opinion, Bangladesh could not sustain the necessary level of exports to supply America and suggested an upper ceiling of 1,000 animals a year. He also noted that Mol Enterprises had made no move to build a breeding farm as required under the original agreement.

Several hundred rhesus monkeys were exported by Mol Enterprises in 1978, the bulk going to the National Institutes of Health, which sent about 30 males to AFRRI. This was not a wise move. When Shirley McGreal of the International Primate Protection League learned of this, she notified contacts in Bangladesh that AFRRI had some Bangladesh rhesus monkeys. A week later, Bangladesh terminated the Mol Enterprises agreement because Mol had not built the breeding center and because the monkeys had ended up at AFRRI "for neutron bomb radiation experiments" (International Primate Protection League 1979).

The Bangladesh monkey saga continues. According to a Wall Street Journal report (March 26, 1981), the U.S. Embassy has continued to apply pressure to get the trade reopened and a U.S. State Department official was quoted as saying that "aid could be cut off. We don't want to threaten, but there's a stage when this has to come into play." Eventually, two U.S. senators and a presidential science advisor were also drawn into the effort, but without success (Heneson 1982).

AFRRI is not the only Defense Department research establishment that uses monkeys. The School of Aerospace Medicine (SAM) in San Antonio, Texas, has also been using monkeys in radiation and laser beam studies. Donald Barnes, a psychologist at SAM since 1964, began to question the relevance of these studies in 1979 and, in January 1980, he was dismissed from his post, allegedly for not completing assigned tasks. (Barnes was reinstated after he protested his dismissal.) Barnes went public with his concern, relating a gruesome tale of monkeys being trained to perform meaningless tasks by severe electric shock treatment (International Primate Protection League, 1980). Not surprisingly, the School of Aerospace Medicine denies these charges, but disturbing questions remain about the self-perpetuating nature of the studies, about the lack of independent peer review in study approval, and about the lack of utilization of the data from the monkey studies.

Three years after the Indian ban, military research on monkeys has come under fire, but biomedical research has not collapsed. Furthermore, many primatologists now acknowledge that the ban has had a beneficial effect. Domestic breeding programs have been established and projects proposing the use of monkeys are more closely scrutinized. Despite the alarmist rhetoric that emanated from NIH and elsewhere after the Indian ban, the rhesus monkey has been shown to be far less essential than was claimed.

The Polio Vaccine Story. The original Indian ban of 1955 was lifted primarily because of the need for primates in the production and testing of the new polio vaccines. Polio has never been a major killer, but its ability to leave a child struggling in an iron lung and crippled for life horrified the public. As a result, the war against polio was waged in a highly charged, emotional atmosphere that was not helped by media hype and high-pressure fund raising (Wilson 1963). Between 1953 and 1960, well over a million monkeys died, many en route to the laboratories, as Salk, Sabin, and others raced to be the first to develop an effective vaccine. There is no doubt that some monkeys were necessary to develop and produce the vaccine. On the other hand, there is also little doubt that many animals were wasted. Twenty years later the situation has changed dramatically and we are very close to developing the technical capability to eliminate all but a very few monkeys from polio vaccine production and testing.

There are two types of polio vaccine. The Salk vaccine consists of viruses that have been inactivated or "killed" by treatment with formaldehyde. The vaccine is usually administered in three doses, separated by several months. The Salk vaccine dominated the field until the early sixties when it was replaced by the live Sabin vaccine in all but a few countries (e.g., Scandinavia and the Netherlands). The Sabin vaccine consists of live, attenuated viruses that are "too weak" to cause polio but that still elicit a strong immune response. The vaccine can be given orally and in very small doses (1,000 times smaller than the Salk vaccine) because the viruses grow and multiply in the body. As a result, the Sabin vaccine is far cheaper; it also results in a "pass-on" effect as children who have taken the vaccine infect those who have not.

The Sabin vaccine appears to be associated with paralytic poliomyelitis in a few isolated instances (Boffey 1977). The Salk vaccine had some early problems, notably the 1955 Cutter disaster, when more than 200 children contracted polio after vaccination. This was due to inadequate inactivation of the viruses and technical problems in the safety testing. In recent years, however, there have been no failures and no known cases of Salk vaccine causing polio.

Monkeys may be used in two stages in the manufacture of both vaccines. Freshly prepared monkey kidney cell cultures are used to grow the virus for the vaccine batches, while live monkeys are used in the monkey safety test (Salk vaccine) or neurovirulence test (Sabin vaccine). The majority of monkeys have been and still are used in the production stage, although the development of more efficient techniques has steadily reduced the demand. The Salk vaccine and, in most countries, the Sabin vaccine are produced on monkey kidney cell cultures. It is possible to grow Sabin vaccine on human cells, which may be subcultured to produce an enormous number of cells for virus growth substrate. Nonetheless, only Britain, Yugoslavia, and Iran have succeeded in making acceptable live vaccine from human cell lines. Dr. David Magrath of the National Institute for Biological Standards and Control (NIBSC), in London, says:

> I think it is odd. I think they've been unlucky. We don't know enough about what results in a good vaccine to know where other manufacturers have gone wrong. It is certainly true that we have examined diploid cell vaccines from other countries and agree that they were not suitable for license (Marten 1981b, p. 20).

There are distinct advantages to producing Sabin vaccine on standardized human cell lines, because each new batch of monkey kidney cell cultures must be carefully screened to check for extraneous agents. Up to 50% of monkey kidney cell cultures may have to be discarded because of viral contaminants (Beale 1978). It is not, however, economically feasible to produce Salk vaccine on human cell cultures because the yield of virus from human cells is lower for some reason (Beale 1978). Since one needs 1,000-fold more viruses for the Salk vaccine, a high-yield growth substrate is vital.

Several possible ways to increase virus yield from a given volume of culture medium are being followed up. Microcarrier (bead) techniques can greatly increase the surface area of cells in a fixed volume of culture medium but have not been particularly successful to date (Mered et al. 1981). Cell suspension cultures are another possibility (Petricciani, Hopps, and Chapple 1979) although there is some nervousness about using them to produce human vaccines because cells grown in suspension usually have tumorigenic properties. However, the monkey Vero kidney cell line does not appear to be tumorigenic even though it grows indefinitely. The Institute Merieux, in France, has already made Salk vaccine from Vero cells but is waiting for permission to test the vaccine in field trials (Marten 1981b). Use of this cell line could eliminate the need for primary monkey kidney cell cultures in the production of the Salk vaccine.

Monkeys are also used in the safety testing of both Salk and Sabin vaccine (chicks or guinea pigs are also used). There is no immediately foreseeable alternative to the monkey neurovirulence test for the Sabin vaccine, although the number of monkeys required was halved in 1980 when scientists, searching for a way to reduce the need for rhesus monkeys in the wake of the Indian ban, eliminated the intracerebral injection of viruses, keeping only the intraspinal injection.

The monkey safety test (MST) for the Salk vaccine, however, could be eliminated immediately. The MST is a legacy of the Cutter incident in April 1955. Before this, vaccine safety was assessed by a tissue culture test for "live" virus particles and by intracerebral inoculation of monkeys (U.S. Department of Health, Education and Welfare

1954). After April 1955, the monkey test requirements were increased and became cast in stone despite the fact that the tissue culture test was more sensitive (Technical Committee on Poliomyelitis Vaccine 1956). In 1957, Frank Perkins, who was then working for the Medical Research Council (U.K.), demonstrated that the tissue culture test was more sensitive and more accurate in detecting live virus particles than the MST. However, nobody listened, and the report was never published (Marten 1981b).

Today, Perkins is Chief of Biologicals at the World Health Organization (WHO) and a leading proponent of arguments to eliminate the monkey safety test. In 1979, a WHO expert group reviewed the Salk vaccine testing requirements and, as a result, the WHO has issued a recommendation that the MST be dropped. The recommendation will not, however, be binding on any country, and it is by no means certain that Salk vaccine producers will adopt it. The shadow of Cutter lingers on, twenty-five years later. As Hennessen notes: "It seems remarkable that after the accumulation of much evidence by which experts recommended the abandonment of a monkey safety test" for the Salk vaccine, the test is "still required unchanged by national control authorities" (1980, p. 170–1).

Revising the standards for safety testing and the cell substrates on which the vaccine is grown solves only part of the problem. A substantial reduction in the demand for monkeys for polio vaccine production and testing would still necessitate a major shift from the Sabin vaccine—which is used by most countries—to the Salk vaccine. Salk lost the original battle in the early 1960's but has recently reopened the debate (Boffey 1977; Salk and Salk 1977). However, there is no enthusiasm for such a switch. Economics is only part of the problem. (The Salk vaccine is about 25 to 50 times more expensive per dose, using standard production methods, according to Frank Perkins [personal communication 1981].) One expert asked: "Why rock the boat. We are doing so well that to shift now would make me nervous" (Marten 1981b).

While research gradually eliminates the obstacles to the production of a polio vaccine that does not require monkeys, fear of the consequences of a change, bureaucratic inertia, and economic considerations all militate against a change in the near future. The polio story provides an excellent example of an unexploited alternative.

Chimpanzees in the Laboratory. There are approximately 1,000 chimpanzees in laboratories in the United States (Graham and Hodgen 1979). The major colonies include those at Yerkes Primate Center in Georgia; Bastrop (NIH "storage" colony) in Texas; Gulf Research, Louisiana; Alamagordes, New Mexico University; Laboratory for Experimental Medicine and Surgery in Primates, New York; and Southwest Foundation for Research and Education, Texas. Most of the chimpanzees in U.S. laboratories have been imported from West Africa. For example, Franz Sitter and Suleiman Mansaray, the two major Sierra Leone dealers, exported 1,144 chimpanzees between 1973 and 1978 (International Primate Protection League 1979). Of these, approximately 50% went to the United States, and a further 20% to Japan.

However, the supply of wild-caught chimps for laboratories has been sharply reduced in the wake of the Convention on International Trade in Endangered Species and publicity about the wastefulness of the capture techniques used. The most popular method of capture has usually involved shooting mothers and other kin to obtain infants and juveniles of less than five years of age, resulting in the death of four or five animals for every one exported. In 1978, the Interagency Primate Steering Committee of NIH noted that chimpanzee numbers are in sharp decline throughout Africa and that the chimpanzee is already extinct in some regions (National Institutes of Health 1978a).

Faced with the reduction in supply, as well as opposition from conservationists to further chimpanzee export from Africa (Wade 1978a), the Interagency Primate Steering Committee gathered together about forty laboratory primatologists into a Task Force on the Use and Need for Chimpanzees to assess current and future U.S. medical research needs. Their report (National Institutes of Health 1978b) demonstrated absolutely no appreciation for the realities of the situation.

The steering committee's report estimated an annual use of 735 animals with a projected import demand of 300–350 (see table 8.5). By contrast, the discussion draft of the National Primate Plan (1980), which was issued in 1977, estimated that only about 180 chimpanzees would be required annually for biomedical programs. The figures in the IPSC document include not only demands for chimpanzees for totally unjustified research programs (e.g., toxicology), but also grossly inflated estimates for the need for chimpanzees in other research areas.

The report suffers from a number of other shortcomings. First, the task force states that its evaluation has "clearly shown that [the chimpanzee] is absolutely essential for research on several important human diseases." While it is true that the chimpanzee is an important,

TABLE 8.5
IPSC ESTIMATES OF U.S. DEMAND FOR RESEARCH CHIMPANZEES

	Current Use	Future Annual Demand
Behavioral sciences	n.g.*	50
Infectious diseases—hepatitis	156	314
—other	46	46
Neurological diseases	n.g.*	45
Hematology, immunology, immunogenetics	150	50
Toxicology and pharmacology	200	100
Reproductive biology	85	50
Other (aging, aerospace, etc.)	25	80
Totals	662+	735

SOURCE: Adapted from Interagency Primate Steering Committee (National Institutes of Health 1978b).
* Not given

and perhaps essential, research model in some areas, the task force report contains no specific references, only a general bibliography, and certainly does not substantiate its claims with detailed evidence. The reader is asked to accept sweeping generalizations, some of which are incorrect while others provide little perspective on why the chimpanzee is such an essential research model.

Second, the task force report does not adequately consider the implications of its projected demand of 300–350 chimpanzees per year. Current breeding pograms in the United States produce only about 40–50 animals a year (the major chimpanzee facilities contain about 750 animals altogether) leaving a projected annual import demand of 250–300 animals. Given the decline in chimpanzee exports, one would expect the report to provide some specific guidance as to how, and from where, these animals are to be obtained, but none is forthcoming.

Finally, the task force report glosses over such ethical questions as the problem of capture techniques (if chimpanzees are to be imported) and the moral issue of using chimpanzees in the first place (Davies 1980; Prince 1981). The IPSC must address these issues publicly and expand its current role of ensuring adequate supplies of primates for biomedical research programs. If it did this, its publications might begin to read more like scientific documents and less like semitechnical marketing proposals.

The LEMSIP-SFRE Dispute. The Laboratory for Experimental Medicine and Surgery in Primates (LEMSIP) in New York was established in the mid-sixties. From the start, LEMSIP had a different philosophy from the other primate centers. The facility acted more as a service center for those who were interested in using primates in research and did not concentrate on developing a major intramural research program as did the seven named primate centers. However, this did not stop LEMSIP from seeking primate center status, and the associated financial underpinning. Although it was never successful, the laboratory did manage to obtain some core support from the Division of Research Resources (DRR) as well as one or two other major NIH contracts, which allowed the facility to continue to operate.

LEMSIP has been a leader in hematology research and, in 1974, it was awarded a five-year contract from the National Heart, Lung and Blood Institute (NHLBI) to breed chimpanzees for hepatitis studies and to co-ordinate hepatitis research projects. NHLBI was prepared to underwrite the expensive program of breeding chimpanzees for hepatitis research since this is the only disease in which chimpanzee research models are virtually essential (Wade 1978b). By any measure, LEMSIP was very successful in carrying out the NHLBI contract. In five years they had 63 pregnancies from 35 breeding females, 20 of which were on the NHLBI contract. Their record of preventing hepatitis cross-contamination between and among humans and chimpanzees has been superb.

In 1978, NHLBI issued a Request for Proposal (RFP—seeking bids to conduct specified research) for the continuation of the breeding program. The two finalists were LEMSIP and the Southwest Foundation for Research and Education (SFRE), in Texas. According to NHLBI, the facilities were given very similar ratings by the site visit team and therefore the contract was awarded to the lower of the two bidders—SFRE ($505,000 versus $1.1 million from LEMSIP). LEMSIP protested the circumstances of the award, and animal welfare groups argued that the successful breeding program would not survive the move; subsequent reports confirmed that they were correct.

Unfortunately, for both NHLBI and DRR, LEMSIP did not accept the decision. In an unprecedented move, New York University (of which LEMSIP is a part) brought suit against NIH over the issue. This was the climax of a history of strained relations between LEMSIP and the DRR (Sun 1980) in which the chimpanzees were unwitting pawns.

When LEMSIP learned that they had lost the contract, they consulted with John Stanford—the contract officer, and others from NHLBI and proposed the following timetable for removal of the animals. Twelve animals would be shipped on July 30, 13 animals on August 20, and 23 animals (the breeder panel) on September 17, 1979. The remaining 23 animals were all juveniles on research protocols and would be shipped on completion of the investigations, but no later than January 3, 1980. Additional funds would be required for maintenance of the adults and preparing the animals for transport. The 23 juveniles under experiment would have involved no extra expense to NHLBI since their per diem cost would have been assumed by other research budgets.

This proposed timetable was rejected by NHLBI, which ordered all the animals to be moved by August 31, two months after the contract had ended. NHLBI thus forced several research studies to be cut short and justified this move by arguing that they had ordered LEMSIP not to accept any research projects that extended beyond the end of June, 1979. Research is, of course, rarely quite this ordered.

The transport of the animals took place in a highly charged atmosphere. The 71 animals were moved by truck (the journey taking more than 40 hours) in three groups between July 24 and September 8. The second group of animals arrived at SFRE on the morning of Thursday, August 30. All the animals were fed and watered the next day, but some were not fed and watered over the weekend. Apparently, one of the responsible technicians had missed the briefing session and was off duty on that Friday. Therefore, when he came in over the weekend, he did not know that chimpanzees were now housed in three previously empty units. On Monday morning, one adult chimpanzee was found dead in his cage. Three weeks later, another adult was found dead. In both instances, the cause of death could not be determined. Five more adults died between November 16, 1979, and February 12, 1980, and one infant was found dead on February 15.

As predicted, the animals suffered severe trauma as a result of the move. In the first year, according to a special summary report by the SFRE veterinarian, the 71 NHLBI chimpanzees were still in much poorer condition than the 96 SFRE chimps and suffered persistent problems from anemia and parasitism. After two years, the NHLBI colony at SFRE had fallen from 71 animals to 68. SFRE was nowhere near meeting its contract goal of 20 new animals in the two years. It should be noted that these were the same animals which made up the core of the successful LEMSIP breeding group.

This sorry saga illustrates only too clearly how badly animals fare when they become enmeshed in the political battles of human beings. In retrospect, it is clear that either SFRE's lower estimate for the contract was inadequate or the manner (and speed) in which the animals were removed from LEMSIP resulted in such severe trauma that the breeding colony never really recovered.

The Primate Research Centers. The seven Primate Research Centers in the United States (table 8.6) are the centerpiece of primate research in this country but they have been dogged by mismanagement and overmanagement. In 1981, a comment that "it is an open secret that the primate center program has fallen far short of its proposed potential and that it is an expensive white elephant" (Rowan 1981a, p. 41) drew the following response from the chairman of the IPSC:

> The primate center programs have continued to withstand the scrutiny of peer evaluation, and there are a number of reports which attest to their value. Rowan chose to cite two critical reports. One was published in 1976 by two former staff members of the British Medical Research Council following a brief visit to the United States five years earlier in 1971. The length of their visit limited the number of personal contacts and time available for a careful review of those programs. His other citation takes statements out of context from an NIH-sponsored study. . . . I would prefer to take the view of various study sections, councils and the Congress, which . . . have concluded that these are important centers meriting the expenditure of funds for their support (Held, 1981, p. 10).

Study sections and Congress have been known to make mistakes and, in any case, must rely almost exclusively on material and input from the very NIH bureaucrats who are being criticized for poor management. The above arguments are, therefore, not particularly overwhelming. Furthermore, scientists outside the primate research centers have continued to express dissatisfaction about the program, as noted by a recent NIH-sponsored study (JRB Associates 1979). We need, however, to provide some background.

In 1960 and 1961, a few years after a visit to the Sukhumi primate center in Russia by an NIH official, Congress was persuaded to appropriate funds to establish a primate research center program (Whitehair and Gay 1981). By the end of 1965, seven centers had been constructed and had become fully operational (table 8.6).

TABLE 8.6
Regional Primate Research Centers

Name and Address	Major Research Areas
California Primate R.C. Univ. of California Davis, CA 95616	Perinatal biology Respiratory diseases
Delta Primate R.C. Tulane University Covington, LA 70433	Microbiology Parasitology
New England Primate R.C. Harvard University Southborough, MA 01772	Pathobiology Psychobiology Nutrition
Oregon Primate R.C. Oregon Health Sc. University Beaverton, OR 97005	Reproductive biology
Washington Primate R.C. Univ. of Washington Seattle, WA 98195	Developmental biology Endocrinology
Wisconsin Primate R.C. University of Wisconsin Madison, WI 53706	Primate behavior Reproduction Neuroscience
Yerkes Primate R.C. Emory University Atlanta, GA 30332	Great ape reproduction Physiology Behavioral research

The objectives of the program as established in 1960 were these (Goodwin and Augustine 1975):

1. Pursue basic and applied biomedical research directed toward solution of human health problems
2. Establish a resource of scientists in many disciplines who are trained in the use of primates and can help maintain both continuity and high scientific quality in research
3. Provide opportunities for research and training that might not otherwise be available to visiting scientists, research fellows, and students
4. Determine which problems of medical research are best pursued with nonhuman primates and which species are superior for particular studies
5. Develop improved breeding practices in order to increase the supplies of pedigreed, disease-free primates for research
6. Study the natural diseases of primates and techniques of importation, housing, and management, which influence the animals' well-being and suitability for studies

7. Develop new methods and equipment for primate studies
8. Supply biological specimens to qualified investigators
9. Disseminate the findings of studies done at the centers to primate users and others.

While success stories for each of the nine objectives can undoubtedly be found, the true test must rely on an overall cost-benefit evaluation. Two recent government sponsored reviews deal with the primate center program, by Bolt, Beranek and Newman, Inc. (1976) and JRB Associates (1979). While both noted that the primate centers had succeeded to some extent they also pointed to many deficiencies. Perhaps the most important was the fact that the centers, in general, had not achieved the reputation of being "the place to be" in the scientific community (JRB Associates 1979, p. 4). The Bolt, Beranek and Newman, Inc. report notes also that the research has not always been of high quality, although there are exceptions. Furthermore, not all centers have served sufficiently well as regional resources. The use of the centers by outside scientists has declined even further since 1976, according to JRB Associates.

It would be surprising if the Primate Research Center program had been totally successful, given the diversity of the tasks assigned to it. However, the indications are that it has suffered from a number of shortcomings and that the research is expensive, considering its quality. For the amount of money expended, one would expect a better overall product. Over 70% of the total laboratory animal resources budget is now spent on the primate centers and it is by no means clear that such a concentration of resources is either desirable or cost-effective. The animal welfare movement (via Mobilization for Animals) is highlighting the primate center program, and calling for major changes, but there are one or two specific questions about the concept and its implementation that need answering.

First, should the primate centers develop their own core research, funded by noncompetitive grants under the close (too close?) aegis of the Division of Research Resources, or should they become service centers for the local research community, as exemplified by LEMSIP?

There is no question that LEMSIP has serviced good research. This has been acknowledged by DRR and others. A 1971 British review of the U.S. program noted that LEMSIP "runs on a fraction of the budget of the Regional Centers and yet is generally acknowledged to produce excellent results and give good value for money, especially to visiting workers" (Hobbs and Bleby 1976, p. 37).

LEMSIP is certainly cheaper. In the 1975 financial year the primate centers received $12.5 million of DRR funds and supported $12.3 million of outside research. (Bolt, Beranek and Newman, Inc. 1976, p. 7). By comparison, LEMSIP received only $0.2 million of DRR funds but supported $6.5 million of outside research. However, DRR does not approve of such service orientation and has deprived LEMSIP of funding because it does not have a theme for its research (Sun 1980).

The primate centers do have themes for their research but the true value of what they produce would only be identified if there were a program of steady reductions in their core support, thus throwing their efforts open to market forces. Researchers would be required to recover costs in their grant proposals, including allocations for their own time on a project and the full cost of animal care and maintenance. If this were done, we would have a better measure of just how essential primate research in the centers really is. For example, is it really *that* important to find out why human males go bald or lose sexual vigor as they grow older (Whitehair and Gay 1981)?

Another shortcoming in the Primate Reseach Center program has been the stated long-term commitment to domestic breeding with little or no movement toward such a goal until the last few years. In addition, mortality in the primate centers has been and remains very high (table 8.7), raising questions about the manner in which the centers have sought to understand and control primate diseases. In spite of testimony before Congress on 1982 DRR appropriations, where it was stated that "less than 1% of the deaths were the result of fighting, disease problems, etc," the figures in table 8.8, taken

TABLE 8.7
MORTALITY IN THE PRIMATE RESEARCH CENTERS, 1975 AND 1979

	Holding on Jan 1, 1975	Deaths	% Mortality	Holding on Jan 1, 1979	Deaths	% Mortality
California	1811	237	13.1	1816	243	13.4
Delta	905	250	26.3	2222	662	30.0
New England	1135	316	27.8	1379	299	21.7
Oregon	1760	232	13.2	2540	389	15.3
Washington	1474	530	36.0	1532	596	38.9
Wisconsin	922	123	13.3	1114	108	9.6
Yerkes	1421	188	13.2	1285	154	12.0

SOURCE: Adapted from International Primate Protection League 1978, p. 14; Annual Reports of Primate Centers

from the annual reports of the primate centers, demonstrate these claims to be false.

Most centers lose about 10% or more of their holdings every year to incidental diseases and other causes of mortality that are not related to experimental procedures. Yerkes has the best record, although even 7% losses are probably too high and there should be a general policy of trying to get such mortality down below 5% per annum.

Conclusion

The use of primates in research has generated a great deal of controversy; it is an area in which a representative, national group could probably serve a useful function. The Bolt, Beranek and Newman, Inc. (1976) report recommended the establishment of a body to serve as a primate study authority.

At present, the Interagency Primate Steering Committee and the primate subcommittee of the Animal Resources Board perform some of the suggested functions. However, these committees either do not consider ethical cost-benefit issues, or do so in an inadequate manner. At the very least, any primate study authority should be composed or representatives from relevant Federal agencies and medical primatologists (both supporters *and* critics of Federal programs), as well as public representatives from conservation and animal welfare organizations. A primate study authority should have the authority to deal with a wide variety of questions and to formulate policy. It

TABLE 8.8
MORTALITY OF TOTAL STOCKS NOT ASSOCIATED WITH EXPERIMENTS
(ACTUAL NUMBERS DYING)

	1975		1977		1978		1979	
	%	No.	%	No.	%	No.	%	No.
California	16.4	(116)	11.6	(184)	8.4	(153)	10.0	(203)
Delta	14.5	(131)	*		20.9	(451)	*	
New England	11.7	(133)	*		13.4	(161)	12.7	(175)
Oregon	7.3	(129)	*		9.9	(217)	9.1	(232)
Washington	14.8	(218)	*		24.4	(348)	*	
Wisconsin	8.7	(80)	7.2	(75)	*		*	
Yerkes	8.9	(126)	*		6.9	(88)	*	

SOURCE: Adapted from International Primate Protection League 1978, p. 14; Annual Reports of Primate Centers.

* Breakdown not available.

should also have the confidence of both the research community and interested members of the public (in so far as that is possible). It would be simple to broaden representation on existing committees to include a wider range of concerns and, best of all, it would cost no extra money.

CHAPTER 9

Animal Behavior and Psychological Research

The study of animal behavior and its application to human problems goes back to the beginning of reflective thought and the telling of allegorical stories, such as Aesop's fables or even earlier verbal myths. Long before Darwin's theories upset the Victorians, human beings had tacitly believed that animal behavior could help to explain the human psyche. However, it was not until the end of the nineteenth century that academics began to move away from anecdotes of clever animals and anthropomorphic descriptions to a systematic study of animal behavior.

The early "experimental psychologists" had first to set standards that would minimize anthropomorphic wishful thinking. For example, eminent academics allowed themselves to be fooled by Clever Hans, a horse that purportedly could answer questions requiring mathematical and other knowledge by tapping out the answers with his hoof. However, Hans was not clever, merely an astute observer. He was reacting to unconscious cues from the questioners and would thus stop tapping when they indicated that he had reached the correct answer. If the questioner did not know the answer, then "Clever" Hans became confused and frustrated (Wade 1980). To avoid further problems of this sort, Morgan (1894) introduced the idea that no action should be interpreted as being due to a higher behavioral function if it could just as easily be explained by reference to a lower function. Morgan also urged the introduction of experimental methods, as opposed to the common observational and anecdotal methods. Morgan's canon served a useful purpose, but his principle of parsimony was taken too far.

In 1913, John Watson initiated the behaviorist tradition. He argued that, if psychology ever wished to take its place in the world as a natural science, it would have to discard all reference to consciousness. Psychologists, especially from the mentalist school, should not delude themselves into thinking that they were making mental states the object of their observations. Watson proposed observations on, and behavioral measurements of, intact organisms. He provided the main impetus toward research with animals, although Thorndike had been conducting learning studies on animals since 1898, and other psychologists had also dabbled in animal research. Watson felt that the nonverbal nature of animals indicated the absence of cognition (Franchina 1979), thus helping to perpetuate the Cartesian tradition. Watson also proposed that the behaviorist should recognize no dividing line between human and animal, and that animal behavior research was of interest in its own right regardless of any application to the human condition.

Griffin (1981) notes that rejection of introspection and romantic mentalism at this time was meant to be a temporary measure that was based on sound scientific reasons. At the time, psychologists had no meaningful techniques for studying such mental processes as consciousness, feelings, and the like. Griffin comments that, unfortunately, later generations of behaviorists first forgot the reason for the rejection—and then finally lost sight of the fact that anything had been forgotten in the first place. Whatever the eventual impact, behaviorism flourished and psychology began to overcome its anecdotal beginnings.

In 1923, Watson introduced Pavlov's work on the conditioned reflex to the United States and indicated how Pavlov's techniques permitted observations that could be measured and duplicated. This enabled investigators to study sensory processes in an objective manner. In fact, there were some who even suggested that thought processes could be studied via the motor habits of the larynx since speech is a mode of thought. Pavlov provided more than a technique that produces measurable and repeatable data. Because his discoveries were developed from a base of psysiological research, behavioral scientists were encouraged to think that a truly "scientific" psychology could now be developed.

Subsequent leaders in experimental psychology increased and extended the use of animals to investigate learning, memory, motivation, mother-infant interactions, language, and psychopathology.

Rats, in particular, became very popular as research animals, and their growing use coincided with a big jump in the number of papers on conditioning and learning (Beach 1950). Nevertheless, relatively little psychological research actually involves animal studies. In 1979, only 7.5% of the articles abstracted in *Psychological Abstracts* involved animal research (Gallup and Suarez 1980). These authors also deny claims by Bowd (1980b) that work with animals holds a particularly prestigious position within the psychological profession.

The use of animals in psychological research has not usually been perceived as a major ethical problem. The situation is changing now as a result of increasing pressure from animal welfare groups. However, too frequently experimentation on animals is justified simply because we cannot do to people the things we do to animals (Franchina 1979; Waters, Rethlingshafter, and Chadwell 1960). There are many things that we cannot do to people but this does not mean that they can all be done to animals. The general guidelines developed by the American Psychological Association (1979) and other professional groups are usually little more than platitudinous endorsements of avoiding animal suffering where possible. They provide little specific assistance to those who wonder about particular techniques, such as food deprivation. For example, is it appropriate to reduce animals to 80% of their free-fed weight by restricting food intake, or should we establish 85% of free-fed body weight as the lower limit? This is the type of question that needs to be addressed before we can even begin to claim that we have adequate guidelines for animal research.

It cannot be denied that animal behavior research has led to new knowledge and that some of it has been applied to broaden and improve the therapies available for disturbed individuals. Adams, for example, outlines a range of new knowledge derived from animal research.

> The majority of what we know about how people learn began years ago in psychological research laboratories based on studies using animal subjects. Such everday concepts as reinforcement and reward emerged from carefully controlled animal studies that would not have been appropriate for human subjects, but that clearly have helped the human condition (1981, p. 441).

Adams notes that biofeedback, or the conscious control of what are usually considered to be automatic bodily functions, such as blood flow, heart beat, and muscle position, has been successfully employed to treat such diverse problems as curvature of the spine, high blood pressure, migraine headaches, insomnia, and low back pain. This all started when psychologists began to investigate conditioning of the autonomic nervous system in the rat.

Of behavior modification and behavior therapy (approaches to changing how an individual acts in certain situations), Adams comments:

> The techniques would not have come to being without early and continuing psychological research on what influences animal behavior. Today, both have been documented literally hundreds and perhaps thousands of times in improving the lives of hospitalized mental health patients and in developing effective therapies for psychological disorders. The techniques also are gaining notoriety because of their successful application to problems of obesity, alcoholism, and drug addiction.
>
> What has been less publicized is the effect of such behavioral programs in the industrial sector. For example, Emery Air Freight Company recently reported that a behavior modification program with its employees has increased its use of productive capacity from 45 to 90 percent, with savings of more than $2 million over three years (*Organizational Dynamics,* 1973. 2, Winter, 41–50).
>
> A behavioral program also has been used to teach job finding skills to the unemployed of our country. The cost of placement in this *Job Finding Club,* as the program has been called, was an incredibly low $167 per person *and* the participants in the program were twice as likely to secure and retain employment as those using other employment programs (*Behavior Research and Therapy,* 1975, 13, 17–27). The Job-Finding Club concept has now raised considerable interest in the Department of Labor for use in placing clients who otherwise would be eligible for welfare (U.S. Department of Labor, Report No. DLMA-51-17-76-04, 1978). Not only does this Club concept stem directly from principles of learning first investigated through animal research, but the job club's developer is one of the foremost animal learning psychologists in this country (Adams 1981, pp. 442–3).

The concept of learned helplessness and its application to the study and treatment of depression is also mentioned as an important breakthrough stemming from psychological research on animals. It was shown that when an animal is placed in a stressful situation from which it cannot escape and which it is unable to control, it quickly gives up and displays "helplessness." If the animal is later given the chance to escape, it will not do so unless forcibly shown that it can avoid the stressor. The animal studies of learned helplessness have earned the opprobrium of animal welfare activists, but the information has even been used to support animal welfare arguments (Fox 1982a), thus raising some difficult animal welfare questions (Fox 1982b). In fact, Fox (1982b) notes that he finds learned helplessness studies morally repugnant but that "even so, such research is of value in convincing those who, in treating animals as unfeeling things, can cause unnecessary suffering" because it is only objective, controlled laboratory data that can convince scientists that animals are sentient.

Other advances also mentioned by Adams include chimpanzee language acquisition research, phobia desensitization resulting from basic learning studies on animals, and Roger Sperry's demonstration that the two hemispheres of the brain are separate and communicate with each other only through a connecting band of nerve fibers. This last research has led to major advances in the understanding and treatment of epilepsy, stroke, language disorders, and brain damage. In memory research, disorders of remembering were commonly thought to result from injury to memory traces (i.e., parts of the brain that are modified by learning and experience). However, animal research indicates that few, if any, injuries destroy memory traces, and the majority of memory failures are due to impairment of access to memory traces that are latent, but intact. According to Adams, this discovery has important implications for memory loss in the elderly.

While animal research has, therefore, led to advances in our understanding of human behavior and psychology, the behaviorist tradition has come in for particular criticism. Thus, Kitchener (1972) and Rollin (1981) argue that behaviorism has not led to any important new theoretical insights (this is, of course, disputed by behaviorists). Whatever the merits of either side in this debate, behaviorism has certainly produced techniques that have proved useful in a range of situations. It has also indirectly stimulated a resurgence of interest in the concepts of animal awareness (Griffin 1981) and animal mind (Gallup 1982) as techniques were developed that could possibly be used to investigate these issues.

Nevertheless, there are those who see no use in animal studies. Bannister (1981) argues that animal experimentation cannot be valid for a psychology which seeks to define itself in terms of what we think being human is all about. Experimental psychologists have tended to confine research to those topics or phenomena that can be studied in animals. These phenomena are, he claims, not particularly useful when discussing human psychology because they tend to deny feelings, emotions, reflective thought, and self-awareness. Therefore, in the case of those behaviorist studies that deny animals such mental states, Bannister would probably support the idea that behavior studies on planaria would be just as satisfactory as studies using mammalian models (Best 1973).

Koch (1981), too, questions whether psychology can be a "science" and categorizes much of the development of psychological research and knowledge as scientific role playing. In support of this, he refers to a 1979 Americal Psychological Association (APA) initiative that sought to achieve scientific legitimacy via legal and legislative means, and ridicules the implied attempt to prounounce psychology a "true" science by legislative decree. This sort of initiative can obviously be ridiculed, but that does not imply that one can neatly categorize all psychological research on animals as nonsense and a waste of time. It is not. However, animal research in psychology can be criticized and some of it deserves to be.

Criticism of Animal Research

Several psychologists have criticized animal research from an ethical perspective in the last few years (Bannister 1981; Bowd 1980b; Fox 1981, Heim 1979a; Ryder 1975; Sperlinger, 1981), and the animal welfare movement has begun to focus on the discipline as an easy target. Others (Griffin 1976; Lockard 1968; Menzel 1967; Moore and Stuttard 1979) have questioned the mechanistic assumptions inherent in some psychological research. Thus, Griffin (1976) observes that behavioral scientists are uncomfortable with the very thought of mental states or subjective qualities in animals. When such notions intrude on scientific discourse, there is a tendency to shield reductionist egos and terms such as "fear", "pain" and "pleasure" behind a respectability blanket of quotation marks.

Ten years earlier, Menzel had argued that we tend to be too situation- and technique-oriented in defining what we mean by science and fail to address the primary problem of what sort of questions we want answered. When this primary issue has been settled, then we must ensure an accurate perspective. According to Menzel:

> The more I see of primate behavior both in the laboratory and in the field, the more I feel that psychology is doing everything it can to cover up and hide its real problems in a welter of tests, techniques, statistical machinations and *a priori* assumptions as to what is important in behavior (1967, p. 172).

Menzel argues that the real problem is relating the phenomena of animal and human behavior as such, and achieving the correct perspective to see what is really there. Thus, Guthrie and Horton's (1946) studies on cat learning were hopelessly compromised because they did not recognize that the task in question required behavior that was also the species-specific greeting behavior (Moore and Stuttard 1979). The cat was required to jostle a vertical rod in the cage as part of its task. However, cats will rub up against a vertical surface as part of their greeting response. This reaction, as any cat owner knows, is readily elicited by the sight of a human, including the investigators in the 1946 studies.

This sort of ignorance should be eliminated among psychologists who work with animals. However, too many students are taught to perceive the animal as little more than a reaction mechanism, and many seem unable to overcome this initial training. Heim (1979b) was particularly scathing in her presidential address to the Psychology Section of the British Association for the Advancement of Science. She castigated researchers for oversimplification of inconveniently complex data, for ignoring mental phenomena in animals, and for hiding behind a welter of mechanistic jargon.

Across the Atlantic, Bowd (1980b) has voiced similar criticisms and has specifically commented on the need for more consideration of ethical questions in psychological research projects that are likely to cause pain or suffering. Gallup and Suarez (1980), while agreeing with the need for more attention to ethical issues, denied some of Bowd's allegations. For example, they note that a strictly mechanistic approach to animal behavior has been pretty much abandoned by all but a few Skinnerians. Mason (1976) allows that the great apes have mental experiences, and there is a growing interest in the concept of animal awareness and animal mind (cf. Griffin 1981; Dawkins 1980; Gallup 1982). Nevertheless, psychology journals contain too many papers that treat animals as reacting devices and data generators rather than sentient and suffering beings. Of course, animals are both reacting mechanisms and sentient beings (certain simple human reflex arcs can easily be described as reacting mechanisms—and, presumably, data generators. The sentient natures of research animals need to be recognized by more behavioral scientists and experimental psychologists, and research protocols modified accordingly, to respect the capacity for animal suffering and feeling.

The recent landmark anticruelty case involving the care of monkeys in neurophysiological-cum-behavioral research provides some classic examples of mechanistic thought. The animals were used in deafferentation research, in which the nerves carrying sensations from the arm of a monkey were severed so that it had no feeling. A number of monkeys had attacked their own deafferentated limbs, resulting in severe mutilation. However, those defending the research have commented that the animals do not feel pain because the afferent nerves have been cut. The question of awareness and of the mental states of such animals is just not admitted as being pertinent (see Rowan 1982a).

Response of Professional Societies to Ethical Issues

The growing concern over the ethical issues of using animals in psychological research have filtered through to both the British Psychological Society (BPS) and the American Psychological Association. In Britain, a strongly worded resolution at the 1977 BPS Annual Meeting, calling for an inquiry into the ethics of animal research, was only narrowly defeated. As a compromise, the BPS undertook a general study of how animals are used in psychology (British Psychological Society 1979), but their findings and subsequent activities have not satisfied some of their more outspoken members (Heim 1979a).

The BPS study reported that psychological research accounted for approximately 8% of the annual British use of laboratory animals. Over 80% of the 43,000 animals used were rats. Mice, pigeons, and other birds comprised most of the remainder. The monkey was also an important research animals but was used in relatively small numbers. Approximately 50% of the animals were used in observational studies involving little or no intervention. Of the remainder, 15% were involved in drug studies, 15% in relatively severe deprivation protocols, and 10% each involving surgery or electric shock treatment.

The report noted that British psychologists appeared adequately committed to the need for technician and student training in specialist techniques and specific behavioral adaptations of the species under study. In student exercises, most of the teaching departments indicated that students could, on conscientious grounds, opt out of courses involving live animal work. However, the inquiry found that students are frequently not informed of this option.

The BPS report also suggested three general principles that should be used to guide the researcher who uses animals. First, the researcher should always apply the criterion of likely human benefit (admittedly a matter of subjective judgement) when deciding between different research strategies. Second, psychologists should beware of carrying out animal experiments merely because they are possible, rather than because they contribute to knowledge. Third, the psychological experimenter should ensure that no alternatives exist that involve a lower ethical cost.

On the question of ethics, the BPS committee determined that psychological research on animals raises no unique ethical problems. However, this conclusion is incorrect. Most individuals believe that the important properties setting us apart, in moral terms, from other animals are our mental functions such as rationality, self-awareness, ability to suffer pain and pleasure, and linguistic ability (philosophical arguments notwithstanding). Factors such as similarities of biochemistry, physiology, hair form, and color do not carry any such moral connotations. Therefore, in determining the ethical constraints on different research projects, we are guided, not by biochemistry or physiology, but by the functional capacity of the nervous system. As a result, the psychologist must confront ethical questions that stem from the *essential* elements of his or her research, unlike the biochemist or physiologist, who may be interested in muscle function—and no one considers mobility a criterion for moral consideration. Of course, the particular muscle being studied may be in an animal with a very complex nervous system carrying many human functions and, therefore, there will be major ethical questions. Nevertheless, the moral issues do not stem from the organ system under study as they do in psychology research.

We thus come to the psychologist's paradox. Since we should, if consistent, confer moral worth according to some property (or properties) of the organism's nervous system, then the more suitable the animal is as a model of the human psyche, the greater should be the attention to the ethical issues relating to the research. The paradox boils down to this—the better the animal is as a model of the human psyche, the more restricted its use should be. As a result of this paradox, psychologists using animal models to gain insight into human psychology must show:

1. That the animal is being studied in a manner that does not raise moral issues, using human criteria as a guide but not necessarily as absolute standards; or

2. That the animal is sufficiently different from human beings in its psychological and mental makeup to create no moral problems *and* that it is still a relevant model for learning about a particular question in human psychology; or

3. That the animal's psyche has relevant similarities to the human psyche, but that this does not create a moral problem.

If the last option is chosen, one needs more than a statement of opinion. The reasoning behind the opinion should also be given. The situation is, perhaps, a little different for those behaviorists who do not believe in animal (or human?) mind, but then one must identify the bases for discriminating between humans and animals and show how these affect the moral consideration accorded the animal.

There have been relatively few detailed attempts to justify the use of animals in experimental psychology, but a contribution by Marcuse and Pear (1979) stands out, as does a more recent discussion by Davis (1981). The Davis argument is particularly interesting in that if focuses specifically on the ethical problem of aversive stimulation in humans and animals. He comes to no easy answers but does quote some intriguing research results in which animals appeared to invite electric shocks rather than avoid them as they could have done.

Marcuse and Pear are much more dogmatic than Davis in stating that "animal research is not only desirable but is ethically mandatory" since our knowledge of factors producing human suffering "is so limited that if animal research has even the vaguest possibility of contributing to the human field, it should be done." It is perhaps not surprising that they should come to this conclusion since they argue that social conditioning accounts for our ethical behavior, such as it is, and that the relevant social conditioning arises out of evolutionary selection, which encourages a group to act in ways that promote its survival. This reasoning falls into the classic trap of the naturalistic fallacy, namely, that what *is, ought* to be. They go further and suggest that behavioral science will, in time, explain precisely how values originate, how they interact, and how they relate to the survival of the culture. These are grand claims but the notion of a "science" of ethics, which is implied, seems a little too far-fetched.

Marcuse and Pear do not, on the other hand, dismiss humane concerns. They recognize that the issue of "talking" animals raises peculiar moral issues and suggest that a culture that treats its own members well will tend to give good treatment to members of other species exhibiting "intelligence" or humanlike behavior. In addition, they note that "strong emphasis should be placed on giving animals the best treatment that is compatible with other considerations" regarding the good of the culture.

Silverman (1978) has also raised ethical issues, in a student text, arguing that, while it is legitimate to use animals in behavioral research, the experiments had better be good. In addition, he questions the all too prevalent use of intense and inescapable shock in routine animal psychology studies and classroom exercises, studies on shock-induced aggression in rats, and prolonged immobilization of primates in restraining chairs. He notes that a cost-benefit analysis is necessary when planning an experiment and suggests that the researcher should ask, "How great is the likely benefit to mankind at large? What is the private benefit to the experimenter, in terms of money, prestige, or the Ph.D.? *And what is the cost to the animal?*" (p. 28; emphasis added). One can, of course, continue to debate the moral issues surrounding psychological research, but I only wished to raise the issue before discussing a few specific examples.

Case Studies

Harlow's Research. Most animal welfare literature that addresses psychological research on animals focuses on Harlow's studies on "mother-love" and separation in rhesus monkeys. Terms describing some of the devices used—for example, the rape rack, the well of despair, and monster mothers—are quite evocative enough in themselves to bring a flood of scathing criticism and condemnation from animal welfare and antivivisection quarters. On the one side, animal welfare publications condemn Harlow for the extent and grotesqueness of his deprivation and separation techniques. On the other side, psychologists point to Harlow as one of the major figures in experimental psychology and attest to the importance of his work.

The problem posed by Harlow's work is a perennial one. In the bright light of hindsight, it is difficult to explain why some work is very important while other studies seem to be ignored. Those not steeped in the subject under discussion will have even more difficulty gaining an accurate historical perspective. On the one side, animal welfare advocates point to the fact that both Bowlby (1960) and Spitz (1945) produced data suggesting the importance of mothering in human children, and this work apparently provided key elements underpinning the primate work.

On the other hand, Horenstein (1977) bemoans the fact that he and his clinical colleagues are ignorant of the potential role of comparative psychology in dealing with complex human problems, particularly child abuse. He indicates that studies by Seay, Alexander, and Harlow (1964) on isolation-reared monkeys have pointed the way to possible therapies—for example, teaching abusive mothers normal maternal behavior and motherliness and providing the abused child with opportunities for normal peer interaction in a supervised nursery setting. To the animal welfare advocate, this hardly sounds like startling innovation (even assuming that one can entice abusive mothers into a training clinic). It sounds a lot more like a common-sense approach to the problem than one requiring either animal research or animal suffering to reach.

Two factors account for Harlow's notoriety among opponents of animal research. The first, and trivial factor, was his flippancy. For example, he once said that because he found monkeys annoying creatures he did not worry about what he did with them. His colleagues contend that this was not true and that he was probably just trying to shock the interviewer. On another occasion, he advised authors of papers in the *Journal of Comparative Physiological Psychology* to use footnotes, giving credit to others for all the ideas in the paper, in order "to protect one's reputation, since most experiments are not worth doing and the data obtained not worth publishing" (Harlow 1962). It is clear from the context of the advice that this was more of Harlow's humor, but the statement has been extensively misquoted in animal welfare literature to support the view that psychological research on animals is useless.

The second, and far more telling, complaint concerns the extent of the intervention with the animals' lives in Harlow's research. There is no question whatsoever that Harlow's research monkeys suffered a great deal, and some have argued that Harlow did not need to use such extensive deprivation and aversive stimulation. Thorpe (1974), a behavioral scientist well-known for his concern for animal well-being, made the following comment on Harlow's work.

> Thus Harlow has developed four basic techniques for producing psychopathic states in monkeys. They are (1) partial and (2) total isolation, (3) repetitive peer separation, and (4) restriction within a vertical chamber. Cruel and horrible as these experiments certainly are, they have had results of great value, since they lend themselves to the study of related biochemical and hormonal factors and to the determination of the efficiency of therapeutic techniques, either chemical or behavioural. And there is a brighter side to the picture. As Harlow says, "We now know that love at every stage of transition may be scientifically seduced *[sic]* and separated; but happier far, the jumbled pieces of the primate jigsaw puzzle may hopefully be reassembled" (p. 236).

Thorpe also notes that the Harlows were shocked by the unexpected and devastating success of their deliberate attempts to produce primate psychopathology. They then followed up this work with studies of re-education and psychotherapy, demonstrating that the condition of "patient" monkeys could be improved by monkey "therapists," and that abusive mothers could become nearly normal mothers if their first infant survived their brutal attentions. Thorpe (1974) noted that these results were surprising when they were produced and that they are "clearly of a greater promise and will perhaps make many of the critics of the Harlows' horrible experiments take a rather different view and look at them with enlarged perspective" (pp. 236). Animal welfare critics are, however, unlikely to be appeased by this. To them, Harlow's research involved just too much animal suffering, and they will continue to ask whether more humane and more natural techniques, such as those used by Hinde (1970), could not have done just as well.

Aggression and Punishment Studies. Electric shock is a widely used aversive stimulus in psychological research. Although psychologists argue that the electric shocks are mild, this is not necessarily so in aggression and punishment research where they can be very severe. For example, Ulrich and Azrin (1962) compared the effects of different frequencies and intensities of shock on the reflex fighting response to aversive stimulation. The intensities were varied from 0.5 to 5 milliAmps. The authors noted that two out of four Wistar strain rats died after exposure to 2 milliAmp shocks, and they also reported that the fighting reflex was very resistant to fatigue. A pair of rats continued to show the reflex fighting response over a period of 7½ hours, during which they were subjected to 18,000 shocks. It is perhaps not surprising that, at the end of this time, the rats were "damp with perspiration and appeared to be weakened physically."

Drewett and Kani (1981), critical of this work, commented that intraspecific fighting "elicited by natural phenomenon could be of scientific interest, but fighting elicited by a wholly artificial stimulus is not necessarily of any interest; still less, of course, are parametric studies of the effects of an artificial stimulus necessarily of any special interest" (p. 185). Ulrich, himself, has now rejected these experiments in no uncertain terms. In fact, in 1977, he wrote to the *APA Monitor* that he was pleased that this early research had been criticized.

> Initially my research was prompted by the desire to understand and help solve the problem of human aggression but I later discovered that

the results of my work did not seem to justify its continuance. Instead, I began to wonder if perhaps financial rewards, professional prestige, the opportunity to travel, etc., were the maintaining factors and if we of the scientific community (supported by our bureaucratic and legislative system) were actually part of the problem . . ." (Pratt 1980, pp. 42–43).

Dr. Ulrich's conversion was supported by at least one of his colleagues, one Dr. Robert Brown, who wrote that he and others "no longer believe that the scientific information derived from the type of experimentation we previously conducted merits the imprisonment, torture and extermination of any member of any human or non-human species, and that continued research of this sort should stop" (Pratt 1980, p. 45). These statements are fairly damning; they make clear that insufficient attention has been paid to the ethical issues surrounding aggression research and whether it is likely to provide any unique insights into clinical problems.

Electric shock is not only used to elicit aggressive behavior, it is also widely used as an aversive stimulus (cf. Davis 1981). R.L. Solomon's work on traumatic avoidance learning with dogs, for example, took aversive control to its virtual limits, and Campbell and Masterson's (1969) studies on the "psychophysics of punishment" have come in for recent criticism. Drewett and Kani (1981) commented that there might well be some scientific justification for a systematic study of detection and aversion thresholds for electric shock, but that determination of the death threshold was an example of work of exceptional cruelty for which there was no scientific justification.

Psychopathology: Animal Models. Gallup and Suarez (1980) note that significant recent developments in the treatment and understanding of such problems as phobias, drug addiction, depression, ulcers, and childhood autism (reviewed in Maser and Seligman [1977]) are tied directly or indirectly to the results of animal experimentation. However, Reines (1982), in a study commissioned by the New England Antivivisection Society, disputes this claim. He notes that current animal models of psychopathology do not come close to meeting the four requirements for validity that were specified by McKinney and Bunney (1969). (Of course, there is a chicken and egg question here since researchers hope that such models will lead to improved understanding of human disorders and hence better animal models.)

These criteria require that the animal model and the human mental illness have similar causes, symptoms, responses to treatments that are effective in the clinical illness, and neurobiological mechanisms. Since our knowledge of human psychopathology is very limited, it is hardly surprising that the animal models and their related human diseases often do not match.

For example, according to Paul:

> The validity of any experimental model of human psychopathology will naturally depend on the similarities between the model itself and the clinical disorder. For this reason, the difficulties inherent in defining schizophrenia as a unitary disorder, or in simply identifying core symptoms, will undoubtedly continue to plague future attempts at developing such a model (1977, p. 384).

Maser and Seligman also indicate that the advent of animal "models" for mental illness has not led to many undisputed clinical advances, nor is there a consensus that they have particularly advanced our understanding of human mental disorders. The advances that can be attributed to this animal research must also be weighed against the animal suffering encountered in studies using models of mental disorders—models that by definition are likely to involve unpleasant initiating or training procedures.

In "learned helplessness," one of the proposed models for human depression syndromes, an animal is shocked under circumstances from which it is unable to escape. It soon "learns" that it is helpless and huddles motionless during the shock treatment. The "conditioned-avoidance" model involves conditioning an animal to press a lever whenever a bell is sounded in order to avoid receiving an electric shock. This model is widely used to search for antipsychotic drugs. Physical restraint, sometimes associated with other noxious stimuli, is used to investigate the psychosomatic components of ulcer formation in animals. These models, in turn, have been criticized on methodological grounds (Mikhail, Kamaya, and Glavin 1978). Experimental "neuroses" are induced in animals by placing the subject in a situation that presumably involves a strong conflict, for example, pairing food with an electric shock.

These are only a few of the ingenious techniques used to create psychopathology in animals. Most involve some sort of aversive stimulation. These stimuli may be powerful or very mild, as in the line of "nervous" pointers developed by Reese (1979) to study human psychopathology. These "nervous" dogs act normally under the antianxiety drug, chlordiazepoxide, and they also interact normally with other dogs. However, in the laboratory in the presence of humans, they will retreat, urinate, and adopt a rigid, immobile position.

Reese proposes that these "nervous" dogs rapidly condition aversively to humans by selectively responding more to negative than to positive reinforcements in the laboratory environment. He also notes that the laboratory received the Lassie Award for excellent treatment of dogs but it is, nevertheless, not a dog's paradise, and certainly many experiences with researchers may be aversive reinforcers. Thus, even in this case where the negative stimuli are very mild compared to others encountered in a psychological laboratory, animal suffering is still a problem.

Despite the animal suffering involved, one certainly cannot characterize all studies of animal psychopathology as useless. However, the serious ethical questions raised by such research have largely been ignored or brushed aside with meaningless platitudes about humane care. No one denies the anguish that mental disease produces in humans. If the animal models replicate some or all of the human syndrome, then this research, and a great deal of other animal research, must be re-evaluated from an ethical standpoint. To date, the Ethical Paradox of the experimental psychologist has been scrupulously avoided by most experimental psychologists.

Conclusion

One psychologist has spoken out (Segal 1982), thereby helping to start the process of ethical review: "We never seem to question our treatment of laboratory animals and the brutalizing effect of some of our practices on ourselves and our students. . . ." She argues that scientists react with contempt for animal welfare advocates who "don't understand science" but that this is too simple a dismissal. Psychologists must "ask about *each* experiment . . . whether the harm we will be doing our animal subjects is balanced by the potential contribution to the welfare of the biosphere" (p. 116).

This is not going to be an easy task. In a first-rate analysis of human attitudes toward animals, Burghardt and Herzog describe the inconsistencies and fickleness of human beings.

> We suspect that currently it is impossible to derive from science, theology, philosophy, or any conceivable source a consistent, universal set of principles to guide humans in dealing with members of other species. But then, no ethical system has been universally accepted for our dealings with conspecifics. And interspecific ethical problems are qualitatively different. There are too many competing biological and economic factors involved, and, more significantly, psychological de-

> mands often preclude rational resolution of the issues. Some of our decisions are based on irrational but often understandable preferences (e.g., cuteness: baby features.)
> That there are serious difficulties in simple or sophisticated extensions of arguments extending "human rights" to other animals does not invalidate the recognition that immense and largely unnecessary mistreatment of other animals is occurring worldwide and especially in modern technological societies. Constructive approaches are possible and should be aggressively applied (1980, p. 767).

Psychologists thus have a very important role to play in helping to smooth out our inconsistent attitudes and behavior, but too few have made the attempt. On a less ethereal and more practical level, many initiatives are possible. Lea (1979) has suggested ten points that would certainly reduce, but not eliminate, animal suffering in psychology research.

1. In physiological psychology, substitute recording for stimulation and stimulation for lesion techniques wherever possible. The point here is to minimise the damage done to the brain; there is no experimental evidence that this does minimise suffering, but it seems obvious that it must, at least on average.
2. Wherever intervention in the brain is contemplated, try to find case histories of humans who have suffered damage to the relevant areas of brain, and find out what distress they were caused; such information may help you choose between techniques that seem superficially similar.
3. Many experiments on learning involve unnecessary degrees of deprivation, conventionally 23 hours' deprivation of food or water. Water deprivation should only be used if thirst is the specific subject of the study: it affects animals' condition much more severely than food deprivation. Rats normally leave only 2–4 hours between meals, and 6 hours' deprivation will get them working for food reward almost or quite as well as 23 hours, at least in Skinner boxes (mazes may be more difficult). The same may well be true of water deprivation, since most animals drink mostly in association with meals. If longer deprivation seems to be necessary, it may be because the experimental situation is frightening, which should in itself be cause to question your procedures.
4. It may be possible to avoid deprivation altogether, by using as a reward a preferred food that is not present in the normal well-balanced laboratory diet. Non-deprived rats will usually work well for sucrose, or for oil; non-deprived hamsters will

run mazes for wheat grains or sunflower seeds, even if they are regularly given seeds in their cages. It is necessary to think before introducing odd rewards, however. Oil rewards can give rats liver trouble, for example.

5. Another way of avoiding deprivation is to take the experiment into the animal's living cage, so that he works for his food as and when he wants it, and any deprivation is self-imposed, as it would be in the wild. This is the "free behaviour" situation: its advantages are discussed by Moran (1975).
6. It is sometimes possible to carry out learning experiments on free-living animals, without sacrificing too much experimental rigor: for two successful examples, both involving pigeons, see Baum (1974) and Morgan et al. (1976).
7. If caged animals must be used, choose your caging arrangements carefully. Social animals like rats should always be housed in groups; individual housing is almost certainly cruel and probably disturbs behavior (it is also inefficient: three rats housed together need no more exercise space than one). Of course, one must make sure that the groups won't fight; often this is just a matter of using a big enough cage. You can't cage pigeons together, for example—but you can keep a hundred in an aviary which takes up much less space than a hundred individual cages.
8. Combinations of these research strategies are better than taking them on their own. For example, Harless (1972), Graft et al. (1977) and Markowitz (1975) have all used free behavior situations with groups of animals living in roomy enclosures.
9. Try to avoid punishment or avoidance tasks, and use positive reward instead. This point is made more on grounds of intuition than experimental evidence, since rats at least seem astonishingly stoical, and often show no visible long term reaction to pain at all; and they will take quite severe electric shocks to find a mate, though not to obtain food unless grossly deprived; see pre-war studies in Warden's obstruction box, reviewed by Munn (1950).
10. If aversion training must be used, consider alternatives to electric shock—loud noises or bright lights can be effective, and so can species-specific threat stimuli. No doubt these are all distressing, but shock is distressing and painful, and so seems clearly worse (Lea 1979, pp. 20–1).

These proposals may not be perfect, but they could at least act as points of departure for meaningful and constructive discussion on more specific guidelines for the use of animals in psychology research. In the final analysis, however, psychological research on animals that results in animal pain and suffering is always likely to evoke intense criticism from at least some animal welfare advocates. At present, there are good grounds for such criticism. Positive, constructive, and responsive action still needs to be taken by the psychology profession. If not, outside regulation or funding cutbacks for animal research as a result of animal welfare protests is a possible outcome by the end of the decade.

CHAPTER 10

The "Pound" Animal Battle

In 1946, the National Society for Medical Research was founded to promote the benefits of animal research. One of their first major initiatives was aimed at the "waste" of pound animals. Shelters and pounds were euthanizing millions of dogs and cats every year and were therefore seen as a major source of supply for the growing number of animals required for research and training. The NSMR, therefore, worked for the passage of state laws and city ordinances requiring shelters, usually only those that received tax dollars, to turn over unclaimed animals when requested. These measures have come to be known as "pound seizure" laws, reflecting humane society outrage at the fact that shelters and pounds are forced to turn over dogs and cats to research institutions.

In the first few years, the NSMR was very successful. The first state law was passed in Minnesota in 1949. Other states followed in short order, and it was clear that the majority of the public supported the practice. In Baltimore, a city ordinance mandating pound animal release was passed in a public referendum by a vote of 2 to 1. In Los Angeles, a similar referendum went in favor of pound seizure by a 3 to 2 vote in spite of the active opposition of the powerful Hearst press.

Rodman (1977) has speculated that the practice of pound *seizure* broke an uneasy forty-year truce between medical research and the humane movement. Whether or not this is true, there is no doubt that laws mandating the release of unclaimed pound and shelter animals have sparked a great deal of opposition from animal welfare and antivivisection groups. This is because pound seizure struck at the very core of the humane movement, namely a suffering-free sanctuary for animals which, at the very least, guaranteed a painless death. There are pounds and shelters that do not meet even this minimal standard, but this fact does not diminish the overall protest against pound seizure by the humane movement. It should also be noted that early negotiations seeking some sort of compromise between research and humane interests were undermined by the NSMR (Stevens 1978).

By 1973, Visscher (1973) reported that Hawaii, Maine, and Pennsylvania had state laws prohibiting release of pound animals, while Connecticut, Iowa, Massachusetts, Minnesota, New York, Oklahoma, South Dakota, Utah, and Wisconsin had laws mandating the release of animals from state-supported and subsidized shelters, on request from licensed research institutions. The other states had no general laws dealing with this issue, although there were numerous local ordinances covering the subject.

The Changing Tide

Although the humane movement had won a few victories in the pound animal battle (viz., the prohibition in Pennsylvania and Hawaii—Maine researchers had no real demand for dogs), the research community held the upper hand until the middle of the seventies. By this stage, the humane movement reformation had passed through its first cycle and many animal welfare groups were protesting against animal research—and the use of dogs in particular. In 1975, *Animal Liberation* (Singer) sparked the beginning of the second cycle in which such protest became increasingly activist and more soundly rooted in sophisticated moral theory.

There were sporadic campaigns against pound seizure all over the country, but the focus of the new thrust against the practice was the Metcalf-Hatch Act, in New York State. In 1952, Article 5 of the New York Public Health Law was amended so that municipal pounds and privately financed shelters with a pound contract or other municipal support were obligated to surrender unclaimed animals to research institutions on request. Immediately after the law came into effect, several humane societies in the state gave up their pound contracts so they could not be forced to release animals. However, the ASPCA, the major humane society in the state, continued the tradition of not opposing animal research and supplied animals requisitioned by laboratories until 1971, when the practice was stopped without serious challenge from the laboratories (Pratt 1976).

Throughout the seventies there was growing pressure to repeal the Metcalf-Hatch Act. This effort was spearheaded by the Society for Animal Rights and by Citizens for Animals; it led, in 1977, to a 110 to 22 vote for repeal by the New York State Assembly. However, the bill for repeal was blocked in committee in the Senate. Then, in 1979, a larger coalition of New York and national groups pushed the repeal bill through both the Assembly and the Senate, in the latter by 44 votes to 13, and it was signed into law by the Governor.

The repeal of the Metcalf-Hatch Act in 1979 had great symbolic importance for animal welfare groups. It is no surprise, therefore, that the victory in New York sparked many other efforts to repeal pound seizure legislation (or to pass laws prohibiting the release of pound animals). In 1980, Governor Grasso of Connecticut signed into law a bill that not only repealed the state's pound seizure legislation but also prohibited the release of animals from shelters in the state to research laboratories. In Wisconsin, a small change in their law, which effectively stopped the release of pound animals, was also pushed through the legislature.

In Massachusetts, there have been repeated efforts over the past few years to repeal chapter 49A (the pound seizure law) and to prohibit the voluntary sale of unclaimed animals in public shelters to research facilities or animal dealers. Nancy Payton, then of Massachusetts SPCA, argued thus in testimony in support of repeal:

> a) Unclaimed shelter animals (many of which are former pets) are the least suitable candidates for research from a humane viewpoint because the research laboratory atmosphere is foreign and threatening;
> b) responsible animal control is undermined by pound seizure laws because many people, believing that animals brought to a public pound may be surrendered for research, will abandon them instead; and
> c) pound seizure encourages the view that laboratory animals are cheap, disposable tools (Payton 1981).

By contrast, representatives of research institutions in Massachusetts argued that they require less than 2% of the 250,000 pound dogs euthanized annually in the state, that the animals are treated humanely, that the financial impact would be dramatic (approximately $200 extra expenditure for each dog), that medical, surgical, and veterinary education would be seriously hampered, and that supplies from alternative sources are not plentiful. The pound seizure bill has so far survived, thanks in part to a vigorous lobbying effort by Harvard University, but observers from both sides are predicting that Chapter 49A will be repealed sooner or later.

In Minnesota, recent efforts to repeal the pound seizure law have been singularly unsuccessful, but a similar initiative in Los Angeles succeeded. In fact, the debate in Los Angeles attracted the attention of scientists all over the country (Rosenfeld 1981), apparently because the original L.A. proposal not only dealt with pound seizure but also included a proposal to create external ethical review boards for *all* animal experimentation. However, the final recommendation from the Department of Animal Regulation to the L.A. City Council was limited to the pound seizure issue. This recommendation proposed that the section of the Municipal Code mandating the release of unclaimed, impounded animals for the purposes of medical research should be repealed, since repeal was necessary to "restore full public confidence in the Department of Animal Regulation and to facilitate the return of lost pets to their rightful owners" (Rush 1981).

On the other side, Dr. Albert Yellin of the University of Southern California School of Medicine argued (*Los Angeles Times,* Jan. 15, 1981) that barring the use of unclaimed pound animals would "raise the cost [of research] at least tenfold." Other researchers were more alarmist. Dr. Michael Kirschenbaum of U.C.L.A. Medical School reportedly warned that the prohibition on the use of pound dogs throughout southern California "will effectively stop research in L.A. County" (*Los Angeles Times,* Nov. 30, 1980). The *Los Angeles Times* supported the medical establishment and hoped that the Council would not be "swept by sentiment" (May 27, 1981). The efforts were to no avail. The City Council voted to stop pound seizure.

At the University of Florida, a group of activists in Gainesville started a campaign in 1982 to halt the flow of dogs from the Jacksonville pound to the laboratories in Gainesville—a practice that had been going on for nineteen years. Jacksonville city officials professed ignorance. After the debate had proceeded for about a month, the university invited Jacksonville officials to tour their facilities. Bob Phelps, a columnist with the *Jacksonville Journal* in the tour party, noted that "the animals appeared to be clean, well fed, relatively free of parasites and healthy. The facilities were excellent, clean and expensive." However, Phelps also felt that the tour lacked credibility. (*Jacksonville Journal,* March 1, 1982).

Phelps obtained permission to visit the laboratory again, returning unannounced to the facilities at the end of March. He found a dog bleeding to death in an unattended cage and called for help, but it was too late. This proved to be the breaking point for Jacksonville city officials. Jack Goldberg, the mayor, announced the suspension of further shipments of animals to Gainesville pending a detailed investigation and report from the University of Florida. Apparently, the trade has now been resumed.

The committee at the University of Florida that investigated the incident reported that, in the case of the particular dog found by Phelps, the researcher concerned had taken it out of the intensive care unit three to four days earlier than recommended in the standard operating procedure. Apparently he was concerned about the animal's being kept in a small cage (this is done purposely so that the animal cannot strain the surgical wounds) and moved it to a larger cage where it would have more room.

A similar battle over pound animal use is developing in Illinois, where the University of Chicago Medical School has recently been attacked for using pound dogs in student exercises. The fight started as a result of a complaint by an anonymous medical student at the university who objected to the training exercises on dogs. The medical school is no stranger to such protests—their introductory practical manual notes:

> Animal experimentation has produced great and lasting benefits to medicine and to mankind, as all educated people know. . . . Students and investigators at this and other universities where dogs are available for teaching and research should realize that this privilege was hard-earned by their predecessors but will be threatened again and must be fought for again in each generation. . . .
>
> Until the passage of laws permitting dogs to be made available from city pounds, medical schools in certain parts of the country were able to use dogs to only a limited extent in teaching, and less extensively in research than they would have desired. Thanks to the efforts of the late Dr. A. J. Carlson, the University of Chicago and other medical schools in Chicago have been able for many years to utilize dogs extensively in teaching and research, greatly to the benefit of all persons concerned. (Medical Biology 303, Laboratory Manual, p. 1, 1982).

It is apparent that the medical profession must once again fight to retain access to the unclaimed animals in the nation's pounds and shelters. However, the public's allegiance has shifted in the last thirty years and the outcome this time may well be very different.

The Random-Source dog

Between 1966 and 1969, the Institute for Laboratory Animal Resources reported tht approximately 400,000 dogs were used every year in laboratories throughout the U.S.A. (Institute for Laboratory Animal Resources, 1966–69). However, only about 70% of the laboratories surveyed sent in returns and it was not clear whether this figure represented total use. The Veterinary Extension Service at Rutgers estimated that 500,000 dogs were used in 1971 (Santamarina 1976). According to succeeding ILAR surveys (1970–71), the use of dogs dropped very suddenly from 400,000 to around 190,000. The data compiled annually by the Animal and Plant Health Inspection Service (APHIS) confirms this figure (table 10.1).

These figures provide little information on the sources of the animals. In the late sixties, about 105,000 animals came directly from pounds, 150,000 came via dealers, and 30,000 were bred specifically for laboratories (Potkay and Bacher 1973). The latest ILAR survey (1980) indicates that 138,000 dogs were random-source (i.e., directly from shelters or dealers) and about 45,000 were purpose-bred. Prices for these animals vary greatly. When institutions buy directly from pounds or shelters, the price ranges from $5 to $15. However, dealers sell unconditioned animals for as much as $85, and conditioned dogs for $120 to $140, while a six-month-old beagle

TABLE 10.1
NUMBER OF DOGS USED BY LABORATORIES
1966–80

Year	ILAR Surveys[a]	APHIS[b]	Other
1966	415,159		
1967	371,024		
1968	409,472		
1969	372,229		
1970	182,728		
1971	192,524		500,000[c]
1972		185,788	
1973		195,157	
1974		199,204	
1975		154,484	
1976		210,330	
1977		176,430	
1978	183,063[d]	197,010	
1979		211,904	
1980		188,783	

SOURCES: [a] Adapted from Institute for Laboratory Animal Resources 1966–69; 1970–71.
[b] Animals and Plant Health Inspection Service 1972–80.
[c] Santamarina 1976.
[d] Institute for Laboratory Animal Resources 1980.

is about $275, excluding transport charges. Older and larger dogs are more expensive.

Random-source dogs include unclaimed strays that have been picked up off the streets by animal control officers, as well as dogs turned into pounds and shelters by their owners. In 1974, the Humane Society of the United States estimated, from a nationwide analysis, that between 13 million and 14 million dogs *and* cats were euthanized in pounds and shelters throughout the country. About 6.5 million of these were dogs, about 60% being adults (Guy Hodge, HSUS, personal communication, 1981). While no subsequent in-depth surveys have been conducted, the trends indicate that fewer dogs are being euthanized annually. HSUS analyses also indicate that 40% of the dogs are turned in by their owners; the remainder are strays (Phyllis Wright, HSUS, personal communication, 1981).

Recently, medical research interests have claimed that 13 million to 15 million dogs are euthanized annually (Frederickson 1981; D'Ver, 1981). This figure is attributed to the HSUS but, as has been shown, it is based on a misinterpretation of the HSUS estimates, which included cats in the overall figure. It is probable that only about 2 million to 3 million adult dogs of a size and condition appropriate for research are euthanized annually in the United States.

Research institutions also prefer animals that are tractable and socialized to human beings. The true stray or feral dog will be fearful and, therefore, likely to bite when approached. Strays do not appear to be an actively self-perpetuating population (Beck, 1973); consequently, most animals that end up in shelters and pounds are probably used to human companionship. This is the basis of the animal welfare claim that "pets" are ending up in the laboratory.

Uses and Conditioning. As might be expected, dogs are used for a wide variety of purposes (see Harmison 1973), including toxicology and pharmacology studies, cardiovascular and renal research, and behavioral studies. In fact, one survey indicated that random-source dogs were used in projects covering 87 different research disciplines and 37 different teaching disciplines (C. Hunter, reported at 1981 American Association for Laboratory Animal Science (AALAS) meeting). The dog is the standard "large" laboratory animal, although more researchers are beginning to use pigs (Institute for Laboratory Animal Resources 1980). Large numbers of dogs are also used in student training programs (e.g., Wood et al. 1980).

Finally, random-source dogs are not unloaded from trucks straight into the laboratory. They are first subjected to "conditioning." That is, they are inspected for symptoms and kept in quarantine until ready to use. The length of quarantine depends on the purpose for which the animal will be used. Dogs scheduled for nonsurvival surgery demonstrations need only be clear of zoonotic symptoms, whereas those for long-term research studies are vaccinated and quarantined for at least a month.

Scientific Issues and Pound Animals. It is often argued that, because humans constitute a random-source gene pool, random-source dogs would not only be adequate but would be even more appropriate than purpose-bred animals. However, Festing (1981), a geneticist with the U.K. Medical Research Council, contends that this is invalid reasoning. If it were not, then there would be no reason for the growing use of defined strains of rodents with known genetic and microbiological background; random-source rats and mice (e.g., from the city dump) would be perfectly adequate. More than three-quarters of the respondents to a recent survey (T. Wolfle, reported at the 1981 AALAS annual meeting) stated that purpose-bred animals would be more reliable, but few gave detailed reasons for their opinion. Where opinions have been given in the literature, they tend to be on the lines of Pritchard's statement:

> . . . the biologist can ill afford to treat animal experimentation in the same naive manner as is currently the fashion. It is all too common to find multimillion dollar research projects, consuming the time of highly talented scientists, based upon studies on animals from city pounds, with little thought given to their suitability for the research being conducted. . . . Countless studies are misleading or totally useless because the wrong animal was selected, genetic variations were not taken into account, diseased or stressed animals were employed (1968, p. 230).

As far back as 1959, some researchers were pointing out the need for closer attention to the health and other characteristics of the so-called normal dog. In an editorial in the *American Heart Journal,* Burch is very critical of the lack of attention paid to the health and psychological status of dogs used in research:

> Too often the requisites of performance of investigators, apparatus, and methods far exceed the requirements for the state of health of the experimental animal. No matter how good the method or the performance of the apparatus, an abnormal animal is not suitable for obtaining results intended to define the normal state of health. True science is concerned with the unknown, *but the conditions of the study should be maximally known* (1959, p. 805 [emphasis added]).

Of course, not all studies necessitate control of *all* the variables, even if this were possible. However, researchers display an unquestioning acceptance of random-source animals as satisfactory research tools and produce circular arguments in their favor. Since most groups use these animals, the bulk of the data is generated from them; thus the succeeding investigation tends to use them as well. Papers reporting the data are reviewed by peers who also use random-source dogs. What criticism there is, is either muted or unheeded. Thus Van Citters (1973) notes that the dog has become the main, large laboratory animal because it is cheap, available, and tractable; he argues that these are hardly good scientific reasons.

The need for better quality data than that obtained from random-source dogs has forced much of the pharmaceutical industry to switch to purpose-bred dogs. Gilmartin (1961) described an instance at Norwich Pharmacal in which work on a trial drug was halted for a number of years because of reports of toxicity in dogs. Later studies on animals of high quality gave the opposite results. Further investigation revealed that the damage attributed to the drug in the initial study was, in fact, caused by a severe distemper infection before the test was started. Underwood and Durbin of the Food and Drug Administration (FDA) also emphasized the dangers of using unwanted foundlings from the streets of large cities, noting that "the use of such animals in research programs often resulted in a succession of questionable symptoms and pathological manifestations, resulting in a mass of unintelligible data when an experiment is terminated" (1963, p. 525).

Of course, considerably more is now known about diseases in random-source dogs and cats (Beaucage and Fox 1979; Binn et al. 1979; Doyle et al. 1979; Holmes et al. 1976; Palmer 1973; Secord and Russell 1973) and they are now usually "conditioned" before entering the research program. But this still does not answer the criticism that random-source animals are poor research models because of their unknown genetic and microbiological backgrounds and the confounding effects of many extraneous variables.

The National Institutes of Health determined some time ago that random-source dogs, even when conditioned, were unsatisfactory for medical research (Palmer 1973; Zinn 1968). NIH has for some years used only purpose-bred animals in intramural research, but they have not tried to persuade grant recipients to do the same. In fact, recently, NIH issued a formal statement that there may be some projects "for which random-source conditioned pound animals are adequate" and that there was "ample justification for the continued use of such a relatively small number of these animals in the quest of new knowledge relevant to human disease and disability" (Frederickson 1981, pp. 15–16).

In Europe, the current tendency is to move toward the use of purpose-bred animals only. Thus, the U.K. Laboratory Animal Science Association "believes that for scientific, economic and ethical reasons all dogs and cats, in common with other animals used for research, should be bred for this purpose" (Laboratory Animal Science Association 1981, p. 405). In Sweden, the law regulating animal research actually specifies that dogs and cats should be purpose-bred. It is reasoned that use of pound animals creates a major public relations problem, and that dogs and cats should not be exempted from the perceived need for better defined laboratory animals in research.

Economics. The main reason for using pound animals is their low cost. This has been confirmed by several informal surveys. Over the past ten years, the cost of dogs obtained directly from pounds and shelters has remained relatively static at about $5 to $15, while the cost of conditioned animals from dealers and of purpose-bred animals has risen sharply. A thirty-day, conditional animal now costs about $120, and a six-month, purpose-bred beagle costs a minimum of $275.

Where the animals are used for student exercises, there is some justification for claiming that the cheap pound animal is satisfactory. One certainly does not need a genetically defined and healthy animal for nonrecovery surgery practice. Furthermore, provided the animal is well treated before use, and is properly anesthetized and then euthanized before recovery, there is little difference between euthanasia in the pound and euthanasia in the demonstration laboratory.

Of course, the situation is rarely this clear-cut. In some cases, the animal will be euthanized by questionable means in the pound or shelter. In others, pound animals supplied to a laboratory for nonsurvival surgery practice only, may be allocated to research programs by mistake. Furthermore, one could question whether properly performed euthanasia in a shelter is equivalent to anesthesia and euthanasia in a laboratory. One could argue—and some will—that the animal should be permitted to die with dignity, and not after some student has hacked at it with a scalpel.

Excluding educational use of dogs, there is no clear indication that the overall cost of using pound dogs is, in fact, less than the use of purpose-bred dogs, despite the large differences in the purchase price.

For example, one study has shown that it may actually be more expensive to use random-source dogs than purpose-bred animals in a chronic research project (Fletcher, Herr, and Roger 1969). The reason for this apparently anomalous result is that more random-source than purpose-bred dogs died during the experimental procedure (27% mortality versus 7%) and thus the researchers had to perform more operations to end up with the same number of study animals. The high costs of the operation (including operating room overhead, surgeon's time, technician's time, and material costs) meant that it was more expensive to prepare more random-source animals than it was to pay the higher price for purpose-bred dogs.

In fact, there are a number of problems when trying to estimate the cost of an animal research project accurately. For one, it has long been recognized that cost recovery for animal care varies widely from research facility to research facility, depending on the cost parameters included. A 1974 nationwide survey of per diem costs, by the Laboratory Animal Resources Center at Michigan State University noted a range of $0.50 (University of Georgia) to $1.97 (University of Southern California, L.A.) for the dog per diem costs (housed individually). The Institute for Laboratory Animal Resources (1980) survey indicated that such costing anomalies have still not been resolved.

Since researchers are often not charged the true cost for the care and maintenance of their research animals, or for their use of research facilities, the economic factor that often appears to be the most important from the grant seeker's viewpoint is the initial cost of the animals. As a result, medical researchers continue to fight for access to dogs from the nation's shelters. Better, and more, information is needed about the true costs of experimental procedures and of animal care, and about comparative survival rates, before any sound conclusions can be reached about the apparent economy of using random-source dogs.

Ethical Issues. The general ethical issues about using pound dogs are no different from those affecting research on any other animal, but there are some specific problems in pound-dog research. If there were no further use of random-source animals by research and teaching institutions, then the supply of purpose-bred dogs would certainly have to be increased from its present annual rate of 45,000 to satisfy increased research demand. Output would probably have to be doubled, or even tripled. The question arises: Is it ethically more desirable to use strays and discarded pets, which will be killed anyway, in research and education, or should one instead breed additional animals specifically for the laboratory? Purists will argue that this is the wrong question, but it points to a realistic forecast of what will happen if pound seizure is prohibited. As an additional wrinkle, the use of dogs will fall, but more rabbits and pigs will be used as replacements.

Researchers tend to argue that it is better to use the strays (after all they only need 5% to 10% of the adult dogs euthanized annually in America), while animal welfare advocates disagree. There are several reasons for this disagreement.

First, animal welfare advocates argue that the release of unclaimed animals to research institutions by pounds and shelters discourages people from turning in strays they have found. This makes it more difficult for owners to find lost animals and exacerbates animal control problems. Systematic data to support this contention is scanty, although Rush (1981), manager of the Los Angeles City Department of Animal Control, has made this claim at public hearings.

Second, there is a strong feeling among animal welfare groups that pets, whether abandoned, turned in voluntarily, or lost, should not be used in laboratories. As long as there is any perception that pets may end up in laboratories, there will be vocal opposition to the use of random-source dogs.

Finally, animal welfare groups usually receive a major share of their support through donations from the public and from legacies. This money is given toward the promotion of animal welfare. Most supporters would argue that humane societies should oppose release of unclaimed pound and shelter animals, in order to meet their obligations as effective promoters of animal welfare.

Is There a Solution? At present, there is little likelihood that the animal welfare movement will compromise on the pound seizure issue. Most of the groups are committed to eliminating all use of shelter animals in laboratories. The history of the practice and their anger at having pound seizure forced upon them by legislative mandate is such that few if any of these groups are likely to modify their resolve and enter into negotiations. As a result, one dog breeder has predicted that the "pound animal will be in scarce supply within four years and prohibited from use entirely within ten years" (D'Ver 1981, p. 25).

The position is further complicated by the lack of data in fundamental areas.

1. How many dogs are used annually for educational exercises and for research, respectively?
2. What are the numbers of different types of dogs used every year?
3. What is the survival rate of random-source and purpose-bred dogs in experimental procedures?
4. What are the true costs, including realistic allocation for overhead and personnel, of a range of different research projects and training procedures?
5. How many dogs of suitable age, health, and demeanour are euthanized by shelters and pounds each year?
6. What is the cost of increasing the supply of purpose-bred animals, and are there alternative species that would be as appropriate?

Even if such data were forthcoming, the humane movement is unlikely to be satisfied. Some laboratory animal veterinarians have also suggested that pound animals are far more trouble than they are worth. David Secord, at the University of Alberta, has suggested that pigs are large enough to take the place of the dog as the standard large animal. Pigs are also cheaper and the public relations problem, although not eliminated, would be much reduced. The dog is, after all, America's "sacred cow" (Beck 1974) and medical researchers are probably making a mistake in fighting over the pound animal issue.

CHAPTER 11

Animal Research: An Animal Welfare Case File

The preceding chapters have dealt with relatively specific fields of research or a particular problem (e.g., the pound animal issue). Animal welfare criticism is not, however, limited to these fields or classes of research activity. In this chapter, some of the other questions are addressed, using examples to breathe life into otherwise general and relatively meaningless criticisms. The issues include (a) criticism of the research itself because of its irrelevance; (b) criticism of the research in light of what may be (or is considered to be) excessive animal suffering, related to the use of improper techniques or compared to the knowledge gained; (c) criticism aimed at inadequate anesthesia or analgesia, leading to excessive pain and suffering; and (d) criticism based on inadequate standards of care for the research animals.

Criticism of the Research Itself

Animal welfare organizations receive a steady stream of letters from their members expressing outrage at some particular piece of research that has been publicized in the media. For example, in June 1982, a public furore was sparked over the proposed use of Nim and Ally (two "talking" chimpanzees) in the testing of hepatitis vaccine. Eighteen other chimpanzees, which had also been used in language acquisition studies at the University of Oklahoma, were also sent to the Laboratory for Experimental Medicine and Surgery in Primates for hepatitis research projects, but the public did not express much, or any, concern over these unknowns. However fickle and inconsistent, the public's voice was heeded and Nim and Ally were soon on their way back to Oklahoma.

In fact, the protests over Nim's and Ally's allocation to a hepatitis program were based solely on disquiet over "talking" chimpanzees being placed in a medical laboratory program. Hepatitis in chimpanzees produces little more than a mild immune response. It is certainly not the serious disease that it is in humans. Also there is an undisputed public health need for hepatitis B vaccine, and the FDA requires that the vaccine be tested in chimpanzees. Although the chimpanzees did return to Oklahoma for a brief period, Nim has now been "warehoused" on a ranch in Texas and Ally has reportedly gone to a New Mexico research lab.

Beagle Testing in the Army. In 1973, a proposal by the Air Force to use 200 "debarked" beagles to test the toxicity of jet fuel, rocket propellants, and environmental pollutants was publicized by Les Aspin, a Wisconsin Democrat in the House of Representatives. In the ensuing uproar, which was fueled by antivivisection protests, the Air Force asked the National Academy of Sciences (NAS) to review its proposed program. The NAS concluded that the research was necessary, that the beagles were well treated, and that "there should be no pain from the experiments" (Holden 1974).

While this report took some of the heat off the Air Force, the public's attention was diverted by a U.S. Army proposal to use beagles to test the toxicity of riot control agents, nerve gas vaccines, and other noxious substances. Congressman Aspin and Senator Hubert Humphrey, both of whom wished to curb chemical warfare research, took advantage of the issue to pressure the Department of Defense. The legislators received vociferous support from antivivisection groups, who ran advertisements in newspapers protesting the army research and flooded the Pentagon with more than 30,000 angry letters.

The controversy was, of course, fueled by the fact that dogs were being used for chemical warfare tests. The dog is a favored animal, and chemical warfare has a negative image—even at the best of times. The period following the Vietnam War was hardly the best of times for the military. In this case, therefore, the protest was directly related to public outrage at the type of research proposed and a general feeling that the use of dogs could not be justified.

Cat Sex Research. While the protest over the army's beagle studies was spontaneous, cat studies at the American Museum of Natural History were the focus of a carefully planned and executed campaign, starting early in 1976. Henry Spira, a New York English teacher and an experienced social activist in such causes as the labor, civil rights, and peace movements, became interested in animal rights in the mid-seventies. Spira noticed an abstract of the museum's cat research project in a list of experiments disapproved of by United Action for Animals.

The item was perfect for a major campaign. The research at the museum was vulnerable because most people would be surprised to learn that such studies were even conducted at the museum. Further, the study involved a species of household pet (cats) and concerned sexual behavior. Both of these elements were guaranteed to raise public passion. In the third place, the museum relied on public contributions and was thus vulnerable to negative publicity. Finally, Spira was able to obtain detailed descriptions of the research through Freedom of Information Act requests (Wade 1976).

The campaign itself proved very successful. The museum at first adopted an aloof attitude that alienated the press. Its director, Thomas Nicholson, argued that the museum should be free to study whatever it chose without regard to its demonstrable practical value. Reporters were at first refused access to Lester Aronson, the principle investigator for the project, and to the laboratories. The museum's public statements were all couched in general terms, while the protestors issued detailed accusations and picketed the museum on weekends. Eventually, the beleaguered museum announced that Dr. Aronson would retire (in August, 1977) and the cat research was terminated in favor of greater emphasis on behavioral studies in natural populations of animals in field research (Pratt 1980).

The protest was based on three contentions: that the animals were inhumanely treated, quite apart from the needs of the experiments; that the manipulations were cruel and ethically unacceptable; and that the experiments were unlikely to lead to any significant new knowledge (Wade 1976). The first charge was never shown to have any substance. The other two charges, however, raised complex issues about the value of basic research and the perceived worth of the cat sex experiments, given the type of manipulations undertaken (e.g., destruction of sense of smell, removal of parts of the brain, castration, and severing the nerves to the penis). The protestors obviously felt that the research was not worth the suffering of the animals, whereas Aronson's supporters argued that the research was valuable (Beach 1977).

Wade (1976) attempted to evaluate Aronson's research by analyzing the number of times his cat research had been cited. He noted that 14 of the 21 papers published by Aronson and his collegues had never been cited, while the remaining 7 papers had been cited an average of 5.6 times over the 11-year period studied. (The average item in the Science Citation Index is cited 1.87 times per year). Wade implied that the lack of citations of Aronson's work indicated that it was not considered particularly important. However, Garfield (1977), the founder of citation analysis, contended that Wade had made a number of errors in his analysis. Garfield concluded that Aronson's work has, in fact, been reasonably valuable to the research community. Nonetheless, Garfield raised some caveats:

> I am perplexed by the assertion that Aronson's work is deemed quite significant by Beach and others when their citation of his work is minimal. And I am increasingly suspicious of generalized claims that we can never know in advance (and often not even in retrospect) what value "basic" research may have in the future. In the days when there were just a few thousand people in the world doing basic research, such assertions were acceptable. But when the world's scientific population exceeds one million persons, we need something more than the bland assertions by established investigators or their peers that basic research pays off (1977, p. 10).

Aronson's work should probably have been judged as "basic" research, that is, research with no immediate practical application to human problems. Drewett and Kani (1981) note that techniques involving induction of brain lesions and the implantation of microelectrodes have produced much valuable and interesting information on neurophysiology, but that the application of this data to human problems has been minimal. They argue that more human and less animal research is required. Nevertheless, there is little evidence that the ethical questions—namely, balancing the likely suffering of animals against the possible gain in knowledge—were fully addressed when Aronson applied for or received grants.

If the public had ever been consulted on this disbursement of their tax monies, there is little doubt what the consensus would have been. As Sachs noted:

> Ten years ago, *Science* rejected, without review, a report by Aronson and Cooper because the editor felt that the sex research on cats, as described in that report, would offend the sensibilities of some *Science*

> readers, including antivivisectionists. Ultimately, *Science* had the report reviewed and published a modified version with no adverse repercussions. Despite the superficial sexual enlightment of the last decade, the current reaction to the sexual aspects of the research of Aronson and Cooper and many of their colleagues indicates that, for many persons, basic research on sexual behavior is still beyond the pale (1976, p. 860).

This is undoubtedly a major reason for the protest over Aronson's research. However, if Aronson had been studying cat sexual behavior in seminatural or natural conditions, it is most unlikely that his research would have attracted Spira's attention or that it would have fueled a major protest by animal rights groups.

Excessive Suffering Versus Knowledge Gained

Many examples of research have been criticized on the basis of excessive suffering balanced against knowledge gained, in the animal welfare and antivivisection literature. Diner (1979) lists many experiments involving physical and mental suffering in laboratory animals but, at times, authors indite themselves by their description of research techniques and the care given to their experimental animals.

Orthodontics Research. Everyone is familiar with the use of braces to straighten crooked teeth in children and young adults. The braces apply a gradual but steady force to the teeth that slowly assume the correct position. In this same vein, Brandt, Shapiro, and Kokich (1979) have studied the potential for treating severe skeletal deformities in the adult by the application of a steady force to the relevant bones. At present, correction of severe deformities usually requires jaw surgery.

The researchers prepared two male and two female adult cynomolgus monkeys for the experiment by fitting them with a mixture of face-bows, splints, and screws fixed in the facial bones. A steady one-pound force was then administered to each side, and the monkeys were kept in restraint chairs throughout the active and retention phase of the experiment "to reduce the possibility of damage to the appliances."

The two males lost weight initially, following their placement in the restraint chairs, but then acclimatized and spent 120 to 205 days, respectively, under force application. The female monkeys, however, were not as robust and did not stand up well to being chaired. They were, therefore, placed in cages, but one female succeeded in removing the appliance and was returned to the restraint chair. Further difficulties led to her being killed after 84 days of force application, while the other female died unexpectedly after 93 days of force application. All animals experienced severe gingival inflammation due to the splint, the forces applied to the splint, and poor oral hygiene conditions.

There seems little doubt that the procedure resulted in animal distress and suffering, but the authors did not address this issue in the paper. As for the scientific value, the authors stated that the results confirmed their theory that the facial skeletal complex can be remodeled in the adult by the application of appropriate forces. However, they state that in "the light of our current level of technology in orthodontics, the clinical application of the present investigation is questionable." Presumably, this could have been predicted before the experiment was carried out and it is, therefore, very difficult to justify the study considering the animal suffering involved. In fact, *any* experimental protocol that involved holding an animal for seven months in a restraint chair would be difficult to justify, no matter what the projected medical benefits.

Car Crash Studies. Animals have periodically been used to test the effects of car crashes on their human occupants. In 1978, the Committee to Save the Baboon Seven was formed to protest experiments using baboons in "impact sled tests" to assess thoracic injury. As Heneson (1980) notes, the objections focused on the validity of the baboon as a model for human response, the moral inconsistency of damning the use of human cadavers but permitting live animal tests, and the actual need for the experiments. Eventually, only one of the seven baboons was used in the study, the researchers claiming that they had obtained sufficient data from the one test. Two years later, in France, another animal study of the effects of simulated car crashes was suspended after the project was publicized in the European press.

The protests against both projects were based on the idea that the experiments would cause much animal suffering for little or no gain in useful and applicable knowledge to protect human car travelers from injury. The scientific argument is that comparative biomedical and biomechanical data are needed to develop a suitable dummy that will provide reliable information to aid the design of safe cars. However, the animal studies do not, themselves, provide data for application to real situations. Human cadavers are considered inadequate because a deteriorated and inert corpse is less suitable than a live, morphologically similar animal.

However, in analyzing the issues, Heneson (1980) questions whether the use of live animals provides significant knowledge in light of the difficulties and imprecise nature of the task of developing adequate safety standards. She notes that Dr. Murray Mackay, head of the accident research unit at Birmingham University, U.K., argued that the French animal studies were of marginal importance since the correlation between humans and animals is poor because of anatomical differences. Even those studies which use primates caution that there are differences in skeletal structure that present severe problems when scaling the test results to human circumsances.

It cannot be denied that we need better information on car crash injuries so that we can design safer cars. However, one can question whether it is ethically justified to use animals to achieve this aim, especially in view of the imprecise nature of the data from such studies. Even if the animals are lightly anesthetized or tranquilized (introducing a further complication, since the reaction of a drugged animal is even further removed from that of a conscious human), the ethical issues remain. Those commissioning and supporting these studies should re-evaluate their programs and include animal suffering and death in the equation.

Oral Radiation Research. In 1956, Quastler, and colleagues described the syndrome of oral radiation death (ORD) in mice. This syndrome is similar to marrow radiation death both in survival time (9 to 10 days) and its lack of variation over a considerable range of doses. Before the animals die, the oral mucosae become swollen and open sores develop. In some cases, the mouth may be sealed shut by encrustation from these sores. In the last 4 or 5 days, the animals lose weight steadily, although starvation was ruled out as a possible cause of death by various experiments, including force feeding of the animals (Quastler, Austin, and Miller 1956).

Recently, Grigsby and Maruyama (1981) published a paper in which they used the ORD as an end point to assess the effects of radioprotective and radiosensitizing chemicals. This drew an outraged comment from Hewitt and Porter who wrote that they had

> read with grief and indignation the paper by Grigsby and Maruyama (1981). It appears that the mice in their experiments suffered, or narrowly escaped, death from starvation and thirst while their mucosae were too sore to permit swallowing. Experimental animals should not be subjected

> to such misery, and it is no credit to the British Journal of Radiology to publish a paper that recommends so cruel a procedure as providing "an excellent endpoint" (1982, p. 168).

In response, the Honorary Editor of the *British Journal of Radiology* offered a contrite apology for publishing the paper.

Grigsby and Maruyama were, however, unrepentant. They argued in response that ORD is not caused by starvation and then noted that animal experimentation has been and will remain paramount in scientific investigation of the potential of new tumor therapies.

> While we agree that inflicting unnecessary discomfort on another creature may be unwarranted, it is a small price for studies potentially leading to alleviating the pain and suffering in humans who are so unfortunate as to develop advanced carcinoma of the head and neck (1982, pp. 250–51).

This response, however, did not address the issue of whether an alternative, less painful, end point might be available to conduct the same type of research. It is this point that most concerned Hewitt and Porter (1982), who had asked whether there might not be a way of doing the research without causing so much animal misery. In fact, this appears to be a definite trans-Atlantic problem: Hewitt and Porter are British scientists who received explicit support for their protest from the *British Medical Journal* (vol. 284:518), while Grigsby and Maruyama are from the University of Kentucky Medical School.

Tumor Therapies. Cancer is one of the most feared diseases of the modern age. As infectious diseases in developed countries were controlled by a mix of public hygiene measures, vaccination, and antibiotics, the average life expectancy increased steadily and now stands at about 70 years. Because cancer is far more common in older people, most people today have had some sort of personal experience with a cancer sufferer. The suffering, pain, and debilitation cancer patients endure, and the severe side effects of attempted therapies, have all contributed to the disproportionate public support, via donations and tax monies, to cancer research. In the United States, the National Cancer Institute's budget comprises approximately 10% of the total funds available for biomedical research and development, and President Nixon declared a much ballyhooed War on Cancer in 1971. Heart disease kills twice as many people, yet it receives less research support.

In spite of this, we are still woefully ignorant of the mechanisms of induction and spread of cancer, and the gains of the past three decades have been very expensive in money, time, and animal suffering. National Cancer Institute research programs (both intramural and extramural), for example, use 6½ million rodents annually (U.S. Congress 1979).

The public will probably continue to support this massive effort to find a cure for the many different types of cancers to which we are subject. Millions of animals will continue to die in cancer research projects around the country. Animal suffering, however, could be considerably reduced without compromising cancer research by establishing and enforcing a few simple guidelines for humane research.

Hewitt (1981) argues that stress attributable to pain or trauma is undesirable since it introduces a considerable number of complications into the interpretation of data (cf. Riley 1981; Rowan 1981b). Hewitt notes that because "a high quality of science goes hand in hand with a high standard of humanity," it is always advantageous to refine a procedure until it is sufficiently innocuous to preclude stress-inducing effects and even the administration of anesthetics. He then suggests the following technical guidelines to reduce animal suffering.

When tumors are transplanted from one animal to another one can either disperse the tumor (in all but a few, rare cases) into its constituent cells and inoculate a cell suspension, or the tumor could be cut up into small pieces and introduced under the skin via a blunt, hollow instrument called a *trochar.* Hewitt favors the first method because one can accurately assess the number of cells inoculated and a fine needle can be used for the injection, thereby causing minimal trauma to the animal. The site of the inoculation is also important. The graft site should not lie over a bony surface such as the spinal column or breast plate. He suggests that the posterior part of the loin is a satisfactory inoculation site. The foot or hind leg is commonly used as a site for a tumor graft, but this can cause considerable discomfort to the animal unless the tumor is kept to a very moderate size.

The size of the tumor is an important constraint, wherever the graft site is located. A growing tumor makes significant demands on an animal's resources and there will come a stage when the animal is in great distress. According to Hewitt: "The experimenter who makes observations on tumor growth or behavior after an animal has reached this moribund cachectic state without regard to its influence on what he is observing or measuring, cannot possibly make valid interpretations of his data" (1981, p. 162). He recommends that tumors should not be allowed to grow larger than one gram in weight (13 millimeters in diameter) in the mouse, with proportionately larger limits for the larger species. (A mouse weighs about 20 to 25 gm). To place this in context, a tumor of proportional size in a human being would weigh 6 to 7 pounds, the size of the average baby. He notes that mouse tumors of 10gm weight have been permitted in some instances (cf. Schabel 1981; DeWys 1972).

In the study of metastatic phenomena (where cells from the primary tumor split away and form nodes of cancer elsewhere in the body), the study must proceed for some time before one can observe the growth of the secondary tumors. If the primary tumor is left in place, it will inevitably grow to a size much larger than that recommended above. Hewitt suggests that the original graft site should be *in the skin* and that when the tumor reaches 0.5 gm in size, it should be excised by cutting away a small piece of the skin. This is relatively simple and is usually far less traumatic to the animal than inoculating the hind leg and amputating the leg when the tumor grows too large. Furthermore, one needs to include a humane end point (not death) into the overall experimental design, such as the reappearance of a palpable tumor at the original inoculation site or signs of sickness in the animal. This practice yielded very satisfactory data in a variety of studies (Hewitt 1976).

The experimental study and evaluation of therapeutic agents (chemicals or radiation) inevitably results in animal suffering because the therapeutic and toxic doses overlap. However, even here it is possible to develop techniques that reduce or limit animal suffering without compromising the quality of the data (Hewitt and Wilson 1959). The "death" end point is generally condemned by Hewitt (1981) as "scientifically unsound and inconsistent with a high standard of humanity." He notes that, to reach an acceptable standard of humanity, the animal experimenter must "devote a large part of his diligence and ingenuity to the design of procedures and end-points which enable the information he seeks to be gained before the onset of distress resulting from interference" (1981, p. 171). In general, this is the same appeal as that promoted by advocates of "alternatives."

All these examples have been provided to indicate that there are good reasons to believe that current biomedical knowledge is being advanced at too great a cost in animal suffering. In some cases, the need for particular research information does not appear to have been adequately analyzed, given the extent of animal suffering involved. In others, the researcher has not used his or her ingenuity to develop techniques that involve less stress. Researchers often claim to be animal lovers who care as much or more for their animals than the animal activists. Unfortunately, a careful and detailed reading of the research literature (and remember, many results never find their way into print) reveals far too many cases where a little more thought would have resulted in a lot less animal suffering.

Inadequate Anesthesia

The Animal Welfare Act requires that professionally acceptable standards of anesthesia and analgesia be used to minimize pain and discomfort in laboratory animals, but no specifics are made available. NIH principles also urge that experimenters avoid all unnecessary suffering and suggest that animals should be rendered *incapable of perceiving pain,* except in those cases where this would defeat the purpose of the experiment (Loew 1981). However, neither the U.S. Department of Agriculture, which enforces the Animal Welfare Act, nor the NIH offer much in the way of specifics (cf. Solomon and Lovenheim 1982). General guidelines are available (see the Canadian Council on Animal Care's guide [1980]), but not everybody uses them. Special problems arise where a full-time laboratory animal specialist is not available.

The sort of questions that arise are illustrated by the example of a recent paper on rat burn studies (the burn being caused by boiling water) in which no mention is made of either anesthesia or analgesia (Nishigaki et al. 1980). The researchers (from Japan) may have used anesthesia, of course, but this should either have been included in the methods section or the paper should have been rejected for publication. This is a relatively clear-cut case, but others are less obvious, particularly those in which paralytic agents are used in neurophysiological studies.

Paralytic agents, such as curare or gallamine triethiodide, block muscle activity without rendering the animal unconscious or insensitive to pain. Even without any painful or noxious stimuli, the paralyzed state presumably causes the animal some, if not, considerable distress. The animal's immobility carries another danger, however. If the effect of the local or general anesthetic wears off, the animal is unable to indicate in any way that it is in pain. This is the major problem with the use of paralytic agents.

For example, Gur and Purple (1978) describe a study on ground squirrels in which a microelectrode was inserted into the eye under general barbiturate anesthesia, and the animals were then paralyzed with gallamine. In most cases general anesthesia was maintained by halothane, but in some experiments, neurons were studied in ground squirrels "emerging from pentobarbital anaesthesia before halothane was titrated in to stabilize anesthetic state." In another example, cats were paralyzed with gallamine and, with their heads held firm in a clamp, the skulls were opened up under local anesthesia for neurophysiological studies (Duffy et al. 1976). There was no way in which the authors could tell whether the local anesthetic was effectively eliminating pain.

A more difficult case concerns a series of experiments on the development of vision in cats in which nitrous oxide and oxygen were used to maintain general anesthesia (e.g., Blakemore and Cooper 1970; Eggers and Blakemore 1978). It has been demonstrated that nitrous oxide is not itself a general anesthetic in cats (Russell 1973), and counterclaims that it satisfactorily maintains anesthesia that is first induced with barbiturates (Blakemore et al. 1974) have also been shown to be incorrect (Richards and Webb 1975). Even though the use of an inadequate general anesthetic is unlikely to be more than a minor problem, the above example does indicate that there may be grounds for criticism even where general anesthesia is described in the published paper.

Inadequate Care

The U.S. Animal Welfare Act grants no authority to the USDA to "interfere" in the actual conduct or design of research, but it does provide for the establishment of minimum standards for the care of laboratory animals. Nevertheless, there are still too many cases of inadequate animal care due in part to lack of commitment to the Act and lack of funds to enforce the Act adequately. From time to time, however, the USDA does charge a facility with an Animal Welfare Act violation. For example, on January 5, 1982, Ohio State University was charged with inadequate veterinary care for about 40 kittens that had been found to have metal chains and identification tags embedded in the flesh around their necks.

In other cases, adverse inspection reports may lead merely to a trail of memorandums and no decisive action. At the University of California, Berkeley, the animal facilities have repeatedly been found to be inadequate, and yet there is little indication that any real effort has been made to enforce proper standards. For example, the animal rooms in the Department of Psychology were found to have major housekeeping problems, on February 27, March 5, and June 3, 1980, and then again on four occasions in 1981. The situation was so bad that the campus laboratory animal veterinarian refused to sign the annual report form. Steps were not taken to correct the situation until a local TV station exposed these deficiencies.

In yet other cases, the inspector may ignore gross violations of the standards. On November 23, 1981, Dr. Edward Taub was found guilty of not providing adequate veterinary care for 6 of 17 monkeys confiscated by the police from his laboratory 2 months earlier. Seven months later, a jury lifted 5 of the 6 convictions because the lack of veterinary care had not actually led to "*physical* pain and suffering" in the monkeys, as required by the Maryland anticruelty statute. Dr. Taub is now seeking to have the final conviction dismissed as well, but whatever happens, the case will remain a landmark in the history of protest against animal research.

Dr. Taub and his supporters have attempted to portray the case as an attack on science, analogous to the persecution of scientists by the Inquisition in the Middle Ages, but the real issue revolves around the question of the standard of care provided for his monkeys.

A further peculiarity of the case was the fact that a number of monkeys were deafferentated (i.e., the nerves carrying sensory information from the arm to the brain had been cut where they enter the spinal column). These deafferentated animals perceive the insensate limb as "foreign" and this frequently leads to severe self-mutilation. No veterinarian was called in to inspect the animals for two years prior to the police action but, in the appeal trial, the jury could not agree on whether a wound on an insensate limb would lead to "physical pain and suffering," as required for a conviction under the Maryland anticruelty statute.

In any case, one thing is clear. The conditions and the standards of care in Dr. Taub's laboratory at the time of the police seizure of the monkeys were definitely inadequate. An NIH review panel considered the laboratory to be grossly unsanitary and, as a result, Taub's NIH grant was first suspended, and then, after an in-depth review, it was terminated. The case has also led to a thorough reevaluation of inspection procedures at the USDA, and quality control checks are being instituted. In addition, as discussed elsewhere (Rowan 1982a; Rowan 1982c), Taub's own arguments and actions about the special treatment regimens required for the care of deafferentated animals were inconsistent, and a number of possible options for improving the situation do not appear to have been thoroughly explored or implemented. As Gianutsos (1975) has documented, deafferentated monkeys can be kept in good shape, but it takes dedicated care and some ingenuity. Furthermore, in one grant application, Taub proposed to spend only 55 cents per day on maintaining each monkey, at a time when the nationwide per diem rates for macaque monkeys in *normal* health ranged between $2.50 and $4.00 (Rowan 1982a).

Whether the conditions at the laboratory were sufficiently bad to convict Taub under the Maryland anticruelty statute, is a matter for the courts to determine. However, the revelations from the events leading up to the trial have been a major embarrassment to both the NIH and the USDA. Their procedures for ensuring that facilities maintain professionally acceptable standards of laboratory animal care were clearly demonstrated to be inadequate. In congressional hearings on the issue, it was suggested that the Taub case was exceptional and that nearly all other research facilities are in compliance with both NIH and USDA standards. But this is the same platitude that has been offered time and again when questions have been raised about one or another research facility. It has never mollified the animal welfare movement, and it is even less likely to do so now.

Conclusion

Animal welfare criticism may, of course, include more than one of the above four general categories, but these probably cover most of the complaints. In general, those defending biomedical research have not recognized such distinctions. Any criticism is perceived to be just another attack on "essential animal research." Thus, Taub and his supporters talk of an attack on scientific freedom and one's ability to do animal research, even though the animal welfare groups have very specifically addressed only the issue of adequate care for Taub's monkeys. Research scientists must start to grapple seriously with some of the specific issues raised above. Only by doing so, can they hope to defuse growing criticism of animal research.

CHAPTER 12

Animal Research: A Case for the Defense

This chapter is unlikely to please many animal activists, but I think it is important to leaven the apparently unending catalog of inappropriate animal research with some indication that animal research has indeed led to advances in biomedical knowledge and also to improved therapies and treatment. I do not, however, wish to add my voice to the general paean of praise for animal research per se. Nevertheless, I believe the practice has produced undeniable benefits. At the same time, improved hygiene and public health programs, clinical discoveries, and epidemiological investigations have also had a major impact. However, none of these activities, including animal research, can be divorced from the overall research process.

Some antivivisection literature has sought to present an extremely negative view of the spinoffs from animal research (e.g., Ruesch 1978). For example, it is claimed that not a single benefit to humans or animals has come from animal research, that all current biomedical information could have been obtained using other means, and that all animal research is painful.

These claims are derived from arguments presented by the nineteenth century antivivisection movement, when they could be made with less fear of rebuttal. In the 1800's, improved hygiene, better public health programs, and higher living standards undoubtedly produced far greater advances in the health of the general population than any esoteric data from basic research. In addition, animal research at the time frequently did involve cutting open live, conscious animals. The growing use of anesthetics and the advent of diphtheria antitoxin, however, marked the beginning of the end for simplistic assertions that all animal research was useless and painful.

There were many medical discoveries prior to the development of diphtheria antitoxin, but either they could not be unequivocally identified as resulting from animal research (e.g., the development of antisepsis and anesthesia for surgery) or they had not yet led to any significant advances in medical therapy (e.g., the development of the germ theory). Diphtheria antitoxin was the first major therapeutic advance that owed its development largely to animal research. The antitoxin was also produced and standardized using animals.

The impact of this new therapy was enormous as, in the last decade of the nineteenth century, the prospect of actually dying after contracting diphtheria was cut from 40% to 10% and the potential benefit of animal research was startlingly revealed (Turner 1980). Prudential Insurance Company statistics indicated that the rate of mortality from diphtheria declined from an average of 96 deaths per 100,000 population between 1890 and 1894 to 21 deaths per 100,000 population between 1910 and 1914 (Keen 1917). The initial, dramatic results with antitoxin were soon overshadowed by the realization that it was very important to use the correct dose. Paul Erlich was the man who solved this problem, employing the "minimum lethal dose" as his basis for standardization. This was the smallest amount that would kill a guinea pig weighing 250 grams within four days, and it was the forerunner to the much disliked LD50 test (see chap. 14).

While the use of diphtheria antitoxin reduced the mortality among those suffering from the disease, it should be noted that the number of cases of diphtheria had already begun to decline in Britain, with a particularly sharp fall between 1865 and 1875, as a result of public health measures. This fall owed little or nothing to animal research.

Other therapeutic advances prior to diphtheria antitoxin also owed something to animal research. For example, it was discovered in the late 1800's that removal of the thyroid gland in monkeys created a syndrome analogous to myxedema, a cretinous condition occurring frequently in middle-aged women. This led to the suggestion that myxedema might be treated by thyroid tissue from animals. Practical applications of this idea worked with spectacular results but it did little to undermine antivivisection sentiment. Antiseptic surgery techniques were also improved via animal research. These, however, suffered from the fact that the initial introduction of antiseptic surgery demonstrated no clear advantages over the work of careful, capable, and famous surgeons, such as Lawson Tait, also an ard[illegible]visectionist, who rejected Lister's methods.

Nevertheless, advances stemming from animal research began to outweigh the objections raised by both the antivivisectionists and the public health advocates and by other sceptics within the medical profession. The discovery and use of adrenalin at the turn of the century provided a drug that appeared to bring heart attack victims back from the dead. As Turner (1980) notes, it was hard to argue against such miraculous cures and few antivivisectionists tried. As the pace of the new Scientific Medicine, which included animal research, picked up, so did more and more evidence of the beneficial outcome of such research accumulate.

Most major research advances have involved a broad mix of approaches. Thus, a catalog of the major discoveries leading to the development of modern electrocardiography includes Benjamin Franklin's demonstration that electricity and lightning are identical, Galvani's demonstration of animal electricity, Sanderson and Page's recording of the electrocardiogram in frogs, His' discovery of the atrioventricular bundle, Wilson's description of the laws of distribution of potential differences in solid conductors, Draper and Weidmann's measurement of transmembrane potentials in individual heart muscle cells using intracellular electrodes, and Scherlag's recording from a bundle of His using a cardiac catheter in man (Comroe and Dripps 1976). The major events thus include animal research, human research, cell research, electromagnetics, and theoretical physics. The above research represents only a fraction of the overall corpus of knowledge that underpins modern ECG, but it is indicative of the complex interplay of different fields of investigation that lead to the advance of knowledge.

Antibiotic Discovery and Animal Research

Animal experimentation played a critical role in the discovery and development of antibiotics (cf. Robinson 1967). Other techniques were also used, but animal studies provided some insights that either could not have been derived in another way, or that would have been greatly delayed without animal research.

The immediate story can be traced back to Paul Erlich, who postulated that one could develop chemical "magic bullets" that would attack and destroy the microorganisms causing specific diseases while leaving the host unharmed. His idea was based in part on the fact that antitoxins, in the correct dose, were harmless to the host and also on the observation that specific dyes could be used to identify specific bacteria. Erlich started screening various compounds in infected animals, and eventually this work led to the development and use in 1911, of arsphenamine, an organic arsenical, against syphilis.

Other active chemotherapeutic compounds were discovered, but the first true "miracle" drugs were not identified until the 1930's when Domagk, a scientist with I.G. Farben Industrie in Germany, discovered that the dye prontosil red controlled streptococcal infections in mice. Prontosil red was inactive against streptococcal infections *in culture,* and it was later discovered that the active antimicrobial entity was sulphanilamide, produced from prontosil by enzymes in the body. Many other sulpha drugs were then fabricated and were used to produce near-miraculous cures for bacterial pneumonia, meningitis, gonorrhea, and bowel and urinary tract infections. Further studies using rats and monkeys identified some of the side effects of the sulfa drugs, and treatment modifications were introduced to guard against them (Robinson 1967).

The discovery of these drugs led indirectly to the development of penicillin and the subsequent antibiotic era. Fleming had made his observations leading to the discovery of penicillin at the end of the 1920's, but its potential as a nontoxic (to mammals) antibiotic was not exploited for ten years. Fleming did investigate penicillin's antibiotic properties, but his attemps lacked enthusiasm and he never worked with a sufficiently pure extract. Fleming may also have been influenced by the opinions of Almroth Wright, his department head, who was not a believer in the germ theory (Dixon 1978).

However, the work of Domagk and his colleagues demonstrated in spectacular fashion that disease resulting from infection by microbes could be treated by antimicrobials. These results renewed interest in penicillin. Florey and Chain purified the antibiotic at Oxford and demonstrated that it was indeed a wonder drug. Massive screening programs were then established to see if other microorganisms produced substances that could be used as antibiotics, leading to the development of streptomycin and the tetracyclines.

In the early days of the search for "magic bullets" against disease-causing organisms, some work could be (and was) done *in vitro,* but the animal studies performed by Erlich and Domagk were vital in demonstrating that successful drugs could be produced, thus stimulating intense research interest. In particular, Domagk's influential discovery of the antibacterial action of prontosil could only have been made *in vivo,* since prontosil is inactive *in vitro.* The benefits of the discovery are undeniable. For example, the number of maternal deaths per 100,000 births fell sharply from 400, in 1930, to 40, in 1960 (Paton 1979).

After the Second World War, many different animal screening systems were developed to search (successfully) for compounds that show activity against a wide variety of diseases, including protozoal infections, allergic syndromes, cardiovascular disease and inflammatory reactions (Robinson 1967). A number of drugs were also discovered without recourse to animal experimentation, but this by no means proves that the animal studies were unnecessary. It is also true that modern medicine has overemphasized cures rather than prevention. But, even if the emphasis had been reversed, there would still be an important role for many of the drugs in the modern pharmacopoeia.

The Discovery and Use of Insulin

The problem of diabetes mellitus had engaged researchers for some time before the discovery of insulin. In 1889 in Germany, Van Mering and Minkowski demonstrated that removal of the pancreas in dogs produced all the symptoms of diabetes. At the beginning of the twentieth century, an American pathologist described degenerative changes associated with diabetes in the groups of cells in the pancreas known as the islets of Langerhans. Sharpey-Schafer, the leading British physiologist of the time, proposed that the islets of Langerhans secreted a substance that controlled the metabolism of carbohydrate. In 1921, Frederick Banting, a young Canadian orthopedic surgeon, and Charles Best, a medical student, succeeded in isolating the elusive hormone after experiments on dogs and named it *insulin.* Since that time, insulin has been extracted from the pancreases of slaughtered cattle and pigs to treat diabetics.

One sometimes sees in antivivisection literature the implication that insulin therapy has failed because people still die of diabetes and because the incidence of the disease has climbed during the twentieth century (Ruesch 1978). These tactics are born of desperation. Since antivivisection protestors cannot deny that insulin therapy was derived from animal experimentation, the therapy itself is denigrated. However, these implications can be fairly easily answered.

Nobody claimed that insulin therapy was the perfect treatment for diabetes. Periodic injections of the hormone cannot maintain the same delicate homeostasis of blood glucose levels as can a healthy pancreas. That is why diabetics carry glucose sweets with them—in case of a dangerous fall in their blood sugar. Thus insulin injections convert a sentence of an early and unpleasant death to one of a reasonably healthy and prolonged life. They do not, however, "cure" diabetes. In 1974, it was estimated that 130 million diabetics had had their lives prolonged by insulin (Best 1974).

The rise in incidence of diabetes is a red herring that has nothing to do with insulin therapy. As the normal life span has been extended and living standards have risen, more people have begun to suffer from maturity-onset diabetes. Thus, the rising incidence of diabetes is partly due to the conquest of the infectious diseases and to higher living standards. Genetic factors may also be involved (diabetics live longer and produce many more children) but the increase is certainly not due to any failure of insulin therapy.

Polio Vaccines

The story of the development and production of the polio vaccines is particularly instructive. Animal research played an important role in the development of basic knowledge about the polio virus (LeCornu and Rowan 1979) but large-scale vaccine production only became a practical reality when it was demonstrated that the virus could be grown in cell cultures (Enders, Weller, and Robbins 1949). This started a race to produce a vaccine among several groups of scientists in which professional pride, commercial interests, and public pressure (Wilson 1963) all contributed to an incredibly profligate use of monkeys.

The polio virus could only be grown successfully in primate tissue, and monkey kidney cell culture became the substrate of choice. Hundreds of thousands of monkeys were imported into the United States between 1955 and 1960, but a large proportion died long before they reached the laboratory. This was due to poor conditions of capture and transport, stress-induced mortality, and inadequate health monitoring. The animal research was certainly a necessary part of the final victory over polio, but monkeys, in particular, were used wastefully. Twenty-five years later, biomedical technology has progressed to the point where the use of monkeys in the production and testing of vaccine could be virtually eliminated, but economic and bureaucratic constraints militate against it (Martin, 1981b).

Surgery

Winterscheid (1967) notes that in no other area of medicine are the benefits of animal research more obvious than in the development of advanced surgical techniques. Certainly, it is difficult to imagine how we could have reached our present state of knowledge on shock, surgery, and anesthesiology without extensive animal research. In the middle of the nineteenth century when Lawson Tait was denigrating both animal research and Lister's ideas of antisepsis stemming from the germ theory, the major applications of animal research to advances in surgery were far in the future. In the nineteenth century, surgery was a last resort, even after the discovery and application of anesthesia abolished pain. This was because the mortality rates of even the best surgeons were very high. One thus only underwent surgery if death were virtually certain without it.

In the twentieth century, one advance after another has improved the patient's chance of recovery. For example, during the American Civil War, mortality from chest wounds was 62.5%, in World War I it was 24.6%, and in World War II it was 12% (Winterscheid 1967). Knowledge of respiratory physiology that was gained from the animal laboratory, and the development and improvement of mechanical respirators, contributed substantially to this decline. In another area, mortality caused by obstruction of the viable and unperforated intestine has declined from 60% to between 2% and 5% since 1940. This reduction is associated with improved techniques of intestinal decompression (Burch 1972) many of which were developed using animals.

The fields of surgery and anesthesia demonstrate a steady and, sometimes, spectacular series of advances in the last fifty years. Significant credit for these advances must be given to animal research. Without animal studies, it is virtually certain that elective surgery would still be the exception rather than the rule and that mortality rates from surgery would still be high enough to make surgery a lif-threatening rather than life-saving choice.

Conclusion

To those who feel that no animal research can be justified, the above arguments are, of course, a waste of time and irrelevant. To most of society, however, there are cases for which both human and animal research can be justified and some of the examples given above indicate fields of endeavor in which justification is certainly possible. This does not mean that every research project must be supported—far from it. However, it does mean that animal welfare protesters must be careful before they vehemently protest a particular project.

There are several good reasons why a particular project may not be acceptable. The project may use an inappropriate animal model. The research may be poorly planned. The research may duplicate other work unintentionally. The research question may not be worth asking. The research question may not be important enough to warrant the animal suffering likely to be caused by the experiment.

There are also good reasons to justify a particular project, when it is properly planned and uses an appropriate animal model. The scientists who do the research are often motivated by a strong belief that the knowledge they are generating will prove of value to both human and animal health and well-being. Compelling ethical arguments can be formulated in their support, especially if one happens to be working in a burn unit where intense human suffering is an everyday occurrance. For example, without the knowledge gained from both animal research and clinical tests, it is probable that Richard Pryor would now be dead and we would never have been exposed to his humorous but moving and eloquent warning of the dangers of cocaine (see the film, "Richard Pryor Live on Sunset Strip").

It is easy to criticize animal research. The practice lends itself to both ridicule (what human being considers himself to be like a rat or mouse, after all?) and to implications of lack of consideration and even cruelty. Most members of the public recoil from pictures of an animal (whether human or not) under surgery, and it is easy to evoke horror with visual images of animal research. However, animal welfare advocates who accept some animal research as justifiable owe it to themselves, to the animals they are seeking to protect, and to society to exercise care before taking aim at an apparently easy target. Perhaps readers will consider me guilty of ignoring my own advice in other parts of this book, but I believe that all the examples of animal research and testing I have cited are open to legitimate criticism on one or another of the grounds already mentioned.

Finally, there are many who fight with conviction and emotion to ameliorate the lot of laboratory animals because they have a capacity for suffering and feeling corresponding to those of human beings. But this argument must be used with care because if one believes that animals are like humans, then one cannot reject the use of animals as models of human behavior and physiology on the grounds that animals are unlike humans. The argument involves situational ethics. Whatever one does, some sentient being is likely to suffer as a result. In these circumstances, we must develop sound and flexible guidelines whereby society as a whole (and not just researchers or animal activists) can be guided to make the most morally acceptable choice.

Part III

TOXICITY TESTING IN SAFETY EVALUATION

CHAPTER 13

Toxicology Testing and the Use of Live Animals

The fact that some substances are poisonous and others are not has been common knowledge for all of recorded history. Poisons and poisonous animals and plants played an important role in early human affairs (as exemplified by Cleopatra's asp). Ancient magician-physicians and doctors built up their knowledge of the lethal and medicinal properties of a variety of natural substances, using this knowledge effectively to maintain their power in society. In modern society, the role of toxicologists is somewhat different! Their power has greatly diminished compared to earlier times. They are now only responsible for maintaining and advancing our knowledge of the toxic actions of both natural and man-made chemicals, and for helping to protect us from unknown hazards arising from the use of toxic substances, such as modern drugs and pesticides.

Even this role is relatively recent. Thirty years ago, the public perception of a toxicologist would probably have been limited to Agatha Christie's forensic specialists and to those clinical scientists who concentrated on developing therapies and antidotes for accidental and deliberate poisonings. Today, such work is a relatively minor part of the profession. The emphasis has shifted to developing the knowledge base which allows us to use drugs, pesticides, food preservatives, and industrial chemicals in a safe (or relatively safe) fashion.

Everybody "knows" what a toxic substance or poison is and could reel off a string of examples, such as cyanide, carbon monoxide, and weed killer. However, when one attempts to be a little more rigorous, a precise definition becomes very elusive. If we define a toxic substance as one that, on administration by some route to a living animal or plant, causes some injury or death, can we then compile a list of nontoxic substances? The answer is no, we cannot. Even distilled water, when administered in sufficient quantities, will kill rats (Boyd and Godi 1967). Admittedly, the dose must be very large (equivalent to a grown man drinking a gallon every twenty minutes up to a dose of seven gallons) but this demonstrates that, ultimately, the toxicity of a substance depends on the dose given and the manner in which it is given. As a result, chemicals are usually classified according to the dose required to produce a toxic or lethal effect, thus reflecting Paracelsus' dictum that "all things are poison and none are not and that only the dose determines that a thing is not poison."

Many classification schemes have been devised. One of them grades substances into six classes, starting with *supertoxic* and ending with *practically nontoxic* (table 13.1). The supertoxic substances are those that require only a few drops to kill a 70 kg man; they include some pesticides, cyanide, strychnine, and nicotine. *Extremely toxic* substances (one teaspoonful may be lethal) include drain cleaners, amphetamines, and morphine. Most cosmetics and alcohol fall into the *slightly toxic* class (lethal dose of one quart) while foods, candles, kaolin, and liquid petrolatum are *practically nontoxic.* The most toxic substances of all, however, are some of the natural toxins. Botulinus toxin, for example, has an estimated lethal dose for man of less than one-millionth of an ounce. Even the most potent manmade pesticides are at least a thousand times less toxic.

In the last twenty years, there has been a steady increase in public concern about the effects of our new chemically based society. Rachel Carson (1962) highlighted the problem of unforeseen pesticide effects, generating a groundswell of public concern that eventually led to the establishment of the Environmental Protection Agency and the passage of the Toxic Substances Control Act, and similar legislation in other developed countries. These laws usually required the premarket testing of new chemicals. A year before *Silent Spring* was published, the thalidomide tragedy had brought the dangers of the powerful new drugs of the pharmaceutical industry into tragic focus (The Insight Team of the *Sunday Times of London* 1979). This disaster led to a demand for much more thorough safety evaluation of new drugs.

Unfortunately the task set for toxicologists is far beyond the capacity of the crude, unreliable, and time-consuming testing tech-

TABLE 13.1
GRADING OF TOXIC SUBSTANCES

Grade (lethal dose per kg bodyweight)	Dose Required to Kill	Examples
Supertoxic less than 5mg/kg	A few drops	A few pesticides, cyanide, nicotine
Extremely toxic 5–50 mg/kg	A few drops to a teaspoon	Drain cleaners, morphine, amphetamine
Very toxic 50–500 mg/kg	One teaspoon to one ounce	Disinfectants, degreasers, aspirin, boric acid
Moderately toxic 0.5–5 gm/kg	One ounce to one pint	Polishes, hairdyes, bleaches, kerosene, methanol
Slightly toxic 5–15 gm/kg	One pint to one quart	Most cosmetics, soap products, ethyl alcohol, saccharin
Practically nontoxic	More than one quart	Foods, candles, kaolin, talc

SOURCE: Adapted from Encyclopedia Brittanica, 15th Edition, "Poisons and Poisoning" Vol. 14, p. 619.

nology presently available. There have been a few recent improvements but, for the most part, toxicology was and still is ill prepared to cope with the demand for more detailed safety evaluation of drugs, pesticides, and other chemicals. But the problem is very real.

According to the American Chemical Society's registry, there are over 4 million known chemical entities, and the number is increasing by 6,000 per week. It has been estimated that approximately 63,000 chemicals are in commercial use (Maugh 1978a) and that 1,000 new chemicals enter the market each year (Maugh 1978b). Dr. David Rall, Director of the National Toxicology Program, stated during the 1979 budget hearings that, between 1940 and 1977, the annual production of synthetic organic chemicals rose 300-fold to 306 billion pounds. Furthermore, 10,000 chemicals are produced in significant commercial quantities, with a backlog of 8,000 chemicals that need to be evaluated. However, a basic two-year study costs around $500,000 dollars and, even if the money were available, we do not have enough skilled personnel to evaluate the new compounds coming onto the market, let alone those already in commercial use (Ames 1979). Where adequate data are available, the knowledge seems to raise more questions than it answers. According to one toxicologist, "The 1970's may well be characterized as the era in which toxicology created more problems than it solved" (Stevenson 1979).

A thorough analysis would require at least one book—and probably more. Therefore, this chapter can only give a rough idea of the problem. As an initial step, it is important to place the hazards in some sort of social perspective. Therefore I begin with an outline of the question of risk assessment.

Risk Assessment

No society is risk free. We are constantly forced to make explicit or implicit choices between different types of risk, often on little or no data. For example, for many years, the risk of botulism poisoning was reduced by using nitrites in preserved meat. However, evidence has accumulated that nitrites combine with natural substances to form nitrosamines, many of which are potent carcinogens. Nitrite, itself, may be a carcinogen. Therefore, we are faced, in this scenario, with the choice of exposing ourselves to a possible increased risk of cancer or to fatal incidents of botulism. Of course, few situations are restricted to only two choices, and this is no exception. But this simplistic description of a single problem does give some idea of the difficult trade-offs with which we have to grapple.

In any discussion of risks and safety, it is important to recognize the differences between *risk* and *hazard* and the role these play in safety evaluation. *Risk* is the probability that something undesirable will happen. Risks can be estimated from a scientific understanding of the relationship between exposure and effect. *Hazard* is, by contrast, an intellectual construct and the level of hazard may be perceived quite differently by different parties. Thus, the hazards of nuclear power are considered acceptable by government authorities, whereas many local communities in the vicinity of proposed nuclear reactors may disagree sharply. The reverse is true of tobacco smoking: the government stresses the health dangers to smokers, most of whom are content to take their chances.

These examples touch on another problem in the perception of hazard. Catastrophic events create a far greater perception of hazard in the public psyche than more frequent but less dramatic incidents. For example, a substantial minority of the public refuses to fly but is more than willing to risk life and limb in a motor car. If one calculates the risks on the basis of passenger miles traveled, air transport is 2 to 3 times safer than travel in a motor car. Nevertheless, a single accident involving 100 deaths is perceived as a greater tragedy than 100 accidents each of which produces a single fatality.

(It should be noted that risk analysis is complicated by the units chosen. If one estimates transport risks on the basis of the number of journeys undertaken, instead of miles traveled, then fatal air accidents are 30 to 50 times more likely [Council for Science and Society, 1977]. The change is the result of the fact that air journeys are about 100 times longer than car journeys.)

The acceptability of hazard is also related to the amount of personal control one has over the level of exposure. Hang gliding and motor racing are very hazardous pastimes but many accept the dangers. Risks resulting from personal indulgence and convenience are often allowed to persist at quite disproportionate levels (for example, cigarette smoking). When a hazard is encountered involuntarily, then public acceptance is far lower. The lay person does not, in fact, rate risks according to the number of fatalities. Instead the public tends to regard new or unfamiliar activities and imposed technologies as risky *a priori.* If the hazard is perceived as a "major hazard" (defined as one that has a low probability of realization, combined with the likelihood of great harm if the hazard is realized), then the public's acceptance will be even lower. Of course, the actual perception that some factor is a major hazard may not arise until after the hazard is recognized. Thus, the thalidomide tragedy altered the public perception of the dangers of new drugs.

Disasters associated with other chemicals (e.g., Seveso and Love Canal) have tended to push chemicals into the category of potential major hazards, but the issue is confounded by our level of ignorance of the effects of many chemicals on the environment and ourselves. This ignorance has serious consequences when we move from a discussion of risks and hazards to the concept of *safety. Safety* is a policy issue that involves the weighing of potential risks and benefits. The simple notion that safety means freedom from harm is, unfortunately, not tenable when regulating exposure to chemicals. At the present time, we just do not know enough to identify the risks of new chemicals, and regulatory decisions are based on data that are usually grossly inadequate.

This ignorance, which is far worse at the level of the individual since few of us have the time or inclination to study the toxicological data on household chemicals and drugs, renders incomplete Lowrance's definition that a thing is safe if its risks are judged to be acceptable (Lowrance, 1976). Instead, the definition should read: "A thing is *provisionally categorized as* safe if its risks are *deemed known, and in the light of that knowledge* judged to be acceptable" (Council for Science and Society 1977, p. 13). This is certainly a more accurate definition of the safety evaluation process as applied to the regulation of chemicals (e.g., drugs, pesticides, cosmetics, and household products).

Most of our knowledge of the toxicity of a new chemical and the associated risks of human exposure is derived from animal tests. However, animal tests are very insensitive. Even in a trial using as many as 1,000 test animals and a statistical confidence limit of 90%, a negative result could still conceal a real cancer incidence of 2 tumors per 1,000 animals. If this incidence were applied to the human population of the United States, it would mean 400,000 cancers. Reducing this upper limit of risk to 2 tumors per 1 million would require more than 3 million animals (Lowrance 1976). The suggested test for carcinogenic potential uses only 800 animals, but the test's sensitivity is increased by using very large doses, which is also a controversial solution.

There is no doubt that our knowledge of the risks to humans of most chemicals is very inadequate. The usual response to this problem has been to call for more animal testing, but this solution has long since passed the point where the returns from additional animal tests justify the extra expense and time. Lederburg comments that "the one or two or three hundreds of millions of dollars a year that we're now spending on routine animal tests are almost all worthless from the point of view of standard-setting. It may be appropriate for setting alarms" (1981, p. 5).

History of Animal Testing

Animal toxicity testing is a very old tradition; it probably dates back to the early days of domestication when primitive man fed a new food to camp dogs or other animals to see if it was poisonous. However, not even this technique was infallible. Some princes increased their chances by using human guinea pigs to test their food for poison. Protection of public health and safety is also an old tradition. The Romans developed a sophisticated public health system that included inspection of foods and guarding the aqueducts against pollution. After the fall of the Roman Empire, public health measures fell into disarray and were not reinstated on a systematic basis until the nineteenth century. However, the *systematic* testing of man-made substances on animals to establish safe levels of use did not begin until early in the twentieth century with the development of vaccines and other biological therapeutics.

One can follow the rise of animal testing in the twentieth century via the annual reports produced under the Cruelty to Animals Act of 1876, in England. In 1921, only 20,000 animals were used in England for testing, mainly vaccines and biological therapeutics. This figure rose sharply during the 1920's and had reached 365,000 animals per year just before the Second World War. After the war, the classifications were changed and the category of "testing" was altered to "mandatory testing of products." Most of the animals used in both the old and the new categories were accounted for by bioassays of insulin, other hormones, and vaccines.

In 1952, a survey of British facilities indicated that the proportion of animals used for the *testing* of chemicals, as opposed to the *bioassay* of vaccines and hormones, was growing. By 1975, the commercial and pharmaceutical use of animals in Britain had grown by 400% to 3.5 million, much of it involved in the search for, and evaluation of, new drugs (see chap. 5). Some of this increase was the result of more toxicity testing. One British pharmaceutical company found that, between 1972 and 1978, they had to increase the number of animals required to test a new drug from 600 to 1,200 and staff time had almost doubled. Another company, Wellcome Research Laboratories, reports that toxicology costs increased by a factor of 3.2 between 1965 and 1979, even after correcting for inflation (Weatherall 1982). New legislation regulating drugs and food additives was part of the reason for these increases.

The U.S. market for pharmaceuticals is very important and, therefore, U.S. testing regulations have a strong influence on international practices. In 1906, the U.S. enacted the first Federal Food and Drug Act, but it did not require manufacturers to show that their products were either safe or effective. In 1937, more than 100 persons died when diethylene glycol was mistakenly used as a solvent in a sulfanilamide elixir. The following year, the Food, Drug and Cosmetic Act of 1938, which required premarketing proof of a drug's safety, was passed. Then, in 1961, the thalidomide tragedy provoked a further round of "standards tightening." The Kefauver amendment of 1962 to the 1938 Food, Drug and Cosmetic Act required that: (a) no new drugs could be tried in humans unless evidence was presented that it was safe to initiate such studies; and (b) that no new drugs could be marketed without first demonstrating that they were effective. Similar initiatives were taken by other developed countries. Some of the pressure for more animal testing is, thus, related to demands for safer drugs and foods.

In the last ten years, concerns about safety have spread from the pharmacy to the environment. The seventies have brought a spate of new laws to regulate the safety of chemicals in the environment and the work place (e.g., the Health and Safety at Work Act, 1974, in Britain, and the Toxic Substances Control Act, 1976, in the United States). In the U.S.A., the Charles River Breeding Laboratories note, in their Annual Report of 1981, that their sales have increased as a result of the demands of the Toxic Substances Control Act, and they forecast further increases. However, figures from the United Kingdom indicate that, after an initial increase, the demand for animal testing of environmental chemicals has stabilized (table 13.2).

Even though the numerical impact (on animals used in toxicology testing) of the new controls on the manufacture and marketing of chemicals has not been as great as had been predicted, these laws have further entrenched the notion that extensive animal testing is necessary to establish "safety."

Animal Testing: Techniques and Scope

The animal testing required under government regulations varies according to the type of chemical being tested. A food additive or a new drug, which is likely to be used over a long period of time, will be subjected to intensive animal and clinical trials. A new chemical that is used only sparingly in the workplace under conditions that involve little human exposure need be subjected to relatively superficial tests. Public pressure, however, has forced companies to use more animals and spend more time on testing, and the economic costs are becoming significant.

TABLE 13.2
EFFECT OF GOVERNMENT REGULATIONS ON ANIMAL TESTING OF CHEMICALS IN THE U.K.

Year	Approximate No. of Animals Used
1977	144,600
1978	159,800
1979	115,500
1980	125,900

SOURCE: Adapted from Home Office 1981.

NOTE: Laws affecting animal testing and the numbers used are:—the Health and Safety at Work Act, 1974; Agricultural Poisonous Substances Act, 1952; and equivalent overseas legislation.

Today, a basic series of animal toxicity tests would involve acute, subchronic, chronic, reproduction, and irritation studies (see table 13.3 for an example of the type of testing regime commonly required). The acute studies are designed to determine the toxic effects of a single large dose or a few closely spaced smaller doses. Subchronic studies evaluate the adverse effects of regularly repeated exposures over periods ranging from a week or two to three (or six) months. A chronic study evaluates the effects of a chemical for periods ranging from several months to several years. The chronic study may include an evaluation of a number of specific effects, such as the chemical's cardiotoxic, neurotoxic, hepatotoxic (liver), and nephrotoxic (kidney) potential, as well as its carcinogenic potential. The reproduction studies will include an evaluation of the chemical's potential to induce fetal deformities (teratogenicity) as well as genetic defects in sperm and ova. The irritation studies will include both ophthalmic and dermal effects.

Mice and rats, and either dogs or monkeys as the nonrodent species, are commonly employed. Rabbits are used to assess tera-

TABLE 13.3
TOXICOLOGICAL TESTING AS REQUIRED UNDER THE U.S. TOXIC SUBSTANCES CONTROL ACT 1976

1. SUBSTANCES INVOLVING INFREQUENT OR SINGLE HUMAN EXPOSURE	
Oral LD50	rats
Dermal LD50	rabbits
Inhalation LC50	rats
Eye irritation	rabbits
Dermal irritation	rabbits
2. SUBSTANCES INVOLVING OCCASIONAL LOW-LEVEL HUMAN EXPOSURE	
The Above Studies, Plus:	
Subacute (10–90 days) oral	rats, dogs
Subacute (10–30 days) inhalation	rats
Subacute (10–21 days) dermal	rats, rabbits
Neurotoxicity	hens
Sensitization	guinea pigs, humans
Mutagenicity	bacteria
Water toxicity	fish
3. FREQUENT LOW- OR HIGH-LEVEL HUMAN EXPOSURE	
All Studies in 1 and 2, Plus:	
Mutagenicity	rats, mice
Teratology and reproduction	rats
Carcinogenesis/lifetime	rats, mice
Long-term wildlife effects	quail, ducks

SOURCE: Adapted from Ellison 1977.

togenicity and irritation, while guinea pigs are used for hypersensitivity (allergenicity) testing. Several different forms of test exposure may be necessary. Pesticides that are applied in liquid form will be put through dermal toxicity studies. Inhalation studies are common for gases and aerosols. As a general rule, acute studies (e.g., LD50, irritancy) account for about 50% of the animals used (Home Office 1981).

As might be expected, these studies are expensive. The choice of the proper animal model (Plaa 1976), the husbandry and maintenance of the animals, the detailed controls required to avoid the many pitfalls in animal testing (Stara and Kello 1979), and the skilled staff needed—all these increase the costs. The current price tag for a comprehensive battery of toxicological tests to assess human risk is probably around $1 million per chemical. A suitable battery of screening tests probably would not cost more than $50,000 to $100,000, however. For example, an acute (oral, inhalation, dermal) test on rodents and rabbits would cost about $50,000 to $60,000 in 1983 dollars (Manufacturing Chemists Association 1975). If a subchronic, oral dog test were included, the cost would increase by $25,000 to $30,000. Drug testing is far more detailed and, thus, far more expensive. Each new drug is estimated to require an overall investment of about $30 million (including dead-end research) before it reaches clinical testing (Katz 1980).

Each toxicity test requires a large investment in human time. Apart from the husbandry needs of the animals used, a wide array of observations may also be necessary. Acute studies generally involve observations on behavior and appearance, the recording of the number of animals dying—and time of death, and cursory histopathology observations. Subchronic and chronic studies require far more detailed pathology studies, along with regular, weekly clinical examinations of all the animals in the test. As a result, properly conducted tests are not only labor-intensive, they require skilled and experienced personnel. Record keeping and storage of samples is another problem. In a standard carcinogen study, one must store the data obtained from weekly clinical examinations on 400 to 800 animals, as well as the pathology slides and original organ samples—20 or more from each animal. Data and sample storage can rapidly become a major problem for an organization that runs such tests regularly.

Many factors affect the integrity of a toxicology test and its application to human exposure (Stara and Kello 1979). The choice of species is often the most difficult. Rodents (rats and mice) have become the species of choice for most studies, but this has been influenced primarily by economic considerations (e.g., relatively low housing costs, ease of production, short life span) and not because the results of rodent studies correlate well with human data. In fact, we know very little about such correlation, and there has been little apparent interest in resolving this deficiency. Primates are often considered to be the best species because they are closest to humans phylogenetically, but in some instances human data do not parallel the data from other primates. In choosing an animal for toxicology testing, it is important to match the metabolic profile of the chemical in the test animal as closely as feasible with the human metabolism of the chemical. Frequently, however, appropriate metabolic studies are only undertaken after extensive animal testing has already been completed.

Life span is an important consideration in selecting animals for chronic studies. A rat has a life span of 3 years, and there is some argument whether this is adequate to model the human experience of 70 years' exposure to environmental pollutants (Stara and Kello 1979). The sensitivity of an animal to a chemical also changes with age—young animals being approximately 2½ times more sensitive (Krasovskii 1976). Body weight, sex differences, the genetic strain of the animal, dose selection, and proper diet are also very important factors in designing appropriate test protocols. The doses selected must include the maximum tolerated dose (MTD) that produces a toxic effect, but no mortality or major functional change, and a "no effect" dose that produces no evidence of toxicity. The MTD is important in carcinogen studies because the use of a high dose is one of the only ways of increasing the sensitivity of the animal test, which is low at best. On the other hand, there has been much criticism of the use of dose levels that do not mimic the human situation—as in the saccharin controversy (Office of Technology Assessment 1977).

These are not the only criteria that must be considered but Stara and Kello (1979) argue that they are the most critical. It is clear that there are many traps for the unwary in toxicity testing. Unfortunately, regulatory authorities have tended to respond to these problems by writing increasingly specific guidelines, incorporating inadequate and antiquated testing techniques, which allow little room for scientific judgment. The process of "intensification" of animal testing may be peaking, however, because economic pressures and public protests have slowed, and perhaps stopped, the swing of the pendulum in this direction.

Criticism of Animal Testing

There is no shortage of criticism of animal testing, or of the apparently relentless pressure to increase the number and extent of animal studies required, with little regard for their usefulness in predicting human hazard. Consider the following excerpt.

> Animals, as well as humans, have been used suboptimally for experimentation with drugs. In pre-Phase 1 testing, academia has participated in (even if it did not initiate) the proliferation of animal models for studies of toxicology. . . . This usually results from the public's emotional feeling that such tests would guarantee safety if and when the drugs were given to humans. *In most cases, the animal tests cannot predict what will happen when the drug is given to man.* Standards for toxicology are often set by officials, such as Federal regulators, who are responding to the pressures of ill-advised but obviously well-intended legislators or consumer groups who may or may not be aware of the futility of increasing the amount of testing required when some tests often have no bearing on how man will respond to the drug. The multiplication of tests in animals, often invalid tests and possibly performed in the wrong species, can only add to the cost of drug discovery and can only limit the range of discovery. *The result is not only a waste of animals but also a waste of a limited scientific resource;* the loss is compounded by the fact that human life will not benefit from drugs whose release is unnecessarily delayed. (Melmon 1976, pp. 125–126 [emphasis added]).

The complaint that excessive testing delays drug development has recently been repeated by Weatherall (1982), and the detrimental impact of bureaucratic demands is a common refrain among toxicologists and industrial scientists (Heywood 1978; Stevenson 1979; Zbinden 1976). Heywood argues that "toxicology is a science without scientific underpinning. . . . The toxicologist has turned his attention to the mechanics of how to carry out studies . . . but (this) will certainly not help to interpret this data" (1978, p. 686). Stevenson argues that toxicology is in the position of having to provide answers when the basic question is so general as to make the task virtually impossible. The bioassay systems now availalbe may not be able to provide the answers, even when the question is defined, yet we try to hide these difficulties by escalating "the size and complexity of experiments without a commensurate decrease in the problems of interpreting the results obtained" (1979, p. 9).

The pressing need at the moment is for more data on mechanisms and the development of a theoretical framework for toxicology within which rational decision making can have a chance. Lederburg (1981) decries "blind" animal testing and calls for the redeployment of resources to raise the status of toxicology as a fundamental science, rather than a scientific arm of government regulators. Heywood (1978) makes the same plea and argues that, if mechanisms of toxicity were known, then choice of species and tests, the interpretation of results, and their appropriate extrapolation to man would be relatively easy. The animal welfare advocate could also throw in the suggestion that the data now being generated should be subjected to a more thorough analysis, and that a few appropriate computer models and analytical tools could lead, at the very least, to valuable insights and a potential reduction in the need for more animal tests.

Another complaint, heard, paradoxically, from both animal welfare critics and industrial scientists, is that the animal tests are either irrelevant to human exposure or insufficiently accurate to be used for regulatory decision making. The animal welfare literature is full of claims that animal tests are useless because side effects were found in humans, despite extensive animal testing. In many cases this is true but, in many others, the potential risk was known in advance and the potential benefits were judged to be sufficient to outweigh the risks. Animal welfare criticism of animal testing on the grounds that humans are not rats may be on the right track, but it is usually too simplistic to make much of an impact on decision makers.

Industrial criticism concerning the lack of relevance of animal testing is usually related to concerns about the economic impact of regulating or banning a product. For example, the National Coffee Association reacted to criticism of the health hazards of coffee by producing a thirty-five page rebuttal, arguing that no basis exists for extrapolating animal results on fetal defects to humans. The association statement quoted Professor S. J. Yaffe of the University of Pennsylvania's Department of Pediatrics and Pharmacology thus:

> Experiments with animals have yielded considerable information concerning the teratogenic effects of drugs. Unfortunately, these experimental findings cannot be extrapolated from species to species or even from strain to strain within the same species, much less from animals to humans. (*American College of Laboratory Animal Medicine* 1980, p. 13).

Another example is the American Industrial Health Council's (AIHC) arguments against proposed Occupational Safety and Health Administration's (OSHA) regulations on carcinogens in the work place. Most of those testifying on behalf of the American Industrial Health Council (1978) recognized that animal tests have been and would continue to be useful. Nevertheless, they highlighted the deficiencies of the animal tests for carcinogens—deficiencies that would make one very reluctant to accept mouse data as applicable to human beings.

A third argument, and one which is usually the exclusive domain of the animal welfare critics, is that the ethical costs of many of the toxicology tests on animals are too high. The underlying reasons for this argument are: (a) that the animal suffering is too great and the knowledge gained too trivial; (b) that the substance being tested satisfies a frivolous human need and therefore does not justify any animal suffering; (c) that the animal test is an established habit and there has been little or no effort to find and promote alternatives that would produce less animal suffering and death; and (d) some combination of the above elements. In the following chapters some of these criticisms are examined with reference to the LD50 and Draize tests as well as carcinogen and teratogen testing.

CHAPTER 14

The LD50 Test

In the 1920's, Trevan, a British biologist, was looking for a way to standardize, with a high degree of precision, such important but potent drugs as digitalis extracts, insulin, and diphtheria antitoxin. The potency of these drugs varied from one batch to another, and it was vital to assess accurately the potency of each batch so that correct doses could be administered to patients. Trevan (1927) demonstrated that the median lethal dose (LD50) could be used as a reliable and reasonably precise measure of potency, provided a sufficient number of animals were used. This is the origin of the LD50 figure (or Lethal Dose—50 percent), a measure which determines the dose which will kill 50% of the target group of organisms.

Over the course of the last fifty years, the LD50 has gained wide acceptance as a measure of the acute toxicity, not only of biological therapeutics but also of drugs, household products, pesticides, and any other chemical on which toxicological studies have been performed. The LD50's original purpose, the standardization of biological potency, has largely been forgotten as improved technology permitted substances such as digitalis to be assayed by physicochemical techniques. (It is still used, however, for the biological standardization of a few therapeutics.) Use of the LD50 as a general measure of toxicity, with a status almost on a par with such physical constants as specific gravity, is totally unwarranted—and is also a needless waste of animals.

It must be emphasized that determination of the LD50 is not the same as determining the acute toxicity of a chemical compound. Our knowledge of structure-toxicity relationships is so limited, and the mammalian system is so complicated, that the use of a few mammals to obtain a rough measure of the lethal dose (or Approximate Lethal Dose) of a chemical and its associated qualitative effects if still necessary. But determination of a precise statistical figure for acute toxicity—that is, the LD50—cannot be justified. There is no useful gain over the determination of an Approximate Lethal Dose.

Animal Welfare Opposition

It is hardly surprising that animal welfare groups object to the LD50 test. The idea of deliberately administering a large enough dose of a substance to poison to death approximately 50% of a target group of animals (the surviving animals are killed and examined two weeks after dosing) is virtually guaranteed to arouse the anger and protest of animal welfare groups. The LD50 test was apparently first highlighted as a problem by United Action for Animals in the 1960's. It rapidly became a favorite whipping horse for the animal welfare community.

For example, one animal welfare claim is that nontoxic test substances are forced down an animal's throat until the stomach ruptures or the breathing passages are blocked. It is true that the test substance for oral studies is usually intubated (i.e., put directly into the stomach via a tube), and it is also true that some toxicologists have been decidely overzealous in their analysis of acute toxicity. The determination of the LD50 of distilled water (469 ml/kg body weight) by Boyd and Godi (1967) is a prime example of gratuitous and unthinking cruelty. Boyd and Godi had methodological problems in this study because administration of more than 280 ml of distilled water (in 70 ml lots) resulted in water being expelled from the anus as fast as it was given intragastrically!

However, stomach rupture is an uncommon form of death in LD50 testing; it is caused by careless use of the intubation device rather than the physical mass of the test material. In addition, most toxicologists are no longer making LD50 determinations on relatively nontoxic substances. If the substance causes no deaths at a dose of 10 gm per kilogram bodyweight (i.e., one-hundredth of an ounce for a mouse), then it is classified as nontoxic and an LD50 is not determined. This is the so-called limit test, in which only a few animals need to be used.

Research done at the Central Toxicology Laboratories of Imperial Chemical Industries (U.K.) has demonstrated that the above dose does not, in itself, cause any discomfort to an animal. In the mouse, an oral dose of 50 gm/kg was necessary to cause stomach distension, while an intravenous dose of 25 ml/kg was associated with hyperpnea. The equivalent dose limits in the rat were 30 gm/kg and 30 ml/kg, respectively (cf. Rowan 1982b).

Pressure applied by the animal welfare movement, led the British Home Secretary to request his Advisory Committee to the Cruelty of Animals Act to review the extent of the use of the LD50 test in Britain and to consider its scientific necessity and justification. The Advisory Committee (1979) found that 4% to 5% of U.K. animal experiments (approximately 230,000 animals) were involved in LD50 testing. They recommended that LD50 tests continue but that, for safety evaluation purposes, a degree of precision which calls for large numbers of animals is not necessary and that, wherever possible, a limit test should be employed.

Not surprisingly, this did not satisfy the animal welfare groups, who had pressed for substantial changes. For example, the Committee for Reform of Animal Experimentation (CRAE) (1977) had called for an immediate abolition of the LD50 in those cases where it is invalid and for a phasing out, over a period of years, of the LD50 in other instances. FRAME (1977) (Fund for the Replacement of Animals in Medical Experiments) had recommended that not more than 10 animals be used for acute toxicity determinations and that not more than 5 gm of a test substance per kilogram body weight be administered to an animal. The Universities Federation for Animal Welfare (UFAW) (1977) had recommended an even lower limit of no more than 1.2 gm of test substance per kilogram body weight, with the stipulation that, if no toxic effects are observed at this dose, the substance should be considered nontoxic.

Certain government departments and industrial associations were also very critical of the LD50 test. The Scottish Home and Health Department stated that the LD50 gives only an *order of magnitude* indication of toxicity and recommended that there should be no mandatory requirement to demand an LD50 test on a particular chemical substance. For innocuous substances the LD50 is likely to be in the order of grams per kilogram and no useful information is going to be obtained from a relatively precise value. The Association of British Pharmaceutical Industry stated that regulatory authorities should be encouraged not to demand unnecessary precision of acute lethality or LD50 estimates.

However, the LD50 test (or at least the term *LD50 Test*) continued to be sanctioned by the establishment, and animal welfare groups continued to press for changes. The most recent flurry of activity was marked by two symposia, in Holland and Sweden, and the establishment of an International Coalition to Abolish the LD50 (Marten, 1981a). According to Henry Spira, one of the co-ordinators of the Coalition, they are aiming at better protection of the public and abolition of a cruel and archaic method of testing for toxicity. The campaign proposed to target companies involved in animal testing on the grounds that such companies have a social responsibility to fund research into alternatives.

For the moment, however, it is clear that the LD50 issue is mainly a political problem and not a matter for scientific analysis and research. There is just too much evidence indicating that a precise LD50, with its standard deviation and requiring at least 50 to 60 animals per test, is unnecessary in most instances. Determination of an approximate lethal dose, using 6 to 10 animals, will usually be more than adequate, especially if we only wish to allocate chemicals to a rough toxicity class (e.g., highly toxic, toxic, moderately toxic, and nontoxic). Bureaucratic inertia and the conservative attitudes of some toxicologists, who grew up believing a precise LD50 to be one of the cornerstones of any toxicological study, still prevent any meaningful action.

Toxicological Factors

Before the development of the LD50 measure, the toxicity of a compound was usually expressed as the lowest dose that had been observed to kill an animal. In 1926, de Lind van Wijngaarden demonstrated that the scatter of values for the minimum lethal dose of digitalis extract in cats followed a normal distribution. In 1927, Trevan injected thousands of frogs with digitalis extract and plotted the mortality percentage against each dose to obtain a sigmoidal curve. From this curve, he determined the LD50 dose as that killing 50% of the animals. It is important to note that Trevan developed this measure for "the accurate *standardization,* by biological methods, of drugs which are not available *in chemically pure form*" (1927, p. 483 [emphasis added]).

Nowadays, the test usually starts with 1 or 2 ranging studies on 10 to 15 animals (usually rats) to determine the approximate lethal range of the test chemical. The final stage involves administration of 4 to 6 doses of the chemical to groups of 10 animals (5 males and 5 females). All animals are inspected frequently for the first 8 hours after dosing, and at least twice a day thereafter. Any survivors 14 days later are killed and inspected. The LD50 is calculated using specially prepared nomograms (Litchfield and Wilcoxon 1949), and the measure is usually expressed as the number of milligrams (milliliters) of the test substance per kilogram of body weight of the test animal.

The LD50 test has not only been widely criticized by animal welfare groups, its usefulness has also been called into question by a number of toxicologists (Morrison, Quinton, and Reinert 1968; Sperling and McLaughlin 1976; Zbinden 1973). In 1960, Barnes stated that too much effort was being spent on producing accurate LD50 figures and not enough on defining acute toxicity effects (Barnes 1960). In 1973, Zbinden, a World Health Organization toxicology consultant, called the LD50 test "a ritual mass execution of animals." On a later occasion he added that "most experts considered the modern toxicological routine procedure a wasteful endeavor in which scientific inventiveness and common sense have been replaced by a thoughtless completion of standard protocols" (1976, p. 333). In 1969, Baker stated that acute toxicity studies "are of little use and are expensive in animals. The main information they give is an indication of the size of dose required to commit suicide" (1969, p. 23).

The LD50 figure is notoriously variable and can be affected by a range of factors, some of which are presented below. More detailed information is available in Morrison, Quinton, and Reinert (1968) and Zbinden and Flury-Roversi (1981).

Marked differences are seen in the LD50 values for different animals, and with a wide variety of substances. For example, there is a 75-fold difference in the LD50 for methylfluoroactate between dogs (0.15 mg/kg) and monkeys (11.0 mg/kg) (Mitruka, Rawnsley, and Vadehra 1976). Tenfold (and greater) interspecific differences in the LD50 figures are commonplace. Large differences can occur even between closely related species. For example, 5-(N-piperidino) 10,11-dihydro-5H-(a.d.)-cycloheptene gave oral LD50 values of 1,160 mg/kg in male albino mice and 6.6 mg/kg in male albino rats. (Morrison, Quinton, and Reinert 1968).

Enormous differences can also exist between different strains of the same species. For example, Dieke and Richter (1945) reported that the LD50 of thiourea in the Hopkins strain of rats was 4 mg/kg, whereas it was 1,340 to 1,830 mg/kg in Norwegian rats. Age and sex may also affect the value of the LD50. Many of these differences are related to specific variations in enzyme content and activity, since so many xenobiotics must be metabolized before they are excreted from the body

Diet can have an important effect on an animal's reaction to a chemical. The time that food is withdrawn from mice can cause a fourfold change in the LD50 value for methohexitone sodium (Quinton and Reinert 1968). Other environmental factors affecting the LD50 include the microbiological status of the animals, the ambient temperature, the time of year, and such social factors as the number of animals per cage.

The multitude of factors that affect the measure explains why the LD50 value for the same substance varies from laboratory to laboratory, even when efforts are made to standardize conditions (Hunter, Lingk, and Recht 1979; Zbinden and Flury-Roversi 1981). For example, an interlaboratory comparison among 65 European laboratories produced four- to tenfold ranges for identical substances (Hunter, Lingk, and Recht 1979). According to the Federal Insecticide, Fungicide and Rodenticide Act, a substance with an oral LD50 of between 50 and 500 mg/kg body weight must carry a warning label. It thus makes a difference to the bureaucracy whether a substance has an LD50 of 350 or 1,280 mg/kg. Yet this was the smallest range found in the Hunter, Lingk, and Recht survey. Obviously, the classification of compounds by their LD50 is a very arbitrary affair and perhaps should be recognized as such rather than camouflaged in a respectability blanket of statistics.

The Proposed Value of the LD50 Test

Various claims have been put forward regarding the need for LD50 values, but for the most part they fail to justify the claimed need for a statistically precise figure. A rough (semiquantitative) measure of the acute lethality of the test substance, combined with *qualitative* data on symptoms and organs at risk is usually all that is required.

The LD50 is useful as a guide in planning further toxicological or pharmacological studies. There are numerous examples in which chronic dosing produces a response pattern very different from acute dosing. Zbinden (1963) reported that the acute toxicity of two isoniazid analogues in mice was the direct opposite of the compounds' chronic toxicity in rats. Sperling and McLaughlin (1976) note that the LD50 is only marginally informative and that it has little prognosticating value for nonlethal toxicity resulting from single or multiple low-level exposures. Morrison, Quinton, and Reinert (1968) comment that the LD50 figure is at best only a rough guide for the toxicologist and pharmacologist because the acute-dose effect may be so different from the chronic-dose effect. Malmfors, of Astra Pharmaceuticals in Sweden, has also recently argued that the LD50 is a waste of animals in planning pharmacological studies (cf. Rowan 1982b). There may be instances in which good arguments can be presented in favor of determining an LD50, but they rarely appear in print. The determination of an LD50 as a routine first step in such studies is, however, slowly falling out of favor (Zbinden and Flury-Roversi 1981).

The LD50 is of value to clinicians and others in poison reference centers. Arguments supporting the use of the LD50 frequently cite the fact that many cases of accidental ingestion of large quantities of chemicals occur, most of which involve children under the age of five. In such cases, the therapy may be unpleasant or dangerous, and it is therefore valuable to know the extent of the risk of poisoning before embarking on a course of therapy.

However, Dr. Birgitta Werner of the Karolinska Poison Information Center, in Stockholm, has argued forcefully that the quantitative data provided by an animal LD50 is virtually useless. She also claims that many of her European colleagues agree with her and that they would rather have qualitative information on symptoms and modes of action (cf. Rowan 1982b). As can be seen in table 14.1, an animal LD50 provides little information on actual human toxic or lethal doses.

The LD50 is of value to regulatory agencies in classifying substances according to their toxicity. Examination of standards reveal that the various regulatory bodies around the world have set up arbitrary

TABLE 14.1
HUMAN ACUTE LETHAL DOSES (LD_{LO}) AND ANIMALS LD50S (ORAL)

Chemical	Human LD_{LO} (mg/kg)	LD50 (mg/kg) Rat	Mouse	Rabbit	Dog
Aniline	350	440	—	—	—
Amytal	43	560	—	575	—
Boric acid	640	2,660	3,450	—	—
Caffeine	192	192	620	—	—
Carbofuran	11	5	2	—	19
Lindane	840	125	—	130	120
Fenoflurazol	—	238	1,600	28	—
Cycloheximide	—	3	133	—	65
Aminopyrine	—	1,380	1,850	160	150

SOURCE: Adapted from Christenson and Luginbuhl 1975; Sunshine 1979.

lines between very toxic, toxic, and nontoxic substances, and that precise LD50 figures are unlikely to provide further clarification. The German Democratic and Federal Republics define very toxic materials as those with LD50s of less than 100 mg/kg; toxic materials as those with LD50s between 100 and 300 mg/kg; and moderately toxic materials as those with LD50s above 300 mg/kg. The Soviet Union has standards set at less than 50, between 50 and 200, between 200 and 1,000, and above 1,000 mg/kg as measures of very toxic, toxic, moderately toxic, and nontoxic materials, respectively (Woodcock 1972). Common Market countries use less than 25, between 25 and 200, between 200 and 2,000, and above 2,000 mg/kg as their standards for very toxic, toxic, moderately toxic, and safe substances (Official Journal of the European Communities 1976). Similarly disparate figures are used as standards by the United States and the Council of Europe (Christenson and Luginbuhl 1975; Woodcock 1972).

As demonstrated by the collaborative study by Hunter, Lingk, and Recht (1979), LD50 values for the same substance can vary substantially, depending on who makes the determination. Therefore, the argument that a precise figure, with its standard deviation, is necessary for classifying chemicals according to toxicity is analogous to claiming that a sow's ear is a silk purse. One may as well base one's classification on approximate lethal values. The use of such figures will, at least, not lead to a false sense of security bolstered by carefully calculated, but toxicologically meaningless, standard deviations.

The LD50 is necessary to standardize some biological therapeutics that cannot be standardized by physicochemical means. As has already been mentioned, the LD50 was developed as a method to standardized biological substances, and it is still used today for this purpose. This is one of the few valid arguments for performing a full LD50 determination. However, there are relatively few substances for which the lethal end point is still required in biological standardization.

The British Pharmacopoeia Commission (1977b) looked at a variety of bioassay systems involving the determination of an LD50 and separated them into three categories. The first category included those in which no alternative to the LD50 test was considered possible—such as in the bioassay of pertussis vaccine, botulinum antitoxin, and clostridium botulinum antitoxin, or in potency tests for rabies antiserum or veterinary vaccines. The second category included those in which alternative systems are in the process of adoption, (for example, the determination of a mild paralytic end point in the bioassay of tetanus antitoxin and tetanus vaccines. The final category included those in which alternatives might be possible but in which further investigation is necessary (as in the case of the bioassay of typhus vaccine, in which instance the vaccine's infectivity in eggs is under investigation as an alternative; or in the measurement of the potency of gas-gangrene antitoxins, in which lecithinase activity might be used as an indicator). The report further noted that the initial expense involved in adequately developing and testing a new method may act as a strong deterrent to such work.

The Development and Use of Alternatives

At the present stage, some animal dosing is required in acute toxicity studies and, therefore, any discussion of practical alternatives must focus on tests that use fewer animals rather than on those systems that involve no animal testing at all. In the long-term future, however, cell-culture systems or computer programs to predict toxicity may become sufficiently developed to provide an adequate measure of acute toxicity. With this in mind, some preliminary studies with these systems are described, as well as some simple technique to effect an immediate reduction in the number of animals used.

The "Limit" Test. When substances are basically nontoxic, there is no point in doing more than confirming that a single dose of, say, 5 gm/kg, does not cause any harmful effects in a group of 6 to 10 animals. There is some argument about the size of this limit dose (ranging from 1 gm to 10 gm/kg) and some standardization will be necessary.

The Approximate Lethal Dose. In the 1940's, two papers were published setting out protocols and evaluation studies for the performance of an approximate-lethal-dose (ALD) determination (Deichmann and Leblanc 1943; Deichmann and Mergard 1948). The ALD is determined by administering graduated doses, each increasing by approximately 50%, to single animals. The spacing of the doses in these increments precludes, in most cases, the possibility of killing an animal with one dose and failing to kill with the next higher dose. The doses are spaced sufficiently close together, however, to allow the determination of the degree of toxicity of a compound within reasonably specific limits. Provided that a suitable starting dose is chosen, this method alows determination of an ALD using as few as 4 but, more usually, 6 to 10 animals.

Deichmann and Mergard (1948) compared the ALD with a statistically precise LD50 in 87 different acute tests, using more than 30 different chemical entities, several different vehicles, and several different animals. The largest differences seen was for o-nitrodiphenyl (25% solution in olive oil given orally to the rat), in which case the ALD exceeded the LD50 by 70%. For most of the remaining compounds, the variations were less than 20%. The overall mean variation between the ALD and LD50 in this study was 1.2-fold. This is hardly significant when interspecific and interlaboratory variations are considered.

When one adds the qualitative data obtained from more detailed observations on the 6 to 10 animals (as opposed to cursory examination of 60 animals), the ALD probably provides more satisfactory data on which to base further toxicity studies or hazard evaluations. However, a suggestion that the LD50 be replaced by the ALD will no doubt be met with significant resistance. Some animal welfare activists will be unhappy about the killing of *any* animals by poisoning, some toxicologists will be unhappy with the proposed gradual disappearance of the LD50, and statisticians will be most unhappy about the lack of statistical rigor.

Statistical Techniques. The "up-and-down" method of Dixon and Mood (1948) and the "moving averages" technique of Thompson (1947) use fewer animals than the usual technique for LD50 determinations and yet give figures of satisfactory precision (Weil, 1952). Molinengo (1979) suggests another possibility in which the relationship between dose and survival time is plotted. He determined the LD50 and the variances for 10 drugs with this technique, using only 6 to 11 mice. The values were in close agreement with figures given in the literature.

Future Possibilities. At present, it is not possible to eliminate animal testing (either acute or chronic) and at the same time maintain an acceptable level of public safety. There are, however, a number of interesting new techniques being developed that establish new measures of acute toxicity. Whether it will be possible to so refine them that they can replace whole, live animals is uncertain, but their potential is being explored.

One obvious possibility is the use of cell cultures to provide a measure of acute toxicity. A number of such systems have been explored. However, it should be noted that the data obtained will not be of the same nature as LD50 data, since *in vivo* metabolism and distribution cannot, at present, be effectively mimicked. The cell-culture approach could involve one of a number of variations on a theme, and a number of studies have explored the relationship between *in vitro* and *in vivo* toxicity (e.g., Barile and Hardegree 1970; Ekwall 1980).

One particularly interesting study by Autian and Dillingham (1978) indicates that the intrinsic cellular toxicity (T_1) observed *in vitro* is a predictively useful measure in the expression of animal toxicity and provides meaningful information with respect to structure-activity relationships. However, the authors cautioned that the study only suggests a direction for the development of good predictive systems.

Computer systems have also been suggested as a possible means towards the goal of predicting LD50s without concomitant animal testing. For the moment, however, some of the suggested computer programs employing multiparameter equations (e.g., Craig and Enslein 1978) have come in for severe criticism (Rekker 1980). The Craig and Enslein (1981) approach in the first place, is characterized as a "dummy-type" parametric analysis in which several important computer-modeling criteria are not met. For example, oral LD50 values are not based on well-defined interactions—they are, instead, a reflection of an extensive set of different and poorly understood interactions between chemical substances and biological systems. Second, the range of substances selected do not come from a series of structurally similar (congeneric) compounds. This is the prime reason for having a large and unwieldy set of parameters. However, this criticism tends to be pedantic carping since there is no reason why, given a large enough set of examples and good substructural keys for the compounds, we should not steadily expand from a narrow band of "congeners" to a much broader band.

Rekker's (1980) critical dismissal of the Craig and Enslein program is supported wholeheartedly by the International Union of Pure and Applied Chemistry's Working Party on Quantitative Structure-Activity Relationships. Despite this, it is clear that computer modeling of quantitative structure-toxicity relationships (QSTR) does hold promise for the future. If QSTR methods could be combined with *in vitro* systems, it is possible that reasonably reliable LD50 estimates could be derived without resort to animal tests. However, such estimates are unlikely to be judged acceptable by regulatory agencies for the foreseeable future.

Conclusion

While there are some research avenues that might lead to the development and validation of methods to reduce the use of animals in LD50 tests, the main problem is political and bureaucratic. We could achieve substantial reductions without sacrificing one bit of human safety merely by shifting the emphasis from quantitative studies to qualitative and semiquantitative studies.

According to Zbinden and Flury-Roversi, the minimum changes required from regulatory agencies are these:

1. In all guidelines and regulations for toxicological studies, it must be stated specifically that the concept of acute toxicity testing (harmful effects off single doses) is not identical with the performance of a classical LD50 test.
2. In all guidelines and regulations for toxicological studies the classical LD50 test carried out with large animals, such as dogs, monkeys, pigs, etc., must be prohibited. In its place, a short-term test on small numbers of animals incorporating a variety of clinical, chemical, and histopathological examinations must be required.
3. In all guidelines and regulations for toxicological studies it must be pointed out that the classical LD50 test with small rodents using large numbers of animals is only permissible if the reason for the desired high precision is clearly stated and scientifically justified. In all cases where high precision of the LD50 determination is not required, a test using small numbers of animals must be used. For this test supplementary clinical, chemical, and histopathological examinations must be required.
4. In all guidelines and regulations for toxicological studies it must be stated that no LD50 test should be done with pharmacologically inert substances. It is sufficient to determine that a single oral dose of approximately 5 gm/kg and a single parenteral dose of approximately 2 gm/kg cause neither acute symptoms nor death in animals.
5. The requirement to conduct a LD50 test in newborn animals must be eliminated from all guidelines and regulations. For the assessment of special risks in newborn humans and infants, clinical-pharmacological and pharmacokinetic studies must be required. These should preferentially be done in human subjects but may be substituted by specifically designed studies in immature animals.
6. For the classification of chemicals with the aim to assign them to a toxicity class in official lists of poisonous substances the approximate LD50 values determined in small numbers of animals by an appropriate method must be accepted. Whenever possible, the classification

> should also consider other relevant data including information obtained through pharmacological, biochemical, and chronic toxicological studies. Modern knowledge and concepts of structure-activity relationships should also be applied (1981, p. 97).

Exploitation of animals for the determination of acute toxicity is considered an unfortunate necessity at present. However, we could do a great deal more to alleviate animal suffering, without sacrificing human safety, by adopting the above recommendations. Researchers also have an obligation to develop a less stressful test to demonstrate that the human commitment to reduce our exploitation of other species is more than an empty statement of intent. Recently, the Pharmaceutical Manufacturers Association (1982) has released a statement on the LD50 in which they note that it is not a necessary part of drug development and that satisfactory data can be obtained using far fewer animals. In fact, it is estimated that changing from the LD50 to a modified test could reduce the use of animals by a substantial amount (up to 20,000 animals per year for some larger companies). This is the sort of initiative that must be implemented and allowed to prosper.

CHAPTER 15

The Draize Test

In a survey conducted in the United Kingdom, the vast majority of respondents objected to cosmetic testing on animals (National Opinion Polls 1974). Several years later, in a BBC television program on animal experimentation, the following question was put to a number of individuals in a group of shoppers: "Would you use a shampoo if it had not been safety tested on animals?" All answered that they would not. The difference in the responses to the two surveys illustrates the complex nature of the problem.

Some argue that society does not need cosmetics, but they offer few constructive suggestions as to how a $10 billion industry should be prevented from innovation in Western "free" market economies. Others argue that the products should not be tested on animals since humanity has no right to subject animals to pain and suffering for the sake of frivolous vanity products. The conclusion is that the consumer should bear whatever risks are associated with the manufacture and sale of cosmetics and toiletries. Indeed, a *Glamor Magazine* reader survey indicates that a majority of those responding would be willing to use a drug that had not been safety tested. This type of thinking, however, is anathema to consumer organizations, who argue that cosmetics and other chemicals should be even more closely regulated (Nader 1974).

Faced with the continuing threat of litigation as a result of adverse reactions, the cosmetic industry is unlikely to retreat from animal testing. It is known that tests do not necessarily protect consumers from all risk, but they will reduce the extent of the risk and will also provide some protection for a company in the event of a large claim for damages.

There is, thus, no immediate prospect that product innovation (requiring safety evaluation of new products) in the cosmetic or other industries will cease, or that consumer pressures for increased safety of such products will abate significantly. There is, however, a third option for those who object to live animal tests. As biological technology improves, more and more safety testing could be done without using living animals. Animal welfare groups, seeking to highlight this possibility, selected the Draize eye irritancy test as the target of a campaign calling for the development of a nonanimal alternative to the test.

The Draize Test: History

The Draize eye test is named after the principal author of a paper that outlined the test's main features, including a numerical scoring system to provide an idea of the irritancy of the tested substance (Draize, Woodard, and Clavery 1944). According to Dr. John Draize, the test was originally intended for use in England. British scientists had asked the U.S. Food and Drug Administration for assistance in testing eye irritants that they were considering for use in chemical warfare. The test was later adopted by the FDA as a more general test for eye irritancy under the authority provided by the U.S. Federal Food Drug and Cosmetic Act of 1938. Because of incidents involving harmful cosmetics (in 1933, a woman was blinded and disfigured by a mascara [Lamb 1936]), this act specifically requires that cosmetics be free of deleterious or poisonous substances, and the Draize test was pressed into service to guard, as far as possible, against one of the hazards.

The test has repeatedly been criticized, however, as crude, unreliable, or inappropriate (Beckley 1965; Buehler 1974; Carter and Griffith 1965; Weil and Scala 1971). It is certainly crude. It distinguishes between irritants and nonirritants essentially on a pass-fail basis, and the cut-off point is set very low (almost any reaction is enough to fail a compound) to provide an adequate margin of safety. Despite this, the test protocol has not been changed in any substantive way and efforts to develop nonanimal alternatives have been few and far between. The situation at the start of the Draize campaign was, thus, as follows.

The Draize Test: Comparative Studies

The parts of the eye most affected by topically applied substances are the cornea, the bulbar and palpebral conjunctivae, and the iris. The corneas of laboratory mammals are very similar in construction (Duke-Elder 1958, p. 452) and variations are, for the most part, minor. The main thickness of the cornea does vary: in man it is 0.51 mm; in the rabbit, 0.37 mm; and in the cat, 0.62 mm.

The rabbit has historically been the animal of choice for the Draize eye test, but this seems to have occurred more by accident than by design. The use of the rabbit eye for predicting human ophthalmic response has been challenged from time to time. It has been suggested that the greater thickness of the human cornea and other anatomical differences may contribute to the rabbit's greater susceptibility to alkali burns of the cornea (Carpenter and Smyth 1946). However, the rabbit is less sensitive than man to some other substances (Marzulli and Simon 1971). Tears are produced in smaller quantities in the rabbit than in man, but the rabbit nictitating membrane may supplement the cleansing effects of tears, ensuring adequate removal of foreign substances.

Proctor and Gamble (1979) produced an extensive critique of the Draize test. They expressed disappointment at the fact that Federal agencies have been singularly unresponsive to widespread criticism of it. They commented on the differences between the human and rabbit eye (Beckley 1965; Buehler 1974) and the fact that the rabbit's response to the test material is greatly exaggerated when compared to human responses (Carter and Griffith 1965). Proctor and Gamble suggest that, when the rabbit result is equivocal, organizations should have the option of using monkeys. The monkey has been proposed as a more suitable model because it is phylogenetically closer to man (Beckley, Russell, and Rubin 1969), but there are still species differences (Green et al. 1978). In addition, use of monkeys for eye irritancy testing is inappropriate, in part because of their diminishing availability. Also, the expense does not warrant the purported fine-tuning involved in the use of monkeys. The rat has also been suggested as an alternative model but has not been investigated in any depth. Studies at Avon indicate that it may be less sensitive than the rabbit (G. Foster 1980, personal communication). If one must use an animal for eye irritancy testing, then the rabbit would appear to be as appropriate as any other species.

It has already been stressed that the Draize eye irritancy test cannot be routinely used to grade substances according to their potential irritancy for human beings but can serve only as a pass-fail test. Weil and Scala (1971) surveyed intra- and interlaboratory variability of the Draize eye and skin test. Twenty-four laboratories, staffed by experienced toxicologists, cooperated on the survey. The results demonstrated that the Draize eye irritancy test produces highly variable results in routine practice. For example, cream peroxide was recorded as a nonirritant by certain laboratories, but as an irritant by others. As a result of this study, Weil and Scala (1971) concluded that the rabbit eye and skin procedures currently recommended by the federal agencies for use in the delineation of irritancy of materials should not be recommended as standard procedures in any new regulations. *Without* careful re-education these tests produced unreliable results. It is pertinent to note that Scala holds that the Draize test can be used to grade irritants, but only by experienced and careful researchers (Scala 1981).

A follow-up study by Marzulli and Ruggles (1973) corroborated the Weil and Scala (1971) data, but the authors interpreted the results differently. They argued that, in most cases, laboratories were able to distinguish an irritant from a nonirritant if that was all that was requested *and* if all four criteria (changes in cornea, iris, conjunctival redness, and conjunctival chemosis) were used for judging in a simple pass-fail procedure. Such a pass-fail test is, of course, a relatively crude discriminatory measure and the "pass" line has, perforce, to be set at the slightest sign of an adverse reaction.

In addition to the problems identified above, the results of ophthalmic tests on rabbits may bear little relation to human responses (Davies, Harper, and Kynoch 1972; Van Abbe 1973). Thus, the technical shortcomings in the Draize eye test include:

1. Lack of fine discrimination
2. Questionable applicability to human situation
3. Questionable reproducibility of results from different laboratories in routine testing

Possible Alternatives

The effect of an irritant occurs initially via direct action on the epithelial cells of the cornea and conjunctiva. (The corneal epithelium is underlaid by numerous nerves, which explains why damage to the epithelial layer is so painful). The irritant may then pass through the cornea and damage the underlying corneal endothelial layer. Since the ephithelial and endothelial cells play a major role in maintaining the cornea as an optically clear organelle, damage to these cell layers has a critical, and possibly irreversible, effect on vision. Although it is argued that one must use a whole, living eye, intact in the body, to test for all the possible cell interactions, it should be possible to develop cell or organ culture systems that can mimic part of the *in vivo* response. In addition, it might be possible to use human tissues to eliminate the problem of interspecific extrapolation.

The use of cell cultures to assess irritancy has been briefly studied at Hazleton Laboratories in Great Britain (Simons 1980). L929 cells, an established line of mouse embryo cells, were used in a cytotoxicity assay of three shampoos, classified as being of high, moderate, and low irritancy in the Draize test (M152, M153, and M154, respectively). A stock suspension of cells was prepared and 7×10^5 cells inoculated into 3 ml of growth medium. After a further 48-hour incubation, the floating and attached cells were collected and the total number of viable cells was counted. The results from the experiments shown in table 15.1 were typical of all the tests.

The test could distinguish between the shampoos of low and high irritancy but not between the moderately irritant shampoo and the others. The author stressed that the results were preliminary and that the discriminatory powers of the test needed to be improved. But the experiment did suggest "that there is a basis for an *in vitro* system for the screening of severe irritants as an alternative to the Draize eye test" (Simons 1980, p. 151). This initial work is being followed up at Beecham Products Research Department, in England, using human buccal mucosa cells (Bell et al. 1979).

On the other hand, other cell culture studies have not demonstrated the same potential. A report from a scientific workshop, sponsored by the Canadian Society for the Prevention of Cruelty to Animals (1980), notes that even with several different parameters (e.g., cell

TABLE 15.1
CELL CULTURE (L–929) IRRITANCY TEST

Shampoo	Total Cell Death End Point (ppm Shampoo/Dish)	95% Confidence Interval
M152	2,690	2,020–3,500
M153	6,020	4,660–7,810
M154	6,920	5,980–8,050

SOURCE: Adapted from Simons 1980.

death, release of cytoactive agents), the correlation between the cell culture test results and animal studies ranged from abysmal to poor. Also, Unilever, after spending over $200,000 investigating cell culture systems, determined that they were not reliable (Johnson 1981). Nevertheless, cell culture protagonists argue that it is premature to dismiss these systems, since the technological advances over the past five years have opened up many new prospects for application to irritancy testing.

Another *in vitro* approach is the use of whole organs, such as bovine eyes obtained from slaughter houses (Carter, Duncan, and Rennie 1973) or human eyes from an eye bank. In eye banks, the epithelium becomes compromised and damaged, but one can study the effects of chemicals on the endothelium, using corneal swelling and thickness as an easily followed parameter of damage. This has been done with some success at Unilever, in the United Kingdom (Burton, York, and Lawrence 1981).

There is no satisfactory nonanimal alternative currently available for eye irritancy testing. Therefore, any modifications that could be incorporated immediately to make the test more humane should be encouraged. Such modifications range from not doing the test at all to the use of smaller volumes or local anesthetics. The following scheme could substantially reduce both animal suffering and the number of animals required.

1. *Do not test substances with physical properties known to produce severe irritation.* For example, it is known that strong alkalis (above pH 12) and acids (below pH 3) produce severe irritant reactions. These reactions would be worse if the test substance has a buffering action. Therefore, there is no need to test such substances—they can be labeled as irritant (or avoided in manufacture) without further ado.
2. *Screen out irritants using* in vitro *or less stressful tests.* The *in vitro* eye preparations described above could be used to screen unknown substances. Irritant substances could either be labeled as such or discarded. One could also utilize results from skin irritancy studies and human patch testing to avoid testing substances that produce trauma, since the skin is likely to be less sensitive than the delicate tissues of the eye.
3. *When the test is conducted in the live animal, smaller volumes should be used.* It has been argued that the use of 10μl, rather than the standard 100μl would be a far more realistic test in terms of assessing possible human hazard (Griffith et al. 1980). The use of smaller volumes would produce less trauma, and one could also do some modest dose-response studies to ensure that a nonirritant has a sufficient margin of safety.

4. *Where it is necessary to test substances that cause pain and irritation in the rabbit, then local anesthetics should be used.* This is recommended by the Interagency Regulatory Liaison Group (1981).

Draize Test: The Campaign

During the last decade, the humane movement has become much more vocal over the issue of testing of cosmetics on laboratory animals. However, with one or two minor exceptions, the campaigns launched against such cosmetic testing have been poorly planned. Effectiveness was undercut by inadequately researched position papers (with the exception of one produced by the Society for Animal Rights) and a dissipation of energy in too many different directions. All this changed when Henry Spira, a New York English teacher and animal rights activist, put together a coalition of more than 400 American humane societies aimed specifically at the use of the Draize eye irritancy test by cosmetic companies.

The Draize test was selected as the specific (and only) target for several reasons. First, the test had been criticized in the scientific literature as being inappropriate. In addition, routine Draize testing produced data that were shown to be unreliable for regulatory purposes (Weil and Scala 1971). Second, the Draize test can cause severe and readily visible trauma to rabbit eyes; this produces a strong reaction from the general public as well as from many scientists. As Henry Spira says: "It's the type of test that people can identify with—people know what it feels like to get a little bit of soap in their eyes" (Harriton 1981). Third, the test has remained essentially unchanged for over thirty years, despite the fact that the prospects for the development of alternatives, as well as modifications, are good. In fact, even Professor Smyth (1978), then chairman of the Research Defence Society, in London, recommended that the Draize test was a good project for research into possible alternatives.

The cosmetic industry was selected as the target because it was vulnerable to the image problem raised by the use of the Draize eye test. The picture of the sultry model advertising a new beauty product is not readily juxtaposed with an inflamed and swollen rabbit eye.

The first step in the campaign consisted of an approach to a major cosmetic company, Revlon, to ask for their assistance.

Revlon requested a formal proposal, and one was accordingly drafted, suggesting that Revlon should (a) approach the Cosmetic, Toiletry and Fragrance Association with a proposal that the CTFA co-ordinate a collaborative effort by industry to seek an alternative to the Draize; and (b) commit $170,000 (0.01% of their gross income) to the project.

Revlon responsed in a letter, dated February 13, 1980, stating that the proposal had been turned over to the relevant CTFA Committee and that "neither Revlon, or any other single company, can give any assurances as to what action, if any, this committee, or any other committee of the CTFA, may take in this matter, except to say that it will receive consideration." Needless to say, this response did not find much favor, and the next phase of the coalition's campaign was set in motion.

This phase consisted of an exhortation to all groups to mobilize their forces to write and protest to: (a) the major cosmetic companies; (b) the relevant U.S. regulatory bodies (the Consumer Product Safety Commission, the Environmental Protection Agency, the Food and Drug Administration, and the Interagency Regulatory Liaison Group); (c) their representatives in Congress; and (d) the media. The Millenium Guild in New York City chose to target Revlon alone, and took out a full-page advertisement ("How many rabbits does Revlon blind for beauty's sake?") in the *New York Times,* on April 15, 1980.

The advertisement itself became news and focused the campaign spotlight on Revlon. It also galvanized other companies into action. The CTFA was soon organizing a closed workshop to discuss the prospects of developing an alternative to the Draize. However, Revlon was not off the hook. Donald Davis, editor of *Drug and Cosmetic Industry,* noted in the June 1980 issue of the magazine that the attack on Revlon "probably has engendered more sympathy in the industry over the company's 'plight' than any other single happening since the founding of the company . . . but . . . there has been a distinct lack of 'volunteers' among industry leaders to help take the heat off Revlon" (p. 35).

By the end of the year, Revlon had grown tired of being the sacrificial lamb and, in a move that came as a major surprise to the rest of the industry, announced that it was making a three-year grant of $750,000 to Rockefeller University to research possible alternatives. As an additional twist, Revlon invited other cosmetic companies to join in supporting such research. Now that the dust has settled, one can determine that the campaign has had a major impact.

Draize Test Campaign: The Results. The Consumer Product Safety Commission (CPSC), which was the only Federal agency with a formal regulatory requirement for irritancy testing, led the way by placing an embargo on all in-house use of the Draize test, on May 8, 1980, pending the results of an investigation into the use of local anesthetics. The study took a lot longer than the three months scheduled, but eventually the CPSC research identified a satisfactory local anesthetic. They found that a double dose of tetracaine abolished the pain response and did not significantly affect the irritancy scores (*Rose Sheet* vol. 2 (17), April 27, 1981). In addition, the CPSC has modified its requirements for Draize testing. For example, if a product contains a known irritant or is itself an irritant in the skin test, CPSC will ask the manufacturer to label it as an irritant. Only if the manufacturer refuses, will CPSC resort to an actual test. According to Richard Gross (personal communication, 1981), the CPSC executive director, the agency would probably reduce its annual quota of Draize testing by about 90%. The Environmental Protection Agency joined the CPSC in establishing an in-house moratorium, on October 1, 1980.

The Food and Drug Administration took no initiative on the Draize test until mid-1981. They then announced that they still considered the Draize test to be the best available technique for assessing irritancy, but that they were "committing funds to allow one of our senior scientists to study a new *in vitro* technique" (U.S. Congress 1981).

Perhaps the most significant initiative was that taken by the Interagency Regulatory Liaison Group (IRLG) (1981). Established to standardize test protocols among five different Federal agencies, they suggested new guidelines for the Draize test that included the following elements:

1. The guide states that "for humane reasons, substances known to be corrosive may be assumed to be eye irritants and should not be tested in the eye. Furthermore, substances shown to be severe irritants in dermal toxicity tests may be assumed to be eye irritants and need not be tested in the eye."
2. The guide recommends that only 3 rabbits (instead of 6 to 9) be used initially and that, only if the results are equivocal, should more animals be used.

3. The guide notes that anesthetics should not be used in most instances. "However, if the test substance is likely to cause extreme pain, local anesthetics may be used prior to installation of the test substance for humane reasons"

As a direct result of the Draize campaign, a number of research proposals and ideas have been suggested and funded, and previously unpublished data have been made available. For example, Johnson and Johnson's experience with the use of serotonin release as an index of response to an irritant was announced at the recent NIH symposium on trends in bioassay methodology (McCormack, 1981).

The search for a satisfactory local anesthetic has been led by the CPSC, which suggests that tetracaine HCl appears to be the most suitable (International Journal for the Study of Animal Problems 1981b). In England, Unilever reports that its scientists have successfully used amethocaine HCl as a local anesthetic when the test substance produced a pain response. Comparative studies with 31 substances demonstrated that, in no instances, did the local anesthetic decrease the irritant response, and in only one case was there a very marked increase in irritancy (Johnson 1981).

New research on the potential of cell culture started with a project at Tufts Medical School, with a $100,000 grant from the New England Antivivisection Society. A relatively direct approach to the problem was outlined. Monolayer cultures of human corneal endothelial cells would be established and characterized and then, the response of the cells to irritants, using a range of end points such as vital dye assays, 51Cr release, and morphometric analysis would be assessed. One of the major concerns proved not to be a problem at all—it transpires that there is no shortage of corneal endothelial cell material from human eye banks.

Joseph Leighton of the Medical College of Pennsylvania has been funded, by an animal welfare consortium, to research the potential of a very different system—the chorioallantoic membrane (CAM) of the developing chick embryo. For the most part, the chick embryo has been used in two fields, virology and cancer transplantation, but the inflammatory response of the CAM to irritating foreign inocula is well known (Leighton 1967). The basic technique involves opening a window in the shell and then dropping the test material onto the CAM. Since the CAM has no demonstrable nerve fibers for pain sensation and fertilized eggs are very cheap (3 for $1) compared to rabbits, the CAM test may be a humane and economic alternative to rabbit eyes. Preliminary results with corrosive substances confirm the promise of the CAM as a bioassay for inflammation, but its true potential will not be known until sensitivity and discrimination is tested with moderate irritants and nonirritants.

The Rockefeller team, with its $750,000 from Revlon, has adopted a four-pronged approach. One member is looking at the response of peritoneal macrophages to irritant-induced release of chemotactic agents. Another is characterizing the cellular pathology of the irritant response, while yet another is looking for biochemical and morphological markers of the irritant reaction in cell cultures of rabbit cornea, human liver, rat liver and mouse fibroblasts. The approach that has so far generated the most data is looking at the effect of irritants on the transport of nucleotides and proteins across fibroblast cell membranes. According to the principal investigator, the results are very encouraging.

The other cosmetic companies did not respond directly to the Revlon appeal to support the Rockefeller initiative. Instead, they opened a fund under CTFA auspices, which was eventually awarded to the Johns Hopkins University School of Hygiene and Public Health to establish a Center for Alternatives to Animal Research. While the center will not itself conduct any research, it has established both an intramural (Johns Hopkins) and extramural research program, and is also acting as an information clearinghouse.

The projects that have been funded range from a study of such basic phenomena as the permeability of epithelial cell tight junctions to an immediate search for a practical end point to discriminate between irritants and nonirritants. Two of the projects will investigate protein distribution in the cells as a function of injury, such as the synthesis of specific, soluble "stress" proteins by rat hepatocytes in response to a challenge by toxic agents. Another three projects propose to investigate correlations between the release of histamine or prostaglandins by cells challenged with an irritant.

Four years ago, David Smyth (1978), Chairman of the Research Defense Society in England, stated that "there does seem to be a good case for a major attempt to find an alternative to the Draize test." He also suggested that, if suitable projects were supported, then the need for anything but the mildest form of *in vivo* eye testing should be greatly reduced within a few years. Considering the promise of some of the projects already mentioned, this prediction may well prove true. It demonstrates once again—and in contrast to the protestations of scientific opponents of the idea of specific support for alternatives (Neal 1981)—that the availability of funding is a potent stimulus to thought. When scientists learned of a possibility of research support to develop an alternative to the Draize test, a number of speculative and creative proposals were produced and circulated.

General Discussion

It has been argued that rabbit eye testing is necessary to protect companies from legal liability. However, in one case where shampoo accidentally splashed into a consumer's eye causing irritation, the court ruled for the manufacturer and against the FDA, who brought the case.

Joan Hughes, the injured person in the case, accidentally dropped a bottle of Beacon Castile Shampoo while bathing and the shampoo splashed up into her eye. The concentrated shampoo caused destruction of the corneal epithelium, as well as burning and pain, but the epithelium was fully restored in three days. In preparing for the case, a full concentration of Beacon Castile Shampoo was tested in both human and animal subjects and the results were entered into the court record.

In 1978, the General Accounting Office (GAO) published a report on cosmetic regulation in which they referred to this case (General Accounting Office 1978). The report specifically noted that the court had ruled in favor of the company because the FDA had failed to show (a) that the shampoo was any more hazardous than similar products on the market and (b) that the results of the tests on rabbit eyes could be extrapolated to humans. From the point of view of animal welfare groups, this was very significant since it apparently undermined the "protection from legal liability" argument for conducting Draize tests. The actual transcript of the judgment (U.S. District Court of the N.D. of Ohio, Eastern Division, No. C–71–53, January 7, 1974, pp. 164–6) indicates however, that the GAO report was not accurate. The judgment was not based so heavily on the issue of extrapolating from rabbits to humans. The judge ruled in favor of the company mainly because the shampoo would not get into the eye in concentrated form under "normal conditions of use." However, he did state that the "rabbit studies, standing alone, do not warrant condemnation of this product."

The Draize test campaign has been successful for a number of reasons. First, the humane movement has campaigned in a co-ordinated and highly directed fashion, thereby applying sufficient political pressure to make it worthwhile for the establishment to move on the issue. Second, while the humane movement has been united, scientists have been divided over the need for the test and the manner in which it is performed. For example, Professor Frederick Sperling, an experienced and well-known toxicologist, has stated that he holds "no brief for this [Draize] test, which is not a good one scientifically. . . . It is deplorable that better testing for *primary* skin and eye irritation has not been developed in the approximately 40 years of its use" (Sperling 1981, p. 481).

By contrast, Dr. T. M. Brody, Chairman of the Michigan State University Department of Pharmacology and Toxicology, responded in typical knee-jerk fashion to a student article criticizing the Draize test. In his response, "Safety before Sanctity," in the *MSU News* (May 8, 1980), he castigated the encroachment on toxicology of uninformed and hypocritical pseudoscientists (spawned by the array of special interest groups in the health field) and then proceeds to justify the Draize test, although he does acknowledge that it is not perfect. However, he then goes on to say that "the suggestion by the authors of the viewpoint that cell cultures may have any utility in assessing the safety of chemicals in the human eye is without any redeeming merit. It clearly indicates the naivete of these students about matters biological."

It is clear from interviews with technicians and scientists involved in conducting Draize eye irritancy tests that the test is unpopular because it causes a great deal of suffering—at least, the behavioral responses of the rabbits imply great suffering. When the coalition then implicitly asked whether the data obtained from the test is worth such suffering and whether there are no other possible alternative techniques for generating data with equivalent powers of discrimination, few scientists were able to answer with an unequivocal no. The public response, on the other hand, has been a very definite and vocal no. As a result, regulatory agencies and targeted companies have gone some way toward answering the public concern.

CHAPTER 16

Chronic Toxicity Tests

The LD50 and Draize tests have received the most attention and criticism from animal welfare groups. Acute tests, of which these are two classic examples, account for approximately 50% of all animals used in safety evaluation; the remaining animals are used in subchronic and chronic studies, and in studies of the metabolism, absorption, distribution, and excretion of foreign compounds (pharmacokinetics and pharmacodynamics). The chronic tests generate more data and are generally much more informative than the acute tests in predicting human risk. However, the long time span of these tests (3 to 30 months) and their high cost ($50,000 to $500,000) means that fewer animals (relative to acute testing) are used.

Two of the better known chronic animal tests are those for carcinogens and teratogens (substances that cause cancer or fetal deformities, respectively). Carcinogen testing has generated the most media attention in recent years as public fears of this unpleasant disease have stimulated consumer concerns. Tumors of various types now account for 20% of all deaths in the United States (approximately 400,000 annually), and increasing attention has been focused on the effect of synthetic and other chemicals on the cancer rates. The need for teratogen testing burst upon the scene with the thalidomide disaster. Some companies were already testing for teratogenic effects if they considered that women of child-bearing age were likely to be exposed to the chemical, but testing for the effects on reproduction and fetal development was not a standard requirement. This has now changed.

Carcinogen Testing: Background

It is widely accepted that at least two-thirds of all cancers are caused by environmental factors, but the proportion of cancers caused by *synthetic chemicals* in the environment is a much-contested statistic (Cottrell 1981). The chemical industry tends to argue that cancer caused by environmental industrial chemicals accounts for no more than 5% of all tumors. Other advocates from the government and the labor movement argue that the incidence is much higher—possibly 40% or more (Epstein 1979). In fact, some appear to assume that the term "environment" refers exclusively to industrial chemicals. However, Higginson (1979), founding director of the International Agency for Research on Cancer and one of the originators of the theory concerning environmental causes of cancer, claims that this is a gross misinterpretation. He uses the term "environment" to refer to the total environment, both cultural as well as chemical, and he estimates that the bulk of environmentally related cancers are caused by tobacco, alcohol, diet, and cultural patterns in life style (table 16.1). For example, cancer of the mouth in Asia represents some 35% of all cancers (in contrast to Europe and North America where it is less than 1%) and is related to the common habit of chewing betel nuts and tobacco leaves.

This issue is important because, if most cancers are caused by environmental factors, be they offshoots of the chemical industry or our own life-styles, then these cancers are theoretically preventable. If we can identify those factors that cause cancer and remove them from the environment then we should be able to reduce the incidence of the disease. This explains the great interest in identifying carcin-

TABLE 16.1
ESTIMATES OF THE PROPORTION OF CANCERS AND THEIR CAUSES

	Female	Male
Tobacco	7	30
Tobacco/alcohol	3	5
Sunlight	10	10
Occupation	2	6
Radiation	1	1
Iatrogenic	1	1
Life style (culture and diet)	63	30
Congenital	2	2
Unknown	11	15

SOURCE: Adapted from Higginson 1979.

ogens. However, there are a number of problems with this idea. First, even when cancer-causing agents are identified (e.g., tobacco use) it may be very difficult to remove them from the environment. Second, two or more substances may act synergistically, causing a much higher incidence of cancer than the sum of the two acting separately. Third, the methods currently used to identify carcinogens are insensitive and inadequate. For present purposes, I will concentrate here on the methodological issues as they affect animal and alternative test systems.

Carcinogen Testing: Animal

The use of animals to study the action of carcinogens dates back to 1916, when tumors were first induced in animals after dosing the animals with chemicals (coal tars). This was followed by the development of the theory of chemical carcinogenesis. However, there were many problems, not the least being the long latent period between application of a chemical and the appearance of tumors. Many of those problems have been overcome or can be minimized in the research laboratory, and this has led to the development of bioassay techniques based on research experience. Unfortunately, research practices were not critically evaluated before they were adopted for regulatory purposes (Gori 1980). The standard bioassay is not necessarily the best approach scientifically; it has also become increasingly expensive. In 1962, the standard NCI carcingoen screening test of a single chemical took as little as 8 months and cost from $10,000 to $15,000. Ten years later, the test involved 2 species, took 30 months, and cost $75,000. Nowadays, the standard test in 2 species may take 5 years and can cost as much as $500,000 (Weisburger and Williams 1981). Cost is not the only problem, however.

Animal tests are not perfect identifiers of human carcinogens. Approximately 7,000 chemicals have been tested for carcinogenicity in animals, about 1,500 of them being reported as carcinogenic. However, at least half of these studies were completely inadequate (Saffioti 1976) and, even today, quality control is a major problem. The testing of unknown samples is not feasible because of expense, and regulators must rely on professionalism to maintain standards. However, there will always be human error in any test on the scale now required (lifetime dosing, hundreds of animals, tens of thousands of slides and samples) and sometimes the errors will be serious. Thousands of tests done at Industrial Biotest Laboratories, in Illinois, have been questioned as a result of information that the results of some of the tests have been doctored (*Wall Street Journal,* Feb. 21, 1978).

The second problem in evaluating the predictability of animal tests is the lack of definitive information on the carcinogenicity of pure chemicals. Approximately 26 chemicals or chemical mixtures are firmly associated with cancer in humans. A further 56 are implicated as human carcinogens, but the evidence is less definitive (Maugh 1978b). As a result, one has a relatively small number of chemicals that can be used to validate the predictability of animal tests, and even with these, there is much room for disagreement (Jansen 1979). However, all of the 26 or so identified human carcinogens, with the exception of arsenic, plus the 56 probable carcinogens have been shown to be carcinogens in animals (but see later).

The correspondence between known human carcinogens and animal carcinogenicity has been put forward as strong support for the value of animal tests in identifying human carcinogens. However, this is a far cry from demonstrating that animal tests will always identify human carcinogens. There are too many cases in which animal tests did not identify a possible human carcinogen, and the fact that human carcinogens are also all carcinogenic in animals does not prove that *all* animal carcinogens will cause cancer in humans.

For example, the Japanese food additive, furylfuramide (AF–2) was tested for carcinogencity in rats in 1962, and in mice in 1971, with negative results in both cases. It was then found to be an extraordinarily potent mutagen in the Ames test (Ames 1979). More thorough testing on AF–2 showed that it was carcinogenic in mice, rats, and hamsters. Ames gives examples of several other chemicals that were first shown to be mutagens in *in vitro* tests and then subsequently confirmed as animal carcinogens in carefully conducted animal tests.

Not only do negative results from animal tests cause problems, the use of positive results to identify human carcinogens is also subject to argument and controversy. It has been argued that mice could be from thirty thousand to one billion times more cancer-prone than humans (Gori 1980), and Jansen (1979) has identified a set of chemicals that cause lung or liver tumors in mice, but are not tumorigenic in other species. Dieldrin, to take one instance, causes tumors in mice but not in rats, hamsters, or monkeys. In addition, it is not mutagenic. In fact, the significance of mouse liver tumors are a particular problem in carcinogenicity testing, especially for organochlorine pesticides, which produce a large proportion of noninvasive neoplasms (Carter 1978).

In fact, the whole biassay program for testing possible carcinogens has recently been called into question by Salsburg (1983). He set out to validate, as best he could, the standard bioassay for identifying carcinogens as specified by the National Cancer Institute. Of the published bioassay data, 170 or more of the reports were appropriate for his analysis for specificity and sensitivity.

Specificity was evaluated by determining how well the standard 2-species, lifetime feeding study performed in identifying human carcinogens. Of the 26 known human carcinogens, 7 were excluded from the analysis since they involved human inhalation exposure. Only 7 of the remaining 19 had been shown to cause cancer in long-term feeding studies using the NCI protocol. This represents a success rate of 36.8%. Sensitivity was evaluated by analyzing the data to see whether the test compound could be identified as causing cancer, protecting from cancer, or both. Salsburg found that, using decision rules apparently specified by the regulatory agencies themselves, 70% of 170 bioassay reports indicated that the test compounds both caused cancer and protected against cancer. At best, these results cast a pall over the reliability of the standard animal bioassay. Any proposed alternative tests apparently need not perform particularly well (anything better than chance would be sufficient) in order to improve on the specificity and sensitivity of the NCI bioassay for carcinogens.

There is undoubtedly some correspondence between human and animal carcinogens, but the correlation is far from perfect. Animal tests have definitely produced false negatives—and most likely false positives as well (Jansen 1979). Given the genetic differences between humans and laboratory animals, and the consequent differences in the metabolic fate of environmental chemicals, it is not surprising that animal tests are not perfect. And yet, the moment an animal welfare critic suggests using (or trying) an *in vitro* alternative, animal testing is suddenly presented as virtually infallible.

Animal test methodology has been taken as far as possible. The insensitivity of animal testing has long been a problem. For example, a negative result using 1,000 test animals (today's standard test employs 400 mice and 400 rats) would indicate (with 99% confidence) that the annual cancer incidence from the test chemical is less than 0.45 (Maugh, 1978c). If the entire population of the United States were exposed to the same level of the chemical, then this result indicates that not more than one million people would get cancer. Obviously this is an unacceptable level.

But there is an additional problem. The above calculations are based on the assumption that the background incidence of tumors in the test animals is zero. This is far from the case. Different strains of rats and mice have different tumor incidences, and there is much debate over whether one should use a "sensitive" or "resistant" strain for carcinogen testing. In addition, the incidence of "spontaneous" tumors in a particular group may vary considerably.

A recent report (Task Force of Past Presidents 1982) discusses the need to use historical controls and gives an example of pheochromocytoma in male rats varying from 0 to 28% over a series of control groups, even though the average incidence in 1,100 animals was 2%. In one study, the incidence of pheochromocytomas in one control group was 8%, while it was 28% in the other. The incidence in the low, middle, and high dose groups was 14%, 18%, and 26%, respectively. Therefore, without the second control group, there would have been an apparently clear dose-response for the chemical and it might easily have been labeled a carcinogen. Given this type of background variation, only potent carcinogens will show up clearly in the animal assay. Since research indicates that there is a millionfold range in carcinogenic potency (Meselson and Russell 1977), the problem could be very serious.

One way in which toxicologists have tried to overcome the problem of insensitivity of the animal test is by increasing the dose administered to the maximum amount tolerated by the animal over its lifetime without producing overt toxicity. This method of overcoming a major problem of the animal test is far from perfect. For example, the large doses employed in some instances (e.g., saccharin) may overwhelm the usual defense mechanisms and cause cancers related purely to a bulk effect rather than the specific properties of the chemical. Nitriloacetic acid (NTA), a highly touted substitute for phosphates in laundry detergents, caused urinary, bladder, and kidney tumors at the maximum tolerated dose. Therefore, it never entered the U.S. market, although Sweden and Canada have both permitted its use. Later studies have shown that NTA formed complexes with essential metals ions at the very high doses used and that this led to interference in the replication of DNA. NTA carcinogenicity appears, therefore, to have been a feature of the bulk properties of the chemical.

Use of such high doses is widely questioned, and a furious battle rages around the "threshold controversy." Some argue that the body's defense mechanisms can cope with a potential carcinogen below a certain level (the threshold) and that tumors will be produced only if the chemical exposure is above the threshold. Others argue that there is no threshold and that a carcinogen will cause some cancer no matter what the level of exposure. Most regulatory decisions involve evaluating the hazard of chemicals at doses far below those used in the animal studies, but there is very little reliable information on the effects of carcinogens at such low doses. As a result, risk estimates can vary enormously, depending on the assumptions made. The estimated human risks from ingestion of 0.12 gm of saccharin a day ranged from less than one case to *10 million cases* per lifetime for the population of the U.S.A. (National Academy of Sciences 1978).

There are many other problems with the animal tests for carcinogens, and regulators are under constant pressure to make decisions based on grossly inadequate data. In fact, regulators often succumb to the easy way out—making decisions on the basis of numbers "since it is always easier to regulate on the basis of numbers (objective evidence) than on the basis of the judgment (subjective evidence) of the toxicologist" (Task Force of Past Presidents 1982).

Carcinogen Testing: In Vitro. In vitro tests for the identification of potential carcinogens are a relatively recent phenomenon, but they have generated a great deal of interest (Hollstein et al. 1979). There are two basic types—those that detect damage to the genetic material (e.g., bacterial mutagenicity, mammalian cell DNA repair, and sister chromatid exchange) and those that use cell transformation (from "normal" to tumorigenic) as the test end point. The first type of system relies on the assumption that most carcinogens are also mutagens. This assumption appears to be true for the large majority of known carcinogens (Jacobs 1979). Some hormones, tumor promoters, solid-state carcinogens and a few other chemical types that do not appear to act directly on the genetic material are the major exceptions currently identified. Of course, there are those who hotly dispute the idea that mutagenicity and carcinogenicity can be related in this way (Rubin 1976) and they may have some good grounds for concern (Cairns 1981).

Cost factors are the main reason for such widespread interest in short-term tests. Compared to the animal test ($500,000 for a 3-year study), a battery of short-term tests is very cheap and very quick ($25,000 for a 3-month study). Because of the speed and relative cheapness of these tests, it would also be a lot simpler to conduct quality control tests. As a result, the reliability of the short-term tests could be checked regularly, unlike the animal tests. The short-term tests are also being subjected to extensive validation, unlike the standard animal bioassay (Salsburg 1983).

Batteries of short-term *in vitro* and insect tests are already being used (Brusick 1980), but there is still some hesitation about employing data from them for regulatory decisions in the absence of any animal data. Nonetheless, there are those who predict that such use is merely a matter of time. According to Brusick (1981) of Litton Bionetics, we should be able to replace the whole-animal bioassay with an appropriate set of short-term tests, coupled with metabolic studies in mammals. In his opinion, short-term systems are already as good as animal bioassays in *detecting* human carcinogenic potential, but we still need *in vivo* data for risk assessment.

An international collaborative study to evaluate various short-term tests, both *in vitro* and *in vivo*, demonstrated unequivocally that the animal tests were both less sensitive and less accurate (De Serres 1981). The Ames bacterial test correctly identified 80% of the 42 chemicals, while a mammalian cell transformation test was 89% accurate. The Ames test result is particularly significant becuase 11 of the 25 carcinogens in the distributed coded samples were selected because they were difficult to detect in bacterial assays. The short-term animal tests produced results that were little better than flipping a coin. In fact, this may be the case for long-term animal tests as well (Salsburg 1983). Commenting on the results, De Serres noted that "batteries of assays can be developed that would detect the majority of chemicals with carcinogenic potential in man in mass screening programs" (1981, p. 232).

Nevertheless, it will not be easy to get regulatory authorities or toxicologists to accept this idea. The animal bioassay, for all its faults, is at least conducted in a whole animal, and this provides the decision maker with both historical and emotional security. Industry is also unlikely to find decisions on short-term tests alone acceptable. At a 1980 meeting of the Council on Environmental Quality to discuss toxicity testing, one of the CEQ staff made a plea for animal welfare groups not to try to push regulators into using short-term test data since they had only just reached the stage where industry was prepared to accept regulatory decisions based on animal test data!

For the moment, animal welfare groups will have to be patient, but change is taking place. Some of those with extensive regulatory experience are prepared to recognize the potential of short-term tests.

> Although they [*in vitro* short-term carcinogenicity, predictive tests] are presently too unpredictable to justify, by themselves, regulatory decisions on the safety of food ingredients, it is only a matter of time before their deficiencies are corrected and they become at least as reliable in predicting human carcinogenicity as animal studies. It is likely, indeed, that in time they will be perfected to a point where they are able to mimic human response far more accurately than animal testing (Hutt 1978, p. 576).

But the majority of regulators are very suspicious of the idea and keep demanding a virtually perfect performance (in predicting human risks) from the short-term tests.

A reasoned approach to this problem is presented by Weisburger and Williams (1981) who argue that we should use a decision-point scheme to test and regulate potential carcinogens. First, one should make structural studies of the chemical, placing particular emphasis on its relationship to known carcinogenic structures. These studies could be greatly enhanced by using structure-activity models, some of which have achieved 85% success rates in identifying carcinogens and noncarcinogens (Morris 1980). Second, *in vitro* tests, including bacterial and mammalian mutagenicity, DNA repair, chromosomal effects, and cell transformation, should be conducted. Positive results in all these tests (cf. Brusick 1980) would, according to Weisburger and Williams (1981), indicate that the chemical "is certain to be carcinogenic." At this point, if further studies are considered necessary, one should move on to limited bioassays in mice and rats. Finally, long-term animal bioassays should be conducted if necessary. This is a sensible proposal but matters should not stop here. We urgently need more basic research and a concerted effort to improve the short-term tests to the point where only the most obtuse will still be able to refuse to accept them.

Teratogenicity Testing

Before 1961, it was already known that chemicals could produce fetal malformations (Baker 1960) and teratogenicity testing was not uncommon. But it was not a major priority. This was dramatically changed by the thalidomide tragedy in 1961, which stimulated a tremendous increase in animal testing requirements for new drugs and a range of other substances. In particular, it also ensured that any new drug likely to be taken by females of reproductive age would be tested for its potential to cause fetal malformations (World Health Organization 1967).

In spite of the urgent need for reliable test methods and intensive research over the last twenty years to improve protocols, teratogenicity testing remains one of the most unsatisfactory of animal toxicity tests as regards application of the data to human risk. For example, S.J. Yaffe, a professor of pediatrics and pharmacology, has recently been quoted thus:

> Experiments with animals have yielded considerable information concerning the teratogenic effects of drugs. Unfortunately, these experimental findings cannot be extrapolated from species to species or even from strain to strain within the same species, much less from animals to humans. Research in this area, and the prediction of toxicity in the human is further hampered by a lack of specificity between cause and effect" (American College of Laboratory Animal Medicine 1980, p. 13; see also Yaffe 1980).

From England, Heywood (1978) asks whether reactions in rats, mice, and rabbits have any relevance to man. In general, human teratogens can be shown to be teratogenic in some laboratory animal. But Heywood notes that only a few human teratogens have been identified, whereas a large number of chemicals have been identified as rat teratogens, including, aspirin, steroids, vitamins A and B, hydantoins, and insulin. Part of the problem may be that rodent and rabbit embryos are not as well protected as human embryos, especially in the early stages of development (Wilson 1975).

There are a number of shortcomings in the currently employed animal test systems. For example, there are the usual problems with interspecific differences in the handling and metabolism of foreign chemicals and the consequent difficulties about extrapolating from animal to man. However, not only are there variations in maternal metabolism, but also placental and fetal metabolisms differ. This adds several additional levels of complexity to the problem. Other factors that also add to the difficulties of extrapolation include the question of just what constitutes a malformation and the variation in response of developing tissues and organs in different morphogenetic situations and gestation periods (Berry and Barlow 1976).

However, if there are problems in the reliable detection of teratogens using whole animal systems, there are even greater problems in attempting to develop an *in vitro* technique sufficiently reliable to be of use, even as a screening technique. Ordinary cell culture is of little use at the present time because the cells do not develop in the progressive manner seen in differentiation. Organ culture has been extensively investigated (Saxon 1976) and a batch of *in vitro* techniques have been reviewed recently (Wilson 1978). Wilson identifies a need for screens for mutagenesis, epigenesis (processes during early differentation), and organogenesis. Mutagenesis screening systems have already been mentioned. Epigenesis and organogenesis *in vitro* screens have been developed, using invertebrate (e.g., sea urchins and insects) and vertebrate embryos or embryonic cultures. For example, Wilk et al. (1980) describe the success of avian embryo cell cultures in differentiating between nonteratogens and teratogens.

One interesting system is being developed at Edinburgh (Clayton 1980), using techniques that may be applicable to general toxicity testing as well as teratogenesis. The method is based on the premise that cell biochemistry, behavior, and morphology are directly related and that the protein profiles of different cell populations will consequently be different. High-resolution protein separation in gels, coupled with autoradiography and staining, forms the basis of the test, and the results so far indicate that the quantitative balance of the protein contents in cells in culture is indeed modified by abnormality. The technique is simple, it can be automated, and it does not require highly experienced pathologists.

Fetal cells are employed as the target cells and several different organ systems are represented—namely, lens epithelium, neural retina, kidney fibroblasts, and limb fibroblasts. The test substance is not added directly to the cell cultures. Instead, it is administered to female animals from whom samples of amniotic fluid are taken for application to the culture. Many problems must still be investigated and much more validation is required. However, using this test system, the investigators not only identified which of two unknowns was teratogenic, they also correctly identified that the teratogen produced phocomelia and cataract formation (Clayton 1980).

Despite these encouraging results, we still appear to be a long way away from developing a viable *in vitro* screen for teratogens. The problem is very complex, and the difficulty is illustrated by the lack of success that investigators have had in attempting to relate teratogenic activity to the structure of different classes of compounds, using computer structure-activity models (Schumacher 1975). More recently, another structure-activity research scientist has claimed to have developed a promising computer model for the prediction of teratogenicity (Enslein 1981).

Conclusion

While tremendous strides have been made in the development of screening systems to detect carcinogens, we still appear to be a long way from developing similar screens for teratogenicity. There are toxicologists, albeit still a minority (Lagoni, Fiebelkorn, and Wormuth 1983), who are prepared to accept *in vitro* screens in carcinogen identification, and we can look forward to further improvements in these techniques. As they improve, we are likely to see a steady change of attitude among the remaining toxicologists and regulators. Unfortunately, there are no similar prospects for suitable screens for teratogenicity, although there is an urgent need for rapid, inexpensive tests. The use of avian embryos has often been proposed but they are far from optimal. At this point, our main need is for more research and a major change in approach, along the lines described in the following chapter.

CHAPTER 17

Toxicity Testing: Proposals from an Animal Welfare Perspective

The applied science of toxicology is currently in serious difficulties. Laboratory techniques have been pressed into service to answer growing regulatory needs with little thought given to the suitability of such techniques or the applicability and range of uncertainty of the resulting data. Empiricism was adequate when regulators were attempting to protect against such gross toxic hazards as the use of the wrong solvent in a drug solution. Today, we can measure contaminants in parts per billion, or even less, and we are seeking answers concerning the effect of a chemical on an individual ten or twenty years hence. Our present crude, expensive, and inefficient bioassays on animals are just not up to the challenge, and something must be done.

Lederburg notes:

> The testing of substances could be greatly improved, improved above all by better understanding of the mechanisms by which these substances work. Right now there is almost no rationale for deciding whether the mouse, the rat, the rabbit, the guinea pig, or the monkey is going to be the better model for effects on human behavior. . . . understand that the one or two or three hundred millions of dollars a year that we're now spending on routine animal tests are almost all worthless from the point of view of standard-setting. . . . the most immediate solution is to redeploy some of our resources (1981, p. 5.).

Animal welfare advocates have also criticized toxicity tests on animals as a major abuse of animals and have joined in the call for a reallocation of resources. They argue that millions of animals needlessly endure the suffering associated with various toxic insults and that the evaulation of human hazard could be accomplished far more efficiently with far fewer animals. A simple scheme for hazard evaluation could, for example, be built on limited testing in animals, extensive testing in animal and human cell cultures, limited clinical studies in humans (where applicable and appropriate), and then prediction of human hazard based on animal *in vivo/in vitro* comparisons and data from human cell culture studies. The effectiveness of such a scheme is limited by our ignorance of toxic mechanisms and the relatively primitive state of cell culture methodology. However, both of these problems could be alleviated by an appropriate reallocation of resources.

Research into mechanisms of toxicity and the development of cell culture methodology will take time. Even if the appropriate priorities in research were changed immediately, it would probably take at least ten years to produce significant results leading to a substantial reduction in the use of animals. Short-term tests for the detection of carcinogens were being investigated at the end of the sixties but they are only now beginning to have an impact on the number of animals used to identify carcinogens (cf. Home Office 1981). But this does not mean that we must wait another ten years to reduce the number of animals used in toxicity testing. Several regulatory changes could be instituted immediately.

Reform of Testing Regulations

The campaign against the Draize eye irritancy test called upon industry and government to conduct research into possible *in vitro* alternatives to the animal test. However, the campaign also proposed some procedural changes that required no new data, only political will and commitment. For example, it was suggested that alkaline substances (pH 12 or greater) should not be tested on animals, since it was already well known that such substances are highly irritant. Substantial methodological changes in animal eye irritancy testing, which should reduce the demand for such testing, have now been accepted by regulatory authorities (Interagency Regulatory Laison Group 1981).

Acute oral toxicity testing is another area in which regulatory changes, which could be put into effect tomorrow, would have an enormous impact on the number of animals used in toxicity testing. For example, suppose the FDA and other regulatory agencies prohibited the determination of LD50s above 10 gm/kg body weight and issued a directive that *any* LD50 data submitted should be accompanied by a justification for an LD50 using 60 to 100 animals as opposed to determination of the approximate lethal dose using 6 to 10 animals. At the present time, LD50 figures are required unless one can show clearly why they are *not* necessary. This modest reversal would probably cut the demand for laboratory animals by 2 to 4 million per year in the U.S.A. alone. At the same time, it would have no adverse affect on human health, since regulators would still have perfectly adequate information on acute toxicity (Zbinden and Flury-Roversi 1981).

Other toxicity tests could be eliminated altogether without affecting the quality of regulatory decisions. For example, oral contraceptive tests on female dogs are useless for regulatory purposes, and yet such studies have been done. Rust (1982) describes a case in which beagles were used for this purpose, commenting that "only the naive will believe that this case is the exception." Unfortunately there are far too many instances of inappropriate animal testing. Regulators tend to protect themselves by requiring all possible toxicity studies, or at least all those tests on the traditional roster. There are few, if any, sanctions against requiring more testing, possibly leading to unjustified animal suffering, but the release of a product that later demonstrates toxic side effects will produce a storm of public protest and an adverse impact on career advancement.

We need to undertake an extensive review of the various toxicity tests that are now conducted and evaluate their appropriateness and applicability. Such a review must include a balancing of potential human benefit against the likely animal suffering. The casual proliferation and lengthening of animal testing must stop. As Stevenson argues, "It is now not only the antivivisectionists who challenge the increasing numbers of animals used, there are also toxicologists who question whether the increase in animal numbers can be justified on the grounds of cost and benefit and for humanitarian reasons" (1979, p. 9). The regulatory process must become more responsive to changing social pressures and new scientific data, and promising areas for further research and alternative test development must be identified and actively pursued.

New Technique Development

For the foreseeable future, some toxicity testing in animals will be necessary for new products, new chemicals, and industrial wastes.

Imperfect as animal studies may be in helping to predict human hazard, they do provide a rudimentary safety net for a wide variety of toxic effects. There have also been numerous attempts to improve animal test methods, but without major success. Animal tests are, according to a previous FDA commissioner, "crude, cumbersome and expensive" when compared to contemporary biotechnology (Kennedy 1978).

Until recently, there has been relatively little interest in attempting to explore new approaches to toxicity evaulation (although see Shanahan [1978]). The improvements already made have involved tightening up the animal protocols rather than exploring the potential of cell culture or structure-activity studies using computer modeling techniques. The traditions and literature of animal toxicology and tissue culture have not overlapped at all (Nardone 1980). In addition, the barrier between animal toxicology and tissue culture scientists has been reinforced by inadequate toxicological training of cell biologists, by ignorance of advances in cell culture techniques among animal toxicologists, and by scientific resistance to animal welfare proposals—proposals that tend to view *in vitro* toxicology as an immediate panacea for all animal testing. Nevertheless, it is becoming "clear that, in time, greater sophistication in using *in vitro* tests may provide enough data to reduce the need for extensive animal studies that are now required" (Forum for the Advancement of Toxicology 1982).

Tissue Culture. In 1954, Pomerat and Leake suggested that tissue culture could be a useful tool in toxicity studies, but progress in the next fifteen years was, at best, sporadic (cf. Dawson 1972). Rofe (1971) noted that animal studies were unlikely to help overcome the difficulty of evaluating human risk from animal data and suggested that "a new kind of multilateral study" would be needed. The advantages of tissue and organ culture would be considerable in such a study since the primary effects (mechanism) of a toxic substance occur within the cell. Subsequent reviews (Nardone 1977, 1980; Worden 1974; Ekwall 1980; Stammati, Silano, and Zucco 1981) indicate that tissue culture can be very useful in toxicity testing but that the advantages of direct manipulation *in vitro* are counterbalanced by the fact that an *in vitro* cell culture does not accurately mimic *in vivo* occurrences. For this reason, tissue culture has been promoted as a useful prescreening system but not as a means of effecting any real reduction in animal testing.

Ekwall (1980) notes that tissue culture studies have suffered from a number of specific problems. First, the wide variety of cell cultures and media that are available means little standardization from one laboratory to another. As a result, each set of studies stands in isolation and cannot be directly compared with another. Second, the questions asked of tissue culture techniques are generally posed in terms restricted to concepts from whole-animal toxicology. This is directly related to the lack of information on chemical injury to basal cell functions—a deficiency that must be corrected before *in vitro* toxicity testing can come into its own.

The use of continuous cell lines that have lost the specialized functions of the parent cells has also been a major disadvantage in *in vitro* toxicity studies. However, this problem either has been or is being overcome by the expanded use of primary or early passage cells and by improved media formulations that extend the periods during which cell cultures exhibit the properties of the original differentiated tissue. In addition, tissues and cells of human origin, and of a quality suitable for toxicity studies, are becoming more widely available. This is very important since the use of human tissues at least overcomes the problems of extrapolating from one species to another, although one must still predict *in vivo* effects from *in vitro* data.

The use of cell cultures to assess toxicity of new biomaterials is one example of a successful *in vitro* test system (cf. Ekwall 1980). Tissue culture has been shown to be more sensitive than any of the animal implantation methods, and it also correlates very well with the results of the animal tests (Pelling, Sharratt, and Hardy 1973).

However, the development of *in vitro* toxicology continues to lag far behind the technological advances in cell culture and biomedicine. Most of the funding agencies appear to be more interested in refining existing animal techniques or solving immediate problems about a chemical's toxicity (e.g., saccharin). Such groups as the Tissue Culture Association's ad hoc Committee on Carcinogenesis, Mutagenesis and Toxicity Testing *In Vitro* do not have enough influence in the right places to effect any meaningful change in approach. In Canada, a panel of toxicologists recommended that organizations supporting toxicological research fund programs with the specific objective of developing and validating nonanimal models for use in safety evaluation (Canadian Society for the Prevention of Cruelty to Animals 1980) but their words appear to fall on deaf ears.

If the potential of cell culture in toxicity testing is to be realized, then we need much more support for basic research into *in vitro* toxicology. We also need the following:

- Standardization of the test systems currently being investigated (Nardone 1977; Ekwall 1980; Stammati, Silano, and Zucco 1981)
- Greater use of human cell cultures
- More sophisticated techniques to signal the onset of cell damage
- More studies to correlate *in vivo* and *in vitro* end points
- A better understanding of the metabolic transformation of xenobiotics and the development of *in vitro* systems to mimic these reactions
- A better understanding of the differences in dose-response caused by static *in vitro* systems as opposed to dynamic *in vivo* systems

As can be seen, there is much work to be done. Most of it has already been started, but the lack of any coherent *in vitro* toxicity program means that many opportunities are lost and progress is haphazard. Animal welfare campaigns have had some effect and some money is now available specifically to explore the potential of *in vitro* techniques as alternatives to animal tests (Holden 1982b). In the United States, the cosmetic industry has established a Center for Alternatives to Animal Testing, at Johns Hopkins University, and, in England, FRAME is supporting research into alternatives at several institutions.

Nevertheless, a comprehensive and expert review of the subject, followed by substantial government support, is the key to any real progress.

Computer Modeling. Progress in the use of computer systems to predict toxicity from structural relations is even less advanced than the use of cell cultures. One of the leading scientists in the field, Corwin Hansch, has stated that trying to apply quantitative structure-activity relationships (QSAR) to predict chemical toxicity is analogous to Congress's saying in 1900 that America would put a man on the moon in ten years. In 1960, such a mandate was conceivable but, in 1900, it would have been little more than a wishful fantasy by Jules Verne.

The development of QSAR for toxicity prediction is also hampered by the lack of reliable biological data for large numbers of chemicals. Part of the problem is the imprecise nature of biological measurement as compared to the physical sciences. However, commercial secrecy also contributes substantially to the difficulties of applying QSAR techniques in hazard evaluation. Nevertheless, there is plenty of potential for using structure-toxicity relationships in the future, especially as we learn more about metabolic transformation and the fate of particular types of chemical structure. There is already much that could be done to analyze the activity of small sets of chemicals with particular structural similarities. For the moment, however, the money available for QSAR studies is more likely to support pharmacological than toxicological research, and there is much suspicion of attempts to predict toxicity from structure-activity modeling (Rekker 1980).

Conclusion

So far, I have not offered much in the way of a specific prescription for an alternative approach to hazard evaluation—namely one that takes animal welfare concerns seriously. This is partly because the fundamental requirement is a change in attitude among regulatory agencies and the industrial laboratories affected. This point can only be stressed a few times before the text begins to sound like a broken record, but it is vital if we are to see any major change. In addition, I am not sufficiently well informed about the possibilities to give precise recommendations. Nevertheless, I can suggest the following.

First, the responsible authorities should establish expert review teams to evaluate current practice, current research, and future prospects. The U.S. Food and Drug Administration, for example, has no formal process for review of new methods. The terms of reference of such teams should include animal welfare issues, as well as human welfare and scientific needs. There should also be a built-in mandate requiring periodic reassessment of the tests in use. One major difficulty that must be overcome by any panel that hopes to achieve real progress is the basic conservatism of the regulators. New tests are usually added to the battery of older tests required, and replacement of one test by another is a relatively rare process that requires lengthy negotiation.

The develoment of some rational decision-making processes within regulatory agencies is also necessary. Cramer, Ford, and Hall (1978), with their decision-tree approach, and Squire (1981), with his proposals for carcinogen risk assessment, have put forward some reasonable suggestions as to how toxicity testing and hazard evaluation might be approached.

Second, we need to develop a major research program in toxicology. It should include support for the development of cell culture technology (especially the growth and availability of a wide range of differentiated human tissues), for a thorough study of metabolic transformation systems, and for computer modeling of structure-toxicity relationships.

The development of cell culture toxicology is already under way, but *in vitro* studies tend to be supported on a piecemeal basis. The government is providing some funds and the interest generated by animal welfare campaigns has focused industry's attention in the last year (Holden, 1982b). Nevertheless, there is still no sign of any planned government program, and the barrier between *in vivo* and *in vitro* toxicology still looms large. This gap must be overcome; only committed action by such institutions as the National Toxicology Program and the Food and Drug Administration will ensure that progress is rapid.

Finally, some way must be found to reduce the detrimental effect of commercial secrecy on toxicology. Scientific development cannot thrive unless there is a free exchange of data and ideas. With the bulk of toxicological data locked up in company and regulatory files, it is hardly surprising that toxicology is only now starting to gain the status of a science rather than having to rely on cookbook recipes.

One possible solution is indicated by the Cosmetic Ingredient Review Committee of the Cosmetic, Toiletry and Fragrance Association. They are slowly reviewing all the data accumulated by various companies on a particular chemical. This approach answers some animal welfare concerns since data already gained by one company will be made available to all CTFA members, thereby reducing duplication (Cosmetic, Toiletry and Frangrance Association 1980). However, this is only a partial solution. Other ideas and initiatives also need to be explored.

It would be most ironic if toxicology were helped in its growth toward a mature scientific discipline by animal welfare critics. Such criticism is often viewed as destructive rather than constructive by many scientists, including industry and academic toxicologists. Nevertheless, animal welfare campaigns could ultimately prove to have a very beneficial effect. Regulators and toxicologists have begun to use the opportunities presented by recent reassessments (stimulated by animal welfare attacks) to assist their moves toward a more rational and realistic approach to hazard evaluation. Ultimately, scientists, consumers, and laboratory animals are all likely to benefit.

Part IV

THE MORAL QUESTION, ALTERNATIVES AND SUGGESTIONS

CHAPTER 18

The Moral Status of Laboratory Animals

The moral status of animals has been debated for millenia. As in most other areas of Western philosophy, the ancient Greeks raised many of the issues that still occupy moral debate today—the main difference being our greater knowledge of biological links between humans and other animals.

The Greeks were divided into four major schools of thought on the animal issue—animism, mechanism, vitalism, and a fourth group who believed that animals were placed on earth for human benefit (Brumbaugh 1978). The animists, led by members of the Orphic religion and the philosophers of the Pythagorean School, held that animals and humans had souls that were indestructible, the same in kind, and interchangeable between animals and humans. The mechanists took the opposite view arguing that both humans and animals were mere machines (they were still alike) and that the "soul" was no more than a physical organ that would decompose on the death of the organism.

The vitalists, epitomized by Aristotle (384–323 B.C.). recognized a difference between animate and inanimate substances. They argued that there was a chain of being in which there was a continuity, but not identity, between different beings. Thus, human qualities included some elements from the "lower" animals. In the opinion of the vitalists, the soul and body were interdependent (contra animism) but different (contra mechanism). Finally, there were those whose viewpoint was essentially nonintellectual and based on a "common-sense" approach to the natural world. They argued that the world had been created for human pleasure and benefit and that we could use animals as we pleased. Presumably, this view was sustained by an assumption that the Creator could be relied upon to keep the system functioning for our benefit.

Among the Romans, the popular attitude toward animals obviously followed this last line of thinking, although there were abstract schools of philosophy that carried on the debate among animists, mechanists, and vitalists far from the common way of life around the Forum and the circuses. In particular, the games beloved of the citizens of Rome demonstrated a clear lack of concern about the moral status of animals. Over the centuries of the Roman Empire, hundreds of thousands of animals were killed in barbaric spectacles where cruelty was the prime attraction (Dembeck 1965). Following the fall of Rome, interest in learning declined, being kept alive mainly through the efforts of Christian theologians. Their impact on our attitude toward animals has been considerable.

The Christian View

There have been various attempts to use the Bible to confirm or deny that there are theological grounds for the notion that animals have rights of some sort. However, modern scholarship has shown that many of the passages that argue against ill-treatment of animals (e.g., do not "muzzle the ox when he treadeth out corn," Deuteronomy 25:4) were directed against pagan practices rather than against cruel behavior (Passmore 1975). Nevertheless, the Old Testament holds that animals and humans share a common life principle, and the New Testament speaks of all things possessing a psyche. Furthermore, the total effect of the scriptures certainly does not indicate that God would be indifferent to animal suffering, quite the contrary (Rimbach 1982).

These biblical ambiguities about the place of animals in creation extended into theological debate. For example, John Chrysostom argued in the fourth century that the saints extend their gentleness unto animals because they are of the same origin as ourselves, while Augustine (354–430, A.D.) denied, in no uncertain terms, that animal suffering could mean anything to human beings (Passmore 1975). Augustine's arguments were based on neoplatonism (Hume 1957) and on the Stoic tradition that animals lack reason and therefore there can be no legal or moral tie of any kind between man and animal. He argues: "We can perceive by their cries that animals die in pain, although we make little of this since the beast, lacking a rational soul, is not related to us by a common nature" (Passmore 1975, p. 197). Augustine's indifference may be shocking to us today but it was hardly out of keeping with the times, considering the savage nature of human existence in Europe during the fifth century.

These ideas may seem to be at variance with the popular view of some famous saints (Waddell 1946), especially Saint Francis of Assissi (1181–1226). The humane movement stresses St. Francis's love of animals and compassion for them (Niven 1967), but the notion of St. Francis as a sentimental animal lover is derided by Roman Catholic biographers, who are instead intent on establishing his orthodoxy (Passmore 1975). Passmore suggests that St. Francis's love of nature was part of a wider love of life and that it is by no means certain that he saw animals as important, except insofar as they glorified God. For example, when one of his disciples cut a trotter off a living pig for a sick compatriot, St. Francis rebuked him, but urged him only to apologize to the owner of the pig for damaging his property.

The thirteenth century revival of Aristotelian science and philosophy brought some problems for the place of animals in theology since Aristotle's ladder of being was not really compatible with the supposed absolute discontinuity between animals and humans. Aristotle also stressed observation of natural phenomena, while Augustine favored introspection. However, St. Thomas Aquinas (1225–1274) resolved these difficulties for the church by distinguishing between affections of reason and sentiment. Drawing on the old Stoic arguments, he noted that, at the level of reason, the treatment of animals was a matter of indifference to the Church since God had given man dominion over the animals. However, at the emotional level, we could certainly pity animals in pain. In fact, this was to be encouraged since those persons who had pity for animal pain were more likely to have compassion for their fellow humans (Passmore 1975).

The question of God-granted dominion over animals has been a contentious issue ever since (Mulder 1979). Some argue that dominion should be interpreted to mean humane stewardship, while others prefer to think of it as domination since this permits humans to use animals as they wish. However, this position is close to the notion of "might makes right" which, if applied widely, would vitiate all morality (cf. Rollins 1981).

A further problem with Aquinas' argument concerns the issue of animal pain and suffering. If one takes as given that God is benevolent and omnipotent, then what is the reason for animal suffering if animals are not to share in the after life where they will be recompensed for their corporeal suffering? A benevolent God would certainly not allow animals to suffer for no reason where there had been no sin (animals did not eat of the forbidden fruit). Augustine attempted to explain this by arguing that there was a lesson for men in animal suffering, while Descartes (1596–1650) and others solved the issue very simply by denying that animals suffer or feel pain and claiming that their cries are no different from the mechanical squeals of an ungreased wheel (Regan and Singer 1976).

In summary, the Roman Catholic Church has followed the teachings of the Stoics, Augustine, and Aquinas. To the present day, it is not particularly sympathetic to animal welfare campaigns. Hume (1957a) has also suggested that the Thomist philosophy is part of the reason for the lack of animal welfare activity in predominantly Roman Catholic countries. This does not mean that prominent Catholics have not lent their support to animal welfare causes. In the nineteenth century, Cardinal Manning was a leading spokesman for the British antivivisection movement. But such support was, at best, idiosyncratic. The establishment position was exemplified by Pope Piux IX (1872–1878), who refused to allow the formation of a Society for the Prevention of Cruelty to Animals because "a Society for such a purpose could not be sanctioned in Rome" (cf. Passmore, 1975).

The Protestant churches tended to be more sympathetic. In fact, Stevenson (1956) argues that Arminianism, especially Methodist teaching, was one of the underlying factors producing a strong British antivivisection movement. Wesley's arguments that animals would share afterlife helped create a social atmosphere in which antivivisection sentiment could flourish. In addition, Stevenson notes that "it is a striking fact that Evangelicals, and those of similar faith and sympathy, occupied almost all of the chief positions in the antivivisection societies" (1956, p. 155). Nevertheless, modern Christian dogma is generally neutral on the status of animals. In fact, the Jewish religion probably has the strongest dogma concerning humane treatment of animals (Cohen 1976). However, in today's secular society, religious influence on our attitudes toward the moral status of animals is unlikely to be a major factor, especially because establishment churches remain aloof from the current controversy.

The 17th to 19th Centuries: Continental Europe versus Britain

The differences that existed between the rationalists of continental Europe—such as Descartes (1596–1650), Spinoza (1632–77), Leibniz (1646–1716) and Kant (1724–1804)—and the empiricists of Britain—such as Locke (1632–1704) and Hume, (1711–76)—are still prevalent today. Descartes held that animals were machines, their reactions explicable in terms of physics and physiology, but that humans were different because of the possession of a human mind, revealed by our freedom of choice and our linguistic abilities. The British philosophers relied more on empirical observations than on edifices built up by reason. They concluded that, on the basis of their observations, animals were not mere machines. The differences between humans and animals could as easily be seen as one of degree rather than of kind. Locke believed that causing pain or destroying animal life needlessly was morally wrong, and Hume argued that, with respect to everyday reasoning, the minds of humans and animals work in the same way.

As a result, our attitude toward animals today is influenced in part by the Cartesians and in part by the followers of Locke and Hume. In scientific research, the animal is perceived to be a physiological mechanism that can be dissected and analyzed. Pet owners and bird watchers, by contrast, perceive animals very differently and have a decidedly Lockean approach. The two approaches cannot be reconciled, and this conflict is undoubtedly one of the problems in attempting to promote a reasonable dialogue between experimenters and animal welfare advocates. In fact, Merchant (1980) argues that the Cartesian influence extended to domination over the female element in nature, and that this led to the subjugation of women. Perhaps it is no coincidence that the bulk of support for animal welfare has come from women.

Later European philosophers did not necessarily agree with Descartes and his mechanistic approach, but neither would they concede that animals have any claims upon human compassion. For example, Kant argued that animals are not self-conscious and, therefore, humans have no duties *to* them. However, he went on to state that we should not abuse animals because we have indirect duties to humanity not to be cruel. This is because the person who is cruel to animals will be predisposed to be cruel to human beings. Thus, Kant resurrects the Thomist argument against cruelty.

Unfortunately, if one could prove that cruelty to animals was not associated in any way to cruelty to human beings, then Kant's arguments would lead to the conclusion that there would be nothing wrong with cruel treatment of animals. Nevertheless, Kant was not a callous person; he maintained that "physical experiments involving excruciating pain for animals and conducted merely for the sake of speculative inquiry (when the end might also be achieved without such experiments) are to be abhorred" (cf. Passmore 1975, p. 202).

In England, Jeremy Bentham (1748–1831) was developing the Utilitarian thesis that we should work toward achieving the greatest happiness of the greatest number (at least, this is a crude interpretation of his philosophy). By placing such a high store on happiness, it is perhaps not surprising that he should perceive suffering as evil. Thus, in 1789, Bentham argued:

> The day has been, I grieve to say in many places it is not yet past, in which the greater part of the species, under the denomination of slaves, have been treated by the law exactly upon the same footing as, in England for example, the inferior races of animals are still. The day may come, when the rest of the animal creation may acquire those rights which never could have been withholden from them but by the hand of tryanny. The French have already discovered that the blackness of the skin is no reason why a human being should be abandoned without redress to the caprice of a tormentor. It may come one day to be recognized, that the number of the legs, the villosity of the skin, or the termination of the os sacrum, are reasons equally insufficient for abandoning a sensitive being to the same fate. What else is it that should trace insuperable line? Is it the faculty of reason, or perhaps, the faculty of discourse? But a full-grown horse or dog is beyond comparison a more rational, as well as a more conversable animal, than an infant of a day, or a week, or even a month, old. But suppose the case were otherwise, what would it avail? *the question is not Can they reason? nor Can they talk? but, Can they suffer?* (Bentham 1962, pp. 142–3, [emphasis added]).

As a Utilitarian, Bentham did not concern himself with the rationality of the moral agent, but with the effect of the agent's actions on sentient beings—that is, beings capable of experiencing pleasure or suffering. If a being had this capacity, then its interests should be *considered* equally with those of other sentient beings, including humans. The suffering of an animal may be less than that of a human but it should still be taken into account. Passmore (1975) notes, however, that Bentham reverted in his later writings to a less radical position.

Despite this retreat, Bentham's statement about suffering has become enshrined in animal welfare literature, and it certainly helped to spur on nineteenth century notions that animals had rights and probably helped the passage of animal protection legislation in both Britain and America. Before leaving the nineteenth century, the impact of Darwin's ideas must be mentioned. Coming on the heels of the social reform movement that included pressure groups for animal protection, it helped to shatter the notion that humans were different in kind from other animals. Considerable resistance to any such idea occurred among religious thinkers eager to stress the discontinuity between human and animal. Nevertheless, the new ideas confirming the ladder of being have found broad acceptance among the public and many religions.

Darwin's theories certainly added fuel to the animal protection fires that had been lit, first in Europe and later in the United States, during the nineteenth century. The notion of animal rights was considered and debated but then lost ground again in the first half of the twentieth century as Europe reeled under the impact of two major wars. In the mid-1970's, however, the debate was revived with a bang with the publication of *Animal Liberation* (Singer 1975). This book provided animal wefare advocates with a clearly articulated and concise argument as to why we should be concerned about animals. The logical and intellectual elements in Singer's arguments were certainly not new (cf. Salt 1892) but they stood in stark contrast to the fuzzy and ill-defined idea of kindness to animals that had been almost the sole basis for the animal welfare message for the previous fifty years.

The Modern Revival

In the last ten years, we have seen a remarkable revival of interest in animal rights. The debate has raged in the halls of academe and in the pages of the scholarly journals. On the one side, Singer (1975), Clark (1977), Rollin (1981), and Regan (1982), all argue that animals are legitimate objects of moral concern in themselves and that they should be accorded greater consideration, or rights of some sort. On the other side, Passmore (1975), Fox (1980) and Frey (1980) argue that animals cannot have rights and that, although we must not cause needless animal suffering, we can continue to exploit animals.

A number of basic factors have been taken as grounds *for making a moral* distinction between humans and animals. As Rollin (1981) notes, we must be very careful about choosing morally important characteristics. Thus, society has determined that it is inappropriate to draw moral distinctions on the basis of intelligence, skin color, and religious belief. Animal rights advocates are now challenging society's belief that we can distinguish between human and animal moral interests on the basic of rationality, linguistic ability, the human soul, a God-granted dominion over animals, or the fact that humans are unique in being moral *agents*, as well as objects of moral concern. Even those philosophers who deny that animals have rights admit that "no one can be very happy, in the atmosphere created by current debate, advocating either man's unrestricted dominion over all living things or the complete abolition of all activities which cause animals suffering or loss of life or liberty." (Fox 1980).

The various criteria mentioned above which have been proposed as conferring a unique moral status on humans, have all been strongly challenged in the last decade. In most cases, I believe, they have been found deficient.

One of the more common arguments for excluding animals from our moral community is that we possess an immortal soul while they do not. Apart from the fact that this claim has, in itself, been the subject of heated debate over the centuries and is still unresolved in the Christian community the question arises as to what the possession of a soul has to do with being an object of moral concern. However, the lack of a soul may even mean that we should treat animals better than humans, since wrongs done to animals will not be redressed in after life. A related point, that God has granted us dominion over animals and therefore we can treat them as we choose, undermines basic morality since it essentially confirms that might makes right. As Rollin (1981) argues, our self-proclaimed position at the "top" of Nature's pyramid does not confer any moral distinction except insofar as it makes us responsible for the well-being of those "below" us.

The question of rationality and linguistic ability are also incapable of standing close scrutiny, even though most people would probably point to our faculty of reason or our possession of an immortal soul as the basis of our moral distinctiveness. First, it is by no means clear that animals are not rational. Even on the linguistic question, which seems much more clear-cut, we are only able to draw a clear distinction between some animals and most humans by raising the requirements for demonstrating the possession of language. Second, there are humans who clearly lack either language or rationality (e.g., infants, the severely brain-damaged, the senile), but they are nonetheless included in our orbit of moral concern. On what grounds do we include these humans and exclude some animals that show clear signs of rationality or linguistic ability?

The social contract argument (only humans are moral agents capable of entering into a contract with both duties *and* concomitant rights) is also subject to the same counterargument. Obviously some humans can neither enter into a social contract nor act as moral agents. Why are they included in our moral community while animals are excluded?

The debate among moral philosophers is an arcane dialectic but there is a basic consensus among such advocates as Regan, Rollin, and Singer that animals should be accorded a higher moral status. This is because animals have a life and/or interests, the satisfaction of which matters to them, and because they are capable of being harmed or experiencing suffering. There appears to be no broad consensus on what is meant by an animal (for example, does the term describe only mammals, all vertebrates, or both vertebrates and invertebrates?), but most would agree that sentience (accepted by many philosophers as the capacity to suffer) is important and is a better requirement for moral consideration than rationality, for example. It is also important to note that Singer, being a Utilitarian, believes in neither human nor animal "rights"; he seeks instead the protection of 'interests."

Before we sink deeper into apparent pedantic sophistry (the above distinctions are important in philosophy), what does all this mean for animal research, and how on earth do we apply these ideas in practice? The answer is that we can do so only with great difficulty. Nevertheless we must attempt to elaborate some consistent framework out of such problems as:

- Where do we draw the line between sentience and the lack of sentience?
- What do we do about conflicting interests between different animals or between animals and humans?
- How do we weigh the interest of a rat against the interest of a human?
- Is killing an animal painlessly as bad as allowing it to suffer but to continue living?

All three of the philosophers I have referred to above do agree that some animal research can be justified within the moral frameworks they have developed, though each would draw the line at a different point. For myself, I would argue that there is a far greater moral problem in experimenting with vertebrates than invertebrates but that, even so, we can justify some experimental use of innocent vertebrates. At this point we must make do with the ususal escapist phrases and fall back on the position that animal experimentation should not be permitted unless substantial benefits are expected (Hoff

1980), and that scientists must justify their need for laboratory animals very carefully, making sure that the work has not already been done or that no alternative is possible.

If an alternative is available, then obviously the animal research cannot be justified. But how strong is the moral obligation to seek out and develop alternatives? The animal welfare movement thinks it should be a major initiative for those in charge of research funds, and certainly there is no doubt that far more vigorous action could be taken. In fact, in the following chapter, it is argued that the development of alternatives will not only benefit laboratory animals, but will also benefit biomedical research.

In conclusion, there are undoubtedly many difficult moral choices in animal experimentation. Weighing present animal suffering and death against possible future human benefit is never going to be amenable to statistical analysis. Nevertheless, we can certainly identify extreme positions and make an attempt to raise the priority of animal suffering in the cost/benefit equations. It is just not adequate for scientists to argue that there is a quantum difference between the moral status of humans and animals if they are unable to give reasons for such a belief and defend their reasons in the arena of modern philosophical debate. It is also clear that the public is concerned about animal research and that, ultimately, the decision as to what is and is not moral in animal research must include public, as well as scientific, animal welfare, and philosophical input.

CHAPTER 19

Alternatives: A Meeting Ground for Science and Animal Welfare

Many scientists are uneasy about the idea of alternatives to the use of laboratory animals. One reason for their tentativeness could be the vigorous promotion of the alternatives concept by traditional enemies of the biomedical research establishment. As a result, innuendo, misinformation, and undue emotion cloud a rational discussion of the topic. Too many simplistic claims have been made by opponents of biomedical research, but defenders of the present level of animal experimentation are also guilty of overgeneralization and faulty reasoning.

The concept of alternatives will not, if enthusiastically applied, result in the immediate cessation of animal experimentation. In many areas of research a problem can only be investigated by means of an intact animal. On the other hand, the number of animals being used in research today could be substantially reduced if more effort and attention were given to promoting the idea of alternatives. At the same time, there need be no threat to the quality of biomedical research or to the advance of biological and medical knowledge.

The concept of alternatives is now fully integrated into the campaign literature of the humane movement, but there are still semantic problems—different groups use the term "alternatives" to refer to different sets of techniques. For example, one group may be referring only to those techniques that lead to total replacement of laboratory animal use, while another will include a broader range, such as techniques that reduce animal pain and suffering. In this book, the term "alternatives" is used to refer to those techniques or methods that: *replace* the use of laboratory animals altogether, *reduce* the number of animals required, or *refine* an existing procedure or technique so as to minimize the level of stress endured by the animal. These three Rs provide a broad-based approach to reducing both laboratory animal numbers and laboratory animal suffering.

This broad definition could include many technical improvements. The use of better defined (microbiological and genetic background) animals (Festing 1981) or improved capture and quarantine methods for primates destined for the laboratory could reduce the demand for laboratory animals and overall animal suffering. Nevertheless, certain techniques have received particular attention in discussing alternatives, and a brief outline of some of them is provided here. Additional details are available in Smyth (1978) and FRAME (1979).

PhysicoChemical Techniques

The physical and chemical techniques now available to the biomedical research worker are far more sensitive and powerful than those used before the last war, and this has resulted in the total replacement of animals in some areas. For example, laboratory animals used to be necessary for the assay of the fat-soluble vitamins, but now, vitamins A, D, and E can be assayed by gas-liquid chromatography and mass spectroscopy (Wiggins 1976). However, one must still use the rat antirachitic assay for the vitamin D content of codliver oil because not even modern GLC techniques can satisfactorily separate the vitamin from the other fats in the oil (British Pharmacopoeia Commission, 1973a). The greater sensitivity of modern machines also means that fewer animals need to be used in other research areas since more assays can be done on smaller amounts of material. The development of sophisticated new diagnostic (noninterventive) tools also opens up interesting future possibilities for reducing the stress and suffering in animals used in physiology research and other studies where whole animals are essential.

Computer/Mathematical Analysis and Modeling

The number of animals required for a series of studies can sometimes be reduced by effective use of statistics and by prior analysis using a computer model (Newton 1977; Harrison and Harrison 1978). However, it is incorrect to state (as has been done on occasion) that such systems can replace all animal experimentation. In fact, Guyton (1981) claims that computer modeling can even increase the demand for animals because one can analyze data so much faster and in much greater detail, thus leading to proportionately more problems to investigate.

Microbiological Systems

Microbiological systems have, in a few cases, totally replaced the use of animals (as in vitamin assays [Gyorgy and Pearson 1967]) but are more commonly employed to reduce the total number of animals required. For example, the Ames test for detecting mutagens (and perhaps carcinogens?), which employs Salmonella detector strains, does reduce the need for animal studies in that initial screening studies can be made in the bacterial system (Ames 1979; McCann and Ames 1975; 1976). These new techniques appear to be having an impact. In Britain, the number of animals used in carcinogen tests has been falling in recent years (from 63,000 to 40,000 between 1977 and 1980) even though the demand for carcinogen screening has, if anything, increased (cf. Home Offce 1981).

Tissue Culture

Tissue culture is the technique for which most has been claimed with respect to the development of satisfactory and practical alternatives. For example, Professor Sergey Fedoroff of Saskatchewan University, a well-known member of the Tissue Culture Association, has claimed that "the application of tissue cultures to biomedical research is limited only by the imagination of the scientists employing them" (S. Fedoroff, personal communication 1976). This may seem a very radical statement at first glance, but not if one interprets it as meaning that tissue culture can be applied to a very wide range of research problems without necessarily replacing the need for animals.

Tissue culture systems have replaced the need for animals in a few cases, notably virus vaccine production and some vaccine potency and safety tests (Petricciani et al. 1977), but in general the technique's main potential lies in its ability to reduce demand. For example, a pharmaceutical virology laboratory reduced its yearly demand for mice from 13,000 to 1,600, between 1963 and 1975. At the same time, they increased the yearly number of compounds screened from 1,000 to 22,000. These changes were due entirely to the employment of cell and organ culture systems as preliminary screening systems before testing the most promising chemicals in the mouse system (Bucknall 1980)

Another example demonstrates that new alternative techniques are not immediately picked up and put into practice, the claims of research scientists notwithstanding. A few years ago, an interesting new *in vitro* technique was developed for assessing the malignancy of cells (Noguchi et al. 1978). The usual assay involves the injection of a known number of the test cells into a mouse or other animal with a compromised immune system (to prevent rejection). If a tumor develops, then the cells were malignant. The *in vitro* method uses chick embryo skin cultures and assesses the invasiveness of the test cells. It appears to be more sensitive than the animal assays (Noguchi 1981), which have other problems as well (Ponten 1976), and yet four years after the method first appeared in *Science*, interest in the technique is still sparse.

Clinical and Epidemiological Studies

The use of human patients, volunteers, or populations is often the final step in the application of a new cure, after extensive animal and *in vitro* studies. There is no doubt that results obtained with human subjects are more relevant than those from animal studies, but there are strict ethical guidelines controlling such experimentation and many research projects are not possible for ethical reasons (National Commission for the Protection of Human Subjects of Biomedical and Behavioral Research 1978). However approximately one-third of NIH-funded projects involve research on human beings (*International Journal for the study of Animal Problems* 1982).

General Refinements in Techniques

Refinements in techniques may lead to reduced stress and can contribute significantly to a decrease in the number of painful procedures. This would qualify as an alternative, and Smyth (1978) has identified reduction of the number of painful experiments as the main area in which advances need to be made. For example, the British Pharmacopoeia Commission (1977a) now specifies a paralytic rather than a lethal end point (British Pharmacopoeia Commission 1973b) for the tetanus antitoxin potency test. The paralysis is mild, involving only minor loss of movement in the hind limb of a mouse, followed by recovery. There is no doubt that this procedure is considerably less stressful than use of the lethal end point.

Development of the Concept of Alternatives

If one includes the ideas of reduction and refinement in one's definition of alternatives, then it could be argued that Marshall Hall, a British experimental physiologist of the first half of the nineteenth century, was one of the first to address the issue of alternatives (cf. Manuel 1981). Hall proposed regulations for animal research that would eliminate unnecessary and repetitive animal research and would minimize suffering. He also recommended the use of lower, less sentient animals and praised the findings of a colleague who demonstrated that an animal that had just been killed could be substituted for a living animal, thereby eliminating pain.

Nevertheless, most people place the beginning of the concept of alternatives with Russell and Burch's *Principles of Humane Experimental Technique*, published in 1959. This book enunciated the three Rs of Replacement, Reduction, and Refinement, although the authors gave them a slightly different meaning than we now use. For example, replacement techniques included not only the use of tissue cultures but also nonrecovery experiments on totally anesthetized living animals. Reduction referred mainly to the use of improved statistical techniques and standardized research animals, leading to the need for fewer animals to make a given point.

Russell and Burch (1959) also introduced the notions of *fidelity* and *discrimination*, two concepts that are most important when discussing the relative merits of alternatives and animal models. An animal model is, as the term applies, a representation of the actual system one is attempting to study. For example, diabetes is studied in rats, not because we wish to develop a cure for rat diabetes, but because we wish to understand the human disease more fully and develop better therapies. For the purpose of one's research, there are two important ways in which the model may differ from the original, namely, in its fidelity and its discrimination. A rat is a reasonably high-fidelity model of a human being, but a chimpanzee is even higher. A protozoan is a very low-fidelity model, but it may be a better model in some studies (e.g., vitamin assays) because of its sensitivity and discrimination.

Russell (1957) argued that progress toward replacement methods is "hindered by an insidious and widespread assumption" that may be called the "hi-fi fallacy." The major premise of this fallacy is that high fidelity is desirable in general. The minor premise is that mammals are of exceptionally high fidelity as models of the human organism and therefore should be used as often as possible. Russell and Burch (1959) disputed this conclusion, describing, as evidence in support of their arguments, a study by Tinbergen and Perdeck (1950) which assessed the response of herring gull chicks to a signal announcing the arrival of food.

The food signal consisted of a parent bird call and the appearance of a model of the adult bird. The model was either an accurate high-fidelity model of the parent's head or a thin red rod with three sharply etched white bands at the forward end. The high-fidelity model elicited only one response to every 1.26 responses elicited by the rod, which carried the three important releaser stimuli for food-begging behavior, namely, elongation, red coloration, and color contrast. Thus, the low-fidelity model had a higher discrimination factor than the high-fidelity model.

This example supports the notion that high-fidelity is not necessary, although there is an important caveat. In order to use a low-fidelity, high discrimination model, one must have some knowledge of the important elements in the system to be studied. Thus, DNA damage appears to play an important role in carcinogenicity and therefore bacterial mutagenicity systems can be used as a screen for potential carcinogens (Ames 1979). Medawar described the problem thus:

> The use of animals in laboratories to enlarge our understanding of nature is part of a far wider exploratory process, and one cannot assay its value in isolation—as if it were an activity which, if prohibited, would deprive us only of the material benefits that grow directly out of its own use. Any such prohibition of learning or confinement of the understanding would have widespread and damaging consequences; but this does not imply that we are for evermore, and in increasing numbers, to enlist animals in the scientific service of man. I think that the use of experimental animals on the present scale is a temporary episode in biological and medical history, and that its peak will be reached in ten years time—or perhaps sooner. *In the meantime, we must grapple with the paradox that nothing but research on animals will provide us with the knowledge that will make it possible for us, one day, to dispense with the use of them altogether* (1972, p. 86 [emphasis added]).

Therefore, as biomedical knowledge increases, we should be able to reduce animal use in the laboratory and there are signs that the decline predicted by Medawar has started (see chap. 5). There is, however, some doubt as to whether the decline in numbers is caused by more knowledge and, therefore, greater use of alternatives, or merely by economic pressures.

The next major landmark in the development and spread of the alternatives concept came in 1962 when the Lawson Tait Trust was founded in England to encourage and support researchers who were not using any animals in their research. By 1965, the idea of alternatives had attracted enough attention to cause a British parliamentary committee of enquiry to question scientific witnesses repeatedly about the prospects for the availability of such techniques (Littlewood Committee 1965, p. 26). The Committee received the stock reply that the search for alternative techniques was being actively pursued and that all possible alternatives were already in use.

In 1967, an American group, United Action for Animals, was formed specifically to promote alternatives, focusing in general on the "replacement" elements. In 1969, a group called FRAME (Fund for the Replacement of Animals in Medical Experiments) was established in England to promote the concept of alternatives, with its major effort aimed at scientific research organizations. They have made steady progress and in 1978, attracted 180 scientists to a symposium on alternatives at the Royal Society (Rowan and Stratmann 1980).

The first major establishment breakthrough came in 1971 when the Council of Europe passed Resolution 621, which proposed, among other things, the establishment of a documentation and information center on alternatives, as well as tissue banks for research. Deliberations on Resolution 621 did not begin until fairly recently and the final Convention is unlikely to support many of the original elements in the Resolution, but there is growing government interest in alternatives. A number of European countries (e.g., Holland, Sweden, Germany) have passed laws regulating animal research that include specific support for the idea of alternatives. The Dutch Minister of Health confirmed his government's support for the concept at the 1979 general meeting of the International Committee on Laboratory Animal Sciences in Utrecht. Sweden has gone further, even allocating a small amount of money for specific support of alternatives research.

Alternatives as Techniques

Even though there is growing government interest in alternatives as a direct result of public pressure on politicians, the general scientific response has been negative. This reaction is understandable in light of some of the exaggerated claims that have been made for alternatives as replacements. However, science policy makers could do much more to promote alternatives, and thus lead to a reduced demand for laboratory animals. In addition, support for alternatives, in the form of reasonable numbers of research grants and practical administrative encouragement, could benefit the advance of biomedical knowledge, the arguments of some alarmists notwithstanding (Grafton 1981).

One of the major problems concerns the place of alternatives in the research process. For example, it is argued that one cannot "throw money" at alternatives because it will lead to substandard research and too much money chasing too few ideas—as happened in the heady days on the War on Cancer. However, the development and promotion of alternatives techniques is very different from the search for a cure for cancer. In the case of alternatives, one is supporting technique development. By contrast, cancer research grants seek to test theories (new or old), solve puzzles, and generate data and, in so doing, scientists employ the techniques that are currently available.

The advance of biomedical knowledge depends on a number of factors, including an adequate reserve of imagination and intuition, as well as sufficient funds, equipment, and manpower for the critical evaluation and testing of new ideas. Imagination and critical review are the basis of the hypotheticodeductive model of scientific advance (Medawar 1969) but two other factors must also be included: luck and technique development. The importance of technique development and availability cannot be overstated. Many awards have been given for the development of new techniques; Rosalyn Yalow, who received a Nobel Prize in 1977 for her part in developing radioimmunoassay, is a recent example. This particular technique has been cited as an alternative because it allows a researcher to assay very small amounts of complex biological molecules which previously could only have been done (if, indeed, it was possible at all) by using living animals (cf. Yalow 1981).

The importance of new technique development is widely accepted (Yalow 1982). For example, Medawar (1969) called his book on the philosophy of scientific discovery *The Art of the Soluble*. Hans Krebs, another Nobel Prize-winner, has also supported the notion. In a letter to Garfield (1982) he wrote:

> Oddly enough, the only paper of mine ever rejected outright by an editor was a purely methodological one. It was a paper on the handling of biological material for metabolic experiments. The editor believed, I think wrongly, that results are more important than methods. The frequent quotation of methods papers unequivocally demonstrates the usefulness of such papers (1982, p. 9).

A listing of a few of the recent technical advances provides ample evidence in support of these notions. Apart from radio-immunoassay, which has opened up many previously insoluble problems in endocrinology, we are beginning to experience the impact of the new techniques in genetic engineering. Another recent development, namely the ability to produce specific antibodies of defined affinity for specific antigens (Scharff, Roberts, and Thammana 1981) also has tremendous potential for research, diagnosis, and disease therapy.

Funding agencies have recognized the importance of technique development to a limited extent. There are some Federal funds available for technique development through the Biotechnology Resources Board (BRB) in the NIH Division of Research Resources. However, Bolt, Beranek and Newman, Inc. (1976), a contract research group in Massachusetts, reported in 1976 that the Biotechnology Resources Board is "substantially underfunded even for its current portfolio." The group also suggested that the BRB "should address the challenges inherent in biotechnology needs by adding activities in new directions. Specifically, support should be given to preresource development of biomedically relevant technologies before they are mature enough to serve a user community" (1976, p. vii–viii). It could be argued that this statement is an exhortation to support some of the proposed alternative techniques, such as cell culture resources, and to start re-evaluating existing research models in light of public concern.

Substantial Federal support is already given to develop and maintain such animal resources as new disease models, diagnostic centers, and breeding colonies. The development and deployment of sophisticated new laboratory hardware is also supported by the Federal government. However, cell culture technology and resources are the poor relation in this particular scheme. Some government money does go to support the American Type Culture Collection and one or two cell science centers, but, despite public pressure to increase support for alternative techniques, no one in the biomedical bureaucracy has yet shown the initiative (or political will) to bring the level of support for cell culture resources up to that enjoyed by the laboratory animal program.

Recently NIH's Division of Research Resources has taken a few tentative steps in the direction of alternatives with the initiation of a Research Models Development Program. The DRR seeks to expand its model development activities by exploring opportunities and limitations in the use of lower organisms, cell cultures, and mathematical simulation in research. While these techniques are basic to the alternatives concept, the term alternatives is not mentioned in the program description, and one cannot help suspecting that this is due to opposition to the very idea from some NIH administrators.

At present, approximately 30% of NIH extramural projects involve nonanimal systems (e.g., cell cultures and computer models), 41% involve mammals, and 36% involve humans as research subjects, including a 12% overlap which use both humans and other mammals. (*International Journal for the Study of Animal Problems* 1982). Research using alternatives is therefore already important, and it is not unreasonable to suggest that more could be done to ensure that appropriate techniques are developed and promoted and that the concept be given administrative support. In fact, there is some evidence that animal research has declined in importance in the last ten years, since the director of DRR testified in 1973, that 57% of NIH-supported research required the use of animals.

Types of Biomedical Programs. Another pitfall in the discussion of the alternatives concept is the fact that the scope for developing and using an alternative varies according to the objectives of the particular laboratory activity using animals. For example, the arguments in favor of using live animals in an educational exercise may well be considerably less pressing than those advocating the use of animals in research to develop a vaccine against poliomyelitis. At the very least, it is probable that the public will respond differently to the two situations. Animal use in the laboratory can be divided into a number of relatively distinct categories, including—but not necessarily limited to—education, diagnosis, toxicity testing and safety evaluation, and biomedical research involving the generation of new data and the testing of hypotheses.

There is little objective evidence that manipulative exercises on live animals are necessary in many educational courses, with the possible exception of certain vocational classes. Certainly, all animal demonstrations involving significant intervention could be excluded from high school and most undergraduate programs without jeopardizing the development of critical, yet imaginative, scientific intellects or the flow of young scientists into research laboratories. This does not mean that the study (as opposed to use) of living animals should be stopped in educational practice—quite the contrary. However, it does mean that adequate alternatives exist in most instances to the idea that biology education must involve the wielding of a scalpel or a hypodermic (see chap. 7).

Diagnosis and toxicity testing are somewhat different activities from basic and applied research. In both diagnosis and toxicity testing, the techniques used are not subject to much change. Thus, the guinea-pig test for tuberculosis is usually carried out according to a set recipe (there is now an *in vitro* alternative to this test [Marks 1972]), while the basic structure of the LD50 test does not vary from one laboratory to another. However, in basic and applied research, the investigator is likely to vary the technical approach considerably from one project to the next. In addition, the investigator may need to use more than one technique to resolve a particular question to the satisfaction of his or her peers.

As a result, it is usually much easier for those who are promoting the idea of alternatives to focus on such areas as diagnosis and toxicity testing. Particular attention has been paid to toxicity testing because so many animals are used in relatively few procedures. LD50 testing accounts for one-quarter of all animals used in toxicity testing (Home Office 1979, p. 9). Therefore, replacement of the LD50 by a test using far fewer animals would have a major impact. Animal welfare groups have thus been prepared to mobilize protests against specific test methods with the aim of generating modifications and research into alternatives. As described in Part 3, this approach has paid off and there is now significant interest among both regulators and scientists (Holden 1982b).

Conclusion

In summary, the notion of alternatives is tied up with biomedical technology. Animal models are usually subject to wide biological variability and environmental modulators, and include many extraneous variables that are difficult to control. Therefore, the development of quicker, cheaper, and more precise techniques will benefit biomedical research. Many such techniques have been developed over the past 100 years, the motivation usually having been the scientist's need for a better technique to resolve the problem directly. The need for improved methodology has been recognized in animal research where animal technique development has received substantial government support. There is, therefore, no reason, other than bureaucratic resistance to change, why specific and equal support should not also be given to alternative technologies.

Opinions within the scientific establishment are changing slowly but they are changing. An opinion poll of German scientists, many of whom worked in the pharmaceutical or chemical industry, were asked whether data from chronic toxicity tests on animal could be replaced by data from carefully conducted clinical trials. Of those respondents who admitted to knowing enough to make a decision on the question, 10% considered complete replacement possible and 55% thought that some animal data could be replaced with data from clinical studies (Fiebelkorn and Lagoni 1981). Another question about short-term mutagenicity testing demonstrated that, in contrast, almost 20% of the knowledgeable respondents were opposed to short-term testing. This indicates that, from the animal welfare perspective, considerable progress is still possible.

Economics is, however, on the side of animal welfare because alternative methods are usually cheaper, especially in some of the toxicity testing protocols. The economic motive has already led to considerable technical innovation on short-term tests for carcinogen testing, and this example is used continuously to indicate that alternatives benefit animals, humans, and politicians. Other scientists have been encouraged to take up the idea of alternatives by the prospect of research grants from animal welfare groups and industry. Thus, the cosmetic industry's money for alternatives research has generated significant interest in the concept of alternatives among those scientists who have suddenly discovered that they may have a project worthy of funding.

The notion of alternatives, especially in safety testing, therefore, has potential as a major bridge between scientists and animal welfare groups. This was noted back in 1969 by animal welfare advocates (Peters 1969) but scientists have responded more slowly. In fact, significant scientific interest has only really been sparked by the promise of research money. The interest of government and industry in funding appropriate research has, by contrast, been mobilized mainly by the threat of disruptive political action.

In the nineteenth century, public health advocates and opponents of animal research found common ground around the idea that better sanitation and clean water would remove the need for most animal research (Stevenson 1955). A century later, the concept of alternatives could provide a similar mechanism for co-operation and collaboration. If so, it means that we are likely to see a powerful coalition of scientists and animal welfare advocates, probably with very different political motives, force political machines to produce some significant initiatives on the question of alternatives before the end of the decade. In fact, the only barrier that could prevent such a development is the historical suspicion of science among animal welfare groups.

CHAPTER 20

Suggestions for the Future

The only certain prediction one can make about the future is that the protests against animal research will continue. In fact, I would forecast that criticism of experimentation on animals will become more vocal and more effective during the rest of this decade. More scientists are joining the animal welfare and animal rights groups and their growing knowledge of research practice has resulted in a definite upgrading of the quality of both the literature and the arguments of the protesters. Sweeping generalizations and misrepresentations are giving way to specific and detailed criticisms of particular programs and practices.

Although the attitude of scientists and scientific organizations to such criticism is beginning to change, there is still a strong and, presumably, natural tendency to react in a defensive manner. Thus, an attack on the use of pound dogs is presented as an effort to stop all animal research. Dr. Taub garners much sympathy by presenting himself as a modern-day Galileo, victimized by anti-intellectual forces, despite the fact that the action against him centered solely on his treatment and care of his monkeys rather than on the merits of his research. The American Psychological Association provided support for Dr. Taub's defense even though the National Institutes of Health terminated his grant (American Psychological Association 1982).

The defensive posture adopted by various biomedical interests is the wrong approach. Nor do biomedical researchers help their cause by arrogantly insisting on their rights to study whatever they wish in whatever manner is deemed appropriate. In so doing, they are promulgating academic license, not academic freedom. Society has already determined that there are some things that should not be done in the name of furthering biomedical knowledge and unlimited freedom for researchers is an illusion. Funding agencies provide support for their research missions, not the whims and fancies of the research scientist.

At the same time, an immediate halt to animal research is a totally unrealistic goal. The public may support some reduction in the use of laboratory animals but only a minority would approve halting all animal research and testing. Therefore, if we are to make any real progress on animal research questions, we must accept the view that simple, and simplistic, solutions, espoused by extremists on either side, are not the answer. Nonetheless, we do need a minirevolution. Government agencies must demonstrate an explicit commitment to animal welfare (the mere presence of a law, regulation, or guideline is not sufficient), and scientists must recognize and confront, in a serious, constructive, and open manner, the concerns of the general public.

How do we effect the necessary change without crippling biomedical research or establishing a vast new bureaucratic infrastructure within the Department of Health and Human Services and the Department of Agriculture? Action is required at many levels—the individual scientist, the professional scientific societies, the journal editors, the research institutions, the funding agencies, and Congress—and some concrete suggestions are presented below.

Congressional Action

Regulation of animal experimentation by legislative mandate has never been a particularly popular notion among scientists and scientific societies. Nevertheless, there is now world-wide recognition that some sort of legislation is, unfortunately, necessary. Self-regulation has either been inadequate or it has not allayed public fears. Therefore, in Europe, the Council of Europe is putting together the final touches to a draft convention on the conduct of research on animals. In England, the prestigious science journal, *Nature,* accepts the need for a major revision of the British 1876 law on animal experimentation (Nature 1981). In Sweden, Switzerland, and the Netherlands, new legislation regulates animal research more closely. In Australia, New South Wales is moving toward the enactment of an animal experimentation law.

In the United States, the animal welfare movement has been promoting legislation to regulate animal experimentation for the last twenty-five years. The Animal Welfare Act of 1966 (amended in 1970 and 1976) is the result, but it deals with custodial and husbandry requirements only and not with the manner in which laboratory animals are used. There is a nodding acknowledgment in the act that pain to research animals must be addressed, but the responsible agency has shown little interest in attempting to enforce even these minimal provisions (Solomon and Lovenheim 1982). As a result, the last five years have produced increasing animal welfare pressure for legislation that would encourage the development of alternatives on the one hand, and control potentially painful animal research on the other.

The optimal legislation to regulate animal research will differ from country to country. A small country with a relatively small research effort could operate a successful regulatory system with relatively little effort. By contrast, the United States, with 1,200 research institutions spread across 3.6 million square miles and accounting for $10 billion of research effort, is a very different prospect.

Probably the most effective approach would be to require institutions to register with a central authority, to submit detailed reports of their activities, and to comply with certain standards of animal care and use. It is important that animal use and the related ethical issues be explicitly included in the mandate. This proposal would also need a knowledgeable inspection service with the will and the means to impose appropriate penalties for noncompliance (e.g., suspension of Federal funding). The inspections need only cover a small proportion of the research institutions every year but they must be unannounced so that no institution will know when it is likely to receive a visit.

As for specifics, one would need a national advisory group to deal with the inevitable problems of interpretation and to provide a formal forum to enable biomedical researchers and animal welfare advocates to work through their differences. There should also be a requirement for all research institutions to establish a committee that would review the ethical aspects of their animal research projects. The committee should have at least one representative, preferably from a local animal welfare group, who is responsible for acting as an advocate for the animals.

The above scheme would have the following advantages (or disadvantages, depending on one's point of view). First, all research institutions would have to register and provide a central authority with sufficient information (open to the public) to indicate how they are complying with the statutory requirements. Second, the inspection service need not be particularly large since only relatively few of the institutions would be inspected in any one year. Nevertheless, because of the random, surprise visits, all institutions would have to keep on their toes. Third, the local institutional committees would address many of the ethical questions that bother the animal welfare movement today. In addition, the presence of a representative from a local animal welfare group will ensure a better dialogue than at present. Finally, the use of a national advisory body as a formal discussion forum for the various protagonists would certainly have a beneficial effect in defusing some of the current controversy.

Obviously, this scheme would not eliminate all animal welfare protest and activism, and there are many research scientists who would view it askance. Commercial enterprises, for example, would not welcome the idea of an outsider reviewing their confidential research projects. However, this could be resolved by withholding commercially sensitive facts that would be irrelevant for the ethical review. Both public and private institutions may hold that the cost of ethical review would be far too great. When human ethical review committees were established, they required over 350,000 person hours of effort (Gray, Cooke, and Tannenbaum 1978). Obviously, a judgment that animal ethical review is worth this will depend on one's point of view, but it must also be seen in relation to an overall biomedical research effort of $8 billion to $10 billion. The relative cost is not large and the Swedes have reportedly found that their ethical review committees have improved the quality of the research proposals submitted for funding.

There is no mention of alternatives in the above proposal but this does not mean that there should not be some congressional initiative on this topic. However, the alternatives issue should not be part of this legislative proposal. Instead, Congress should require Federal funding agencies to take appropriate action. For example, the Division of Research Resources should be required to expand its Biomedical Research Model Development program. Congress is already moving in this direction, but real money is required. The National Toxicology Program should also establish a major alternatives program, rather than squandering money on inconclusive bioassays.

It has been suggested that a National Center for Alternatives should be established. This may be too grand a proposal, but an Interagency Co-ordinating Committee on Alternatives could fulfil a similar function if it were given sufficient authority and funding to conduct the necessary reviews of research practices in the various agencies. Such a committee could play a major role in reviewing animal research techniques and possible alternatives, as well as ensuring proper public accountability for those projects involving animals. As argued earlier, the promotion of alternatives, if done within the appropriate framework of reasoned analysis and review, will bring substantial benefits to biomedical research and will also alleviate a major public concern.

Funding Agencies

While some legislative initiatives will probably be necessary to demonstrate to animal welfare groups that something is being "done" about animal research, funding agencies do not need any new legislative mandate to promote alternatives and tighten up on laboratory animal welfare. For example, NIH already requires an "acceptable" statement of assurance from an institution, that it is "committed to comply" with the NIH Guide for the Care and Use of Laboratory Animals and relevant laws, before NIH will make a grant to the institution for research involving animals. If an instutition fails, in "a material manner," to comply with this requirement, then NIH may refuse to make further awards.

Presumably, NIH implemented this policy when it terminated the grant to Dr. Taub after his conviction for animal cruelty (Cordes 1982). However, if they had been actively enforcing the policy they would not have waited for a conviction. In fact, a more forceful interpretation of the animal research policy would have a major impact on institutional attitudes toward self-regulation of animal research. For example, the laboratory animal veterinarian at the University of California, Berkeley, has publicly criticized the animal facilities at Berkeley and has refused, for the last few years, to sign the annual report required under the Animal Welfare Act. Berkeley has now indicated that it will improve its facilities, but a threat by NIH to cut off animal research funds would have produced far faster action and would have warned other institutions that the statement of assurance is much more than the paper pussycat that it is perceived to be. In fact, NIH shows signs that it is going to tighten up its animal research policies, but animal welfare groups have become skeptical of such statements since past experience indicates that NIH initiatives have not addressed their main concerns.

NIH could also play a major role through its peer review process. The argument is commonly heard that each grant application is subject to rigorous review, including a judgment on the need to use animals and on their welfare, by a committee of scientists who are particularly knowledgable in the area of research under consideration. It is true that this peer review could be a potent force for promoting animal welfare. However, the indications are that animal welfare issues are not properly addressed. For example, one analysis of funded animal research proposals indicated that the grant application just did not contain sufficient information to make any serious judgment on animal welfare (Fox et al. 1979). More recently, a peer-reviewed and approved grant application for a deafferentation project on monkeys quoted a per diem cost for the monkeys of $0.55. Since the average per diem charge for normal monkeys at the time was over $2.00, this should have raised all sorts of red flags for the peer review committee, but did not (cf. Rowan 1982a). Thus, the indications are that the peer reivew process, which by definition reflects rather than challenges the status quo and "normal" science, does not play a major role in promoting animal welfare.

Of course, NIH is not the only Federal agency that supports animal research. The others could also play an important role in upgrading the status of animal welfare in the research laboratory. The Department of Defense, for example, has recently revised its animal research guidelines but it is not clear now much of an impact the revisions are likely to have. The regulatory agencies could also send a strong signal to commercial enterprises by altering some of the safety testing regulations, as outlined earlier. Economic pressures have encouraged pharmaceutical enterprises to switch to *in vitro* systems where possible (Spink 1977) and scientific developments have steadily increased the range of *in vitro* models available (cf. Kolata 1982b). Some unforced movement on animal welfare issues by the regulatory agencies would therefore accelerate the already existing trend to reduce the use of animals in commercial research and testing.

Institutional

Probably the most important control point for laboratory animal welfare in the United States is the local institution. Ethical review of human research has been delegated to institutional review boards (IRBs) and, although the effectiveness of the IRBs has varied considerably from institution to institution, this is probably the most efficient way to regulate research practices in a country such as the United States.

Canada has developed a voluntary system of institutional animal care committees, but it has generated only lukewarm support from animal welfare groups because, they argue, the scheme is voluntary and sanctions for animal abuse are weak or nonexistent. In the United States, institutional committees should be required by Federal statute. A research facility should not be permitted to conduct animal research unless it is registered and has established a suitable animal care and protection committee. If it has not taken these simple steps, then it should be subject to prosecution. Surprising though it may be, failure to register is not a prosecutable offense under the current Animal Welfare Act.

The animal care and protection committee should have at least one member who is specifically charged with looking after the interests of the animals. It should meet regularly and have authority over animal care and husbandry and research projects involving animals. It should also develop (or institute) educational programs on animal welfare and alternatives.

The most contentious of the above will undoubtedly be the review of animal research projects. It has been argued that institutional committees would not have sufficient scientific expertise to make judgments on the wide range of research proposals that would come before them. This is undoubtedly true, but it is by no means clear that they would have to make a judgment on the scientific excellence of the projects in their deliberations on animal welfare. This could presumably be left to the peer review process at NIH and elsewhere. (It should be noted that military research proposals do not necessarily undergo peer review). The committee would focus instead on inadequate justifications for the choice of research animal, the number required, and the proposed research techniques. For example, the committee could ask whether a research project really does require that monkeys be placed in restraint chairs for two months. This type of questioning does not necessarily require knowledge of the scientific validity of the project.

In fact, the most important task the committees could perform is an evaluation of research techniques leading to a steady refinement of methods to reduce animal suffering and distress. One immediate requirement is for a working definition of pain and distress; perhaps along the lines of the one below which has been formulated by an NIH animal care panel.

Pain is awareness of acute or chronic discomfort occurring in varying degrees of severity resulting from injury, disease or emotional distress and evidenced by biological or behavioral changes or both.

Acute Pain results from a traumatic, surgical, or infectious event that is abrupt in onset, relatively short in duration (days to weeks), and generally alleviated by analgesics. Associated distress may be responsive to tranquilizers.

Chronic Pain results from a long-standing physical disorder or emotional distress that is usually slow in onset, has a long duration, and is generally not totally alleviated by analgesics, but frequently responds to tranquilizers combined with environmental manipulation and behavioral conditioning.

Distress is undesirable physical or mental stress resulting from pain, anxiety, or fear. Its acute form may be relieved by tranquilizers, whereas sustained distress requires environmental change and behavioral conditioning, and does not respond to drug therapy.

While these definitions are relatively general, they are better than many others in use (Loew 1981) and they do provide some guidance for researchers and institutional committees. In addition, one can draw up a grading system for various types of procedures. The Swedes have identified six categories, ranging from techniques that cause negligible pain to those that cause extreme pain (see table 20.1). In the U.S.A. the USDA annual report form focuses attention on pain but it gives no guidance; clearly much painful research is not reported as such (Solomon and Lovehein 1982).

This brings us to the problem of specific guidelines. It is all very well to argue that one should not cause unnecessary pain, but what does this mean in terms of specific procedures? Do injections always involve negligible pain? At what point does food deprivation cause distress and suffering? Can tumors associated with cancer research cause pain and suffering? These, and many other specific questions, need to be addressed and guidance provided for both the institutional committees and the individual researchers. In some cases, answers can be provided without further research, but in others, more investigation is necessary. For example, a researcher in England is now looking into the painfulness of such routine procedures as injections (Universities Federation for Animal Welfare 1982, pp. 8–9), and various scientific organizations have offered suggestions as to what constitutes appropriate and justifiable animal research.

The International Association for the Study of Pain has issued guidelines on research using animals. They include the following proposals:

1. Where possible, the investigator should check a painful stimulus by trying it on himself/herself first.
2. The animal's deviation from normal behavior should be carefully assessed on the basis of a wide variety of physiological and behavioral parameters (e.g., the EEG, sleeping/waking cycles, feeding, and motor behaviors).
3. The animal should be able to control the stimuli in studies of acute pain. Animals used in chronic pain pose a particular problem (Sternbach 1976) but even in these instances the investigator can minimize the pain and suffering endured by the animal (Covino et al. 1980).

TABLE 20.1
SWEDISH CLASSIFICATION FOR RESEARCH TECHNIQUES

a.	No pain or negligible pain	e.g., injections, blood sampling, tube feeding, dietary experiments, behavioral observations
b.	Anesthetized animals that are not permitted to revive, or animals killed painlessly	e.g., blood studies, removal of organs or tissues
c.	Surgery under anesthetic from which the animal recovers, the surgery and/or procedure being of such a nature that there will be minimal post-operative pain	e.g., biopsies, transfusions, vascular experiments, pituitary removal
d.	As for (c), but with considerable post-operative pain	e.g., major surgical studies, burn studies, skin graphs
e.	Experiments on conscious animals that cause pain, or experiments in which the animals are expected to become seriously ill and/or suffer pain	e.g., toxicity studies, radiation research, tumor transplants, stress and shock studies, behavioral studies involving aversive conditioning
f.	Experiments on unanesthetized animals paralyzed by curariform agents	e.g., some pharmacology studies

SOURCE: Adapted from Ross 1978.

In cancer research, problems are raised by *in vivo* studies of tumor growth and metastatic phenomena. A 5-gram tumor in a 25-gram mouse will be a significant drain on the animal's resources, and researchers should probably restrict tumor size to no more than 5% to 10% of the animal's body weight. In tumor transplant studies, the transplantation site is also important since significant suffering can be avoided merely by careful selection of an appropriate site.

Suggestions for the Future

Psychological research involves a number of more or less noxious stimuli and treatments, and professional psychology groups could do well to review their research techniques to determine which practices are unacceptable. For example, in food derprivation pretreatment of experimental subjects, should one consider starvation to 80% of body weight as acceptable? Lea (1979) argues that this is unwarranted and suggests that a 6-hour food deprivation for rats is usually just as efficient as a 23-hour deprivation. The use of electric shock should be avoided but, if this is not deemed possible, there is little or no guidance for the concerned psychologist on what levels of shock would be acceptable.

Such questions indicate that there is much that the specialist scientific societies can do to identify painful procedures and help their members to reduce research animal suffering. We can also make some broad classifications immediately (see table 20.2). The classification scheme will vary with the person making it, but table 20.2 indicates in the right-hand column some procedures for which specific justification for the research or testing is required. It should also be noted that even a simple procedure (e.g., blood sampling) can be painful and distressing when done by an unskilled and clumsy individual.

TABLE 20.2
Procedures Classified According to Pain Caused

Minor Pain	Severe Pain/Distress
Administration of anesthetics, immunizations, medication	Behavior studies involving aversive conditioning (e.g., electric shock)
Blood Collection (except intracardiac and periorbital)	Toxicology tests (e.g., LD50, Draize)
Behavior studies without aversive conditioning	Shock and burn studies
Removal of tissue samples	Tumor transplants
Nonrecovery experimental procedures under anesthesia	Infectious disease studies
Injections	Vaccine Challenge testing
Palpations	Restraint/immobilization for more than 12 hours
Diet studies	Radiation toxicity
Recovery surgery involving minor pain (e.g., biopsies, castration, transfusion, catheterization)	Injection of inflammatory or necrotic agent
	Major surgical operations

Some institutions have already begun to experiment with ethical review committees, and there is growing interest in the idea of including an "animals' advocate" on the animal care committee. At the University of Southern California, an Animal Ethics Review Board has been established to review all grants and contracts involving the use of live animals in research and to delineate ethical standards for such research (Blackmore 1982). The Wisconsin Regional Primate Research Center has taken similar action and is busy implementing a new policy statement on the ethical uses of animals which acknowledges that "maintenance and care standards alone do not constitute adequate protection of the well-being and rights of nonhuman animals" (Wisconsion Regional P.R.C. 1982).

Thus, a precedent has already been set for institutional ethical review committees. It is likely that most of the more far-sighted and innovative research facilities will follow suit. The NIH is also moving toward requiring review of animal research protocols by institutional committees (National Institutes of Health 1982).

Individuals

The individual research scientists represent a fourth control point but, because standards vary so widely from person to person, this is unlikely to be an acceptable control from the animal welfare point of view. However, the ultimate protection for laboratory animals is the conscience of the scientific researcher (Ashby 1981). Therefore, we must attempt to raise the level of awareness of that conscience via educational programs.

In England, where individuals must be licensed to conduct animal research, it would be relatively easy to require a training course for all new licensees. In the U.S., it will not be so simple, but some attempt should be made to expose new graduate students and research scientists to the problems raised by animal research.

Editorial Control

Science progresses through a continual exchange of information and argument. The growth of science is clearly demonstrated by the growth in the number of academic journals as scientists "publish or perish." It has been suggested that editors can exercise control over inappropriate animal research by refusing to publish the resulting research reports. However, if this is to become an effective mode of control, the editorial process will have become considerably tighter.

Peters and Ceci (1982) have demonstrated that editors and reviewers cannot even recognize papers that were published no more than 2 to 3 years earlier. This is amply supported by the occasional instance of a plagiarist building up an impressive publication record merely by rewriting already published research. If quality control operates at such a lax level, what hope is there for controlling inappropriate animal research? The answer is, unfortunately, very little.

Even though the editor of the *British Journal of Radiology* accepted that the paper by Grigsby and Maruyama (1981), involving oral radiation death studies in animals, resulted in too much animal suffering, this acknowledgement only came after readers of the *Journal* had drawn the paper to his attention (Hewitt and Porter 1982). In another case involving studies of the effects of hot water scalds on rat lipid biochemistry (Nishigaki et al. 1980), the editor of the relevant journal (in this case *Biochemical Medicine*) refused to accept that the paper raised serious ethical issues. It is, therefore, unlikely that editorial control will ever play more than a small part in the regulation of animal research. Although there are one or two welcome exceptions (e.g., Wall 1975), editors tend to follow fashions rather than make them.

Summary

Briefly, then, we need some enabling legislation to encourage the development and promotion of alternatives; to establish a statutory authority for institutional care and protection committees; and to establish a national body where differences of opinion can be formally debated and perhaps even resolved. Second, we need local institutional care and protection committees with public participants, plus detailed guidelines for research practices. Finally, we need some formal education for prospective animal researchers and animal technicians on the ethics of animal research.

Conclusion

I have proselytized for long enough in this book and it is time to let you, the reader, sit back and make your own decisions about the validity of my arguments and the appropriateness of my suggestions. I have attempted to demonstrate that one can argue for greater consideration of animal welfare without calling upon sentiment or anthropomorphism. I believe that the animal welfare movement raises many questions that deserve serious consideration. I also believe that the cost of the program I have outlined will be more than repaid by the improved science to which it will lead.

Bibliography

Adamiker, D. 1977. Breeding of laboratory animals in Austria. *Wien. Med. Wochschr.* 127: 172–5.

Adams, P. M. 1981. Statement on behalf of the American Psychological Association and the Association for the Advancement of Psychology. Hearings before the Subcommittee on Science, Research and Technology of the Committee on Science and Technology. U.S. House of Representatives, 97th Congress. Washington, D.C.

Adams, R. 1978. *The plague dogs.* London: Knopf.

Advisory Committee. 1979. *Report on the LD50 test.* Advisory Committee to the Cruelty to Animals Act, 1876. London: Home Office.

Altura, B. M. 1976. Sex and estrogens in protection against circulatory stress reactions. *Am. J. Physiol.* 231: 842–7.

Alumets, J.; Hakanson, R.; Sundler, F.; and Thorell, J. 1979. Neuronal localization and immunoreactive enkephalin and B-endorphin in the earthworm. *Nature* 279: 805.

American Anti-Vivisection Society. 1982. *The casebook of experiments with living animals.* Jenkintown, Pa.

American College of Laboratory Animal Medicine. 1980. Continuing criticism of animal testing. *Newsletter* 10(2): 13.

American College of Surgeons. 1935. *Animal experimentation: its importance and value to scientific medicine.* Chicago.

American Family Physician. 1975. Animals in biomedical research. 11(6): 67–68.

American Industrial Health Council. 1978. *Testimony on OSHA's generic carcinogen proposal.* Scarsdale, N.Y.

Ames, B. N. 1979. Identifying environmental chemicals causing mutations and cancer. *Science* 204: 587–93.

American Psychological Association. 1979. Principles for the care and use of animals. APA Committee on Animal Research and Experimentation. Washington, D.C.

American Psychological Association. 1982. Taub loses NIH grant; APA supports his lab. *APA Monitor* 13(10): 3.

Animal and Plant Health Inspection Service. 1972–80. Annual Reports: Animal Welfare Enforcement, 1972–80. U.S. Dept. of Agriculture, Washington, D.C.

Animal Welfare Institute. 1969. More cruelty among teenaged science students. *Information Report.* 18(2): 2–3.

Ashby, E. 1981. How should we protect animals which we use to protect us. *Conquest,* 171: 12–14.

Austwick, P. 1977. The use of experimental animals and in vitro systems in the diagnosis of fungal diseases. In *International symposium on experimental animals and in vitro systems in medical microbiology,* Munich. WHO Collaborating Center for Collection and Evaluation Data on Comparative Virology, pp 203–213.

Autian, J., and Dillingham, E.O. 1978. Overview of general toxicity testing with emphasis on special tissue culture tests. In *In Vitro Toxicity Testing 1975–1976,* ed. J. Berky and C. Sherrod, pp. 23–49. Philadelphia: Franklin Institute Press.

Baker, J. B. E. 1960. The effects of drugs on the foetus. *Pharmacol. Reviews* 12: 37–90.

Baker, J.; Bartlett, F. C.; Hardy, A. C.; Hindle, E.; Hume, C. W.; and Wooldridge, W. R. 1949. Experiments on animals. *Lancet* (2): 259.

Baker, S. B. de C. 1969. The study of the toxicity of potential drugs in laboratory animals. In *The Use of Animals in Toxicological Studies.* Potters Bar, England: Universities Federation for Animal Welfare.

Bannister, D. 1981. The fallacy of animal experimentation in psychology. In *Animals in Research,* ed. D. Sperlinger, pp. 307–317. Chichester: John Wiley & Sons.

Barcroft, H.; Edholm, O. G.; Lane-Petter, W.; and Robertson, J. D. 1951. Animal experiments. *J. Am. Med. Ass.* 147: 1380.

Barile, M. F., and Hardegree, M. 1970. A cell culture assay to evaluate the toxicity of Arlacel. *Proc. Soc. Exp. Biol. Med.* 133: 222–8.

Barnes, J. M. 1960. In *Toxicity Testing: Modern Trends in Occupational Health,* ed. R. S. F. Schilling, p. 20. London: Butterworths.

Baum, W. M. 1974. Choice in free-ranging wild pigeons. *Science* 185: 78–9.

Beach, F. A. 1950. The snark was a boojum. *American Psychol.* 5: 115–24.

Beach, F. A. 1977. Letter. *Current Contents,* 48: 13–14.

Beale, A. J. 1978. The use of tissue culture for testing vaccines. *J. Roy. Soc. Med.* 71: 681–6.

Beaucage, C. M. and Fox, J. C. 1979. Transmissible antibiotic resistance in Salmonella isolated from random-source cats purchased for use in research. Am J. Vet. Res. 40: 849–51.

Beck, A. M. 1973. *The ecology of stray dogs: a study of free-ranging urban animals.* Baltimore: York Press.

——— 1974. The dog: America's sacred cow? *Nation's Cities* 12(2): 29–31, 34–35.

Beckley, J. H. 1965. Comparative eye testing: man versus animal. *Toxicol. Appl. Pharmacol.* 7: 93–101.

Beckley, J. H.; Russell, T. J.; and Rubin, L. F. 1969. Use of rhesus monkey for predicting human responses to eye irritants. *Toxicol. Appl. Pharmacol.* 15: 1–9.

Bell, M.; Holmes, P. M.; Nisbet, T. M.; Uttley, M.; and Van Abbe, M. J. 1979. Evaluating the potential eye irritancy of shampoos. *Int. J. Cosmetic Sci.* 1: 123–31.

Benison S. 1970. In defense of medical research. *Harvard Med. Bull.* 44(3): 16–23.

Bentham, J. 1962. *The works of Jeremy Bentham,* ed. J. Bowring, vol. 1, pp. 142–3. New York: Russell and Russell.

Berry, C. L., and Barlow, S. 1976. Some remaining problems in the reproductive toxicity testing of drugs. *Br. Med. Bull.* 32: 34–38.

Best, C. H. 1974. A short essay on the importance of dogs in medical research. *The Physiologist* 17: 437–40.

Best, J. B. 1973. Learning and neurophysiology of planarians: transphyletic similarities in the organization of brains and psychological systems. In *Behavioral Genetics: Simple Systems,* ed. J. Wilson, pp. 55–84. Denver: University of Colorado Press.

Binn, L. N.; Alford, J. P.; Marchwick, R. H.; Keefe, T. J.; Beattie, R. J.; and Wall, H. G. 1979. Studies of respiratory disease in random-source laboratory dogs; viral infections in unconditioned dogs. *Lab An. Sci.* 29: 48–52.

Blackmore, W. M. 1982. Animal research ethics at the University of Southern California. *Lab. Animal* 11(4): 41–47.

Blakemore, C., and Cooper G. F. 1970. Development of the brain depends on the visual environment. *Nature* 228: 477–8.

Blakemore, C.; Donaghy, M. J.; Maffei, L.; Moushon, J. A.; Rose, D.; and Van Slutyers, R. C. 1974. Evidence that nitrous oxide can maintain anesthesia after induction with barbiturates. *J. Physiol. London.* 237: 39p–41p.

Boffey, P. M. 1977. Polio: Salk challenges safety of Sabin's live-virus vaccine. *Science* 196: 35–36.

Bolt, Beranek and Newman, Inc. 1976. *Assuring the resources for biomedical research. An evaluation of the scientific mission of the Division of Research Resources.* National Institutes of Health (Contract #1-RR-6-2101), Washington, D.C.

Bowd, A. D. 1980a. Ethics and animal experimentation. *American Psychologist* 35: 224–5.

Bowd, A. D. 1980b. Ethical reservations about psychological research with animals. *Psychol. Record* 30: 201–10.

Bowlby, J. 1960. Grief and mourning in infancy and early childhood. *Psychoanal. Study of the Child* 15: 9–52.

Boyd, E. M. and Godi, I. L. 1967. Acute oral toxicity of distilled water in albino rats. *Industrial Med. and Surg.* 36: 609–613.

Brain, L. 1963. Animals and pain. *New Scientist* 19: 380–81.

Braithwaite, J., and Braithwaite, V. 1982. Attitudes toward animal suffering: an exploratory study. *Int. J. Study Animal Problems* 3: 42–49.

Brambell Committee. 1965. *Report of Technical Committee of Enquiry into the Welfare of Livestock Husbandry Systems.* London: Her Majesty's Stationery Office.

Brandt, H. C.; Shapiro, P. A.; and Kokich, V. G. 1979. Experimental and postexperimental effects of posteriorly directed extraoral traction in adult Macaca fascicularis. *Am. J. Orthodont.* 75: 301–317.

Breazile, J. E. and Kitchell, R. L. 1964. Pain perception in animals. *Fed. Proc.* 28: 1379–82.

British Pharmacopoeia Commission 1973a. Biological assay of antirachitic vitamin (vitamin D), pp. A113–114. London: British Pharmacopoeia Commission.

———. 1973b. Biological assay for tetanus antitoxin, p. 104. London: British Pharmacopoeia Commission.

———. 1977a. Biological assay for tetanus antitoxin (Addendum), London: British Pharmacopoeia Commission.

———. 1977b. *A Submission from the British Pharmacopoeia Commission to the Advisory Committee to the Cruelty to Animals Act, 1876.* London: British Pharmacopoeia Commission.

British Psycological Society. 1979. Report of a working party on animal experimentation. *Bul. Br. Psychol. Soc.* 32: 44–52.

Broad, W. J. 1980. Legislating an end to animals in the lab. *Science* 208: 575–6.

Brown & Sons, Alex. 1981. *Charles River Breeding Laboratories,* New York: Alex Brown & Sons.

Brumbaugh, R. S. 1978. Of man, animals and morals: a brief history. In *On the fifth day,* eds. R. K. Morris and M. W. Fox, pp. 6–25. Washington, D.C.: Acropolis Books.

Brusick, D. 1980. *Principles of genetic toxicology.* New York: Plenum Press.

———. 1981. The use of nonanimal assay systems for detection of potential carcinogens. In *Nonanimal research methodologies* ed. A. Posner, pp. 23–29. Washington, D.C.: George Washington University Ethics and Animals Society.

Bucknall, R. A. 1980. The use of cultured cells and tissues in the development of antiviral drugs: In *The use of alternatives in drug research* ed. A. N. Rowan and C. J. Stratmann, pp. 15–27. London: Macmillan.

Buehler, E. V. 1974. Testing to predict potential ocular hazards of household chemicals. In *Toxicology Annual,* ed. C. J. Winek. New York: Marcel Dekker.

Burch, G. E. 1959. Of the normal dog. *Am. Heart J.* 58: 805–806.

Burch, G. E. 1972. Clinical medicine. *Fed. Proc.* 31(6): pt. 2: TF33–TF70.

Bures, J.; Buresova, O.; and Huston, J. 1976. *Techniques and basic experiments for the study of brain and behavior.* Amsterdam: Elsevier Scientific Publishing Co.

Bures, J.; Buresova, O.; and Huston, J. 1977. Teaching vivisection. *New Scientist* 77: 872.

Burghardt, G. M. and Herzog H. A. 1980. Beyond conspecifics: is Brer Rabbit our brother? *Bioscience* 30: 763–8.

Burton, A. B. G.; York, M.; and Lawrence, R. S. 1981. The in vitro assessment of severe eye irritants. *Fd. Cosmet. Toxicol.* 19: 471–80.

Cairns, J. 1981. The origin of human cancers. *Nature* 289: 353–7.

Campbell, B. A., and Masterson, F. A. 1969. Psychophysics of punishment. In *Punishment and aversive behavior,* ed. B. A. Campbell and R. M. Church, pp. 3–42. New York: Appleton-Century-Crofts.

Canadian Council on Animal Care. 1980. *Guide to the care and use of experimental animals,* vol. 1. Ottawa: Canadian Council on Animal Care.

Canadian Society for the Prevention of Cruelty to Animals. 1980. Report of a workshop on alternatives to the use of laboratory animals in biomedical research and testing. Montreal: CSPCA.

Carpenter, C. P., and Smyth, H. F. 1946. Chemical burns of the rabbit cornea. *Amer. J. Ophthalmol* 29: 1363–72.

Carson, R. 1962. *Silent Spring.* Boston: Houghton Mifflin.

Carter, C. J. 1979. NEI votes to protect cold-blooded animals. *Science* 206: 1363.

Carter, L. M.; Duncan, G.; and Rennie, G. K. 1973. Effects of detergents on the ionic balance of permeability of isolated bovine cornea. *Exp. Eye Res.* 17: 409–416.

Carter, R. L. 1978. Long-term tests for carcinogenicity: the pathologist's view. In *Carcinogenicity testing: principles and problems,* ed. A. D. Dayan and R. W. Brimblecombe, pp. 2–15. Baltimore: University Park Press.

Carter, R. O., and Griffith, J. R. 1965. Experimental bases for the realistic assessment of safety of topical agents. *Toxicol. Appl. Pharmacol.* 7: 60–73.

Chamove, A. S. and Anderson, J. R. 1979. Woodchip litter in macaque groups. *J. Inst. Anim. Technicians* 30(2): 69–74.

Cherfas, J. 1982. Lab animals can suffer under Euro-Law. *New Scientist* 93: 495.

Christenson, H. E., and Luginbuhl, T. T. eds. 1975. *Registry of Toxic Effects of Chemical Substances.* Washington: National Institute of Occupational Safety and Health.

Clark, S. R. L. 1977 *The moral status of animals.* Oxford: Oxford University Press.

Clayton, R. M. 1980. An in vitro system for teratogenicity testing. In *The use of alternatives in drug research*, ed. A. N. Rowan and C. J. Stratmann, pp. 153–173. London: Macmillan.

Cohen, N. J. 1976. *Tsa'ar Ba'ale Hayim—the prevention of cruelty to animals.* New York: Philip Feldheim.

Cole, J. R., and Cole, S. 1972. The Ortega hypothesis. *Science* 178: 368–75.

Committee on Medical Research. 1978. Memoranda and tables from Working Group on the Supply of Non-Human Primates for Biomedical Purposes of the Committee on Medical Research. Brussels: Commission of the European Communities.

Committee for Reform of Animal Experimentation. 1977. *The LD50 Test. Evidence submitted to Home Office Advisory Committee (U.K.).* Horsham: RSPCA.

Comroe, J. H., and Dripps, R. D. 1976. Scientific basis for the support of biomedical science. *Science* 192: 105–111.

Conway, W. G. 1965. The availability and long term supply of primates for medical research. Report presented at a conference cosponsored by the N. Y. Zoological Society and the International Union for the Conservation of Nature, May 21–22, 1965, New York.

Cordes, C. 1982. Taub loses NIH grant; APA supports his lab. *APA Monitor* 13(10): 3.

Cosmetic Toiletry and Fragrance Association. 1980. Animal testing: does industry have a choice? Pamphlet. Washington, D.C.: CTFA.

Cottrell, R. C. 1981. Styles of life and death. *Fd & Cosm. Tox.* 19: 785–8.

Council for Science and Society. 1977. *The acceptability of risks.* London: Barry Rose.

Covino, B. G.; Dunbar, R.; Gybels, J.; Kosterlitz, H. W.; Liebeskind, J. C.; Sternbach, R. A.; Vyklicky, L.; Yamamura, H.; and Zimmerman, M. 1980. Ethical standards for investigations of experimental pain in animals. *Pain* 9: 141–3.

Craig, P. N. and Enslein, K. 1978. Extrapolation of LD50's between rat and mouse utilizing chemical structure. *J. Envir. Pathol. Toxicol.* 2: 115–21.

———. 1981. Structure-activity in hazard assessment. In *Hazard assessment of chemicals,* vol. 1, pp. 389–420. New York: Academic Press.

Cramer, G. M.; Ford, R. A.; and Hall, R. L. 1978. Estimation of toxic hazard—a decision tree approach. *Fd. Cosmet. Toxicol.* 16: 255–76.

Cross, B. A. 1981. Currents and portents in biomedical research. *Vet. Rec.* 108: 202–206.

Crowther, J. C. 1969. *A short history of science.* London: Methuen.

Dalton, J. C. 1980. *John Call Dalton on experimental method.* New York: Arno Press. Reprint of *Experimentation on animals as a means of knowledge in physiology, pathology and practical medicine,* 1875, and *The experimental method in medical science,* 1882, New York.

Davies, I. B. 1980. The ethics of studying primates. *Biologist* 27: 228.

Davies, R. E.; Harper, K. N.; and Kynoch, S. R. 1972. Interspecies variation in dermal reactivity. *J. Soc. Cosmetic Chem* 23: 371–81.

Davis, H. 1981. Ethical considerations in the aversive control of behavior. *Soc. Sci. Med.* 15F: 61–67.

Dawkins, M. 1980. *Animal Suffering: the science of animal welfare.* London: Chapman & Hall.

Dawson, M. 1972. The rational use of tissue cultures for drug testing. In *The rational use of living systems in bio-medical research,* pp. 5–17. Potters Bar, England: Universities Federation for Animal Welfare.

Dayan, A. D. 1978. Uses and limitations of primates in the evaluation of drug efficacy and safety. *J. Roy. Soc. Med.* 71: 691–2.

Deichmann, W. B, and Leblanc, T. J. 1943. Determination of the Approximate Lethal Dose with about six animals. *J. Indust. Hyg. Toxicol.* 25: 415–7.

Deichmann, W. B., and Mergard, E. G. 1948. Comparative evaluation of methods employed to express the degree of toxicity of a compound. *J. Indust. Hyg. Toxicol.* 30: 373–8.

deLind van Wijngaarden, C. 1926. Untersuchungen uber die Wirkungsstarke von Digitalis praparaten. II. Mitteilungs uber die Genauigkeit der Digitalissichung an der Katze, *Arch. Exp. Pathol Pharmak.* 113: 40.

Dembeck, H. 1965. *Animals and men.* New York: Natural History Press.

Dennis, C. 1966. America's Littlewood Crisis: The sentimental threat to animal research. *Surgery* 60: 827–39.

De Serres, F. J. 1981. Panel discussion. In *Trends in bioassay methodology: in vivo, in vitro and mathematical approaches,* pp. 230–33. U.S. Department of Health and Human Services (NIH Pub. No. 82 2382).

DeWys, W. D. 1972. Studies correlating the growth rate of a tumor and its metastases and providing evidence for tumor-related systemic growth-retarding factors. *Cancer Res.* 32: 374–9.

Dieke, S. H., and Richter, C. P. 1945. Acute toxicity of thiourea to rats in relation to age, diet, strain, and species variation. *J. Pharmac. Exp. Ther.* 83: 195.

Diner, J. 1979. *Physical and mental suffering of experimental animals.* Washington, D.C.: Animal Welfare Institute.

Dixon, B. 1976. *What is science for?* London: Penguin Books.

———. 1978. *Beyond the magic bullet.* New York: Harper and Row.

Dixon, W. J., and Mood, A. M. 1948. A method of obtaining and analysing sensitivity data. *J. Am. Stat. Assoc.* 43: 109–126.

Doyle, R. E.; Anthony R. L.; Jepson, P. L.; Kinkler, R. J.; and Vogler, G. A. 1979. Missouri researchers find that vaccinating random-source dogs with three-part vaccine pays off. *Lab Animal* 8(2): 39–44, 56.

Drewett, R. 1977. On the teaching of vivisection. *New Scientist* 76: 292.

Drewett, R., and Kani, W. 1981. Animal experimentation in the behavioral sciences. In *Animals in Research*, ed. D. Sperlinger, pp. 175–201. Chichester: J. Wiley & Sons.

Draize, J. H.; Woodard, G.; and Clavery, H. O. 1944. Methods for the study of irritation and toxicity of substances applied topically to the skin and mucous membranes, *J. Pharmacol. Exp. Ther.* 82: 377–90.

Duclaux, E. 1920. *Pasteur, The history of a mind*, trans. E. F. Smith and F. Hodges, Philadelphia: W. B. Saunders.

Duffy, F. H.; Snodgrass, S. R.; Burchfiel, J. L.; and Conway, J. L. 1976. Bicuculline reversal of deprivation amblyopia in the cat. *Nature* 260: 256–257.

Duke-Elder, S. 1958. System of Ophthalmology. vol. 1. *The Eye in Evolution.* St. Louis: C. V. Mosby.

D'Ver, A. S. 1981. The end of the pound dog. *Lab Animal* 10(5): 23–25.

Eggers, H. M., and Blakemore, C. 1978. Physiological basis of anisometropic amblyopia. *Science* 201: 264–6.

Ekwall, B. 1980. Screening of toxic compounds in tissue culture. *Toxicology* 17: 127–42.

Ellison, T. (1977) Toxicological effects testing. In *Guidebook: Toxic Substances Control Act*, ed. G. Dominquez, 8.1–8.22. Boca Raton: CRC Press.

Emmons, M. B. 1980. Secondary and elementary school use of live and preserved animals. In *Animals in education*, ed. H. McGiffin and N. Brownley, pp. 43–46. Washington, D.C.: Institute for the Study of Animal Problems.

Enders, J. F.; Weller, T. H.; and Robbins, F. C. 1949. Cultivation of the Lansing strain of poliomyelitis virus in cultures of various human embryonic tissues. *Science* 109: 85–87.

Enslein, K. 1981. Statistical estimation of toxicological and other biological endpoints using structural/activity relationships. In *Trends in bioassay methodology: in vivo, in vitro and mathemetical approaches*, pp. 315–25. National Institutes of Health (Publication No. 82-2382), Washington, D.C.

Epstein, S. S. 1979. *The politics of cancer.* Garden City: Anchor Press/ Doubleday.

Faupel, R. P.; Seitz, H. J.; Tarnowski, W.; Thiemann, V.; and Weiss, C. 1972. The problem of tissue sampling from experimental animals with respect to freezing technique, anoxia, stress and narcosis. *Arch. Biochem Biophys.* 148: 509–22.

Federation of American Scientists. 1977. Animal rights. *Public Interest Report* 30(8): 1–8.
Festing, M. W. 1981. The "defined" animal and the reduction of animal use. In *Animals in Research*, ed. D. Sperlinger, pp. 285–306. Chichester: J. Wiley & Sons.
Fiebelkorn, J. and Lagoni, N. 1981. *Tierschutz und Tierexperiment—Durchfuhrung, Bewertung, und Aussage von Tierversuchen und alternativen Verfahren.* Bga Bericht—81. Berlin: Dietrich Reimer Verlag.
Fletcher, W. S.; Herr, R. H.; and Roger, A. L. 1969. Survival of purebred laborador retrievers versus pound dogs undergoing experimental heart valve replacement. *Lab Animal Care* 19: 506–508.
Forum for the Advancement of Toxicology. 1982. Workshop on in vitro toxicology testing. *Newsletter* 15(3): 1.
Foster, H. L.; Small, J. D.; and Fox, J. G., eds. 1981. *The mouse in biomedical research,* vol. 1. New York: Academic Press.
Fox, M. A. 1980. On justifying the use of animals for human ends. *An. Reg. Studies* 2: 191–204.
Fox, M. W. 1981. Experimental psychology, animal rights, welfare and ethics. *Psychopharmacol. Bull.* 17: 80–84.
Fox, M. W. 1982a. The show dog syndrome. *Int. J. Study Animal Problems* 3: 3–5.
Fox, M. W. 1982b. Response. *Int. J. Study Animal Problems* 3: 174–5.
Fox, M. W., and Ward, M. A. 1977. Are science fairs fair to animals? *The Science Teacher* 44: 31–33.
Fox, M. W.; Ward, M. A.; Rowan, A. N.; and Jaffe, B. 1979. *Evaluation of awarded grant applications involving animal experimentation.* Washington, D.C.: Institute for the Study of Animal Problems.
FRAME. 1977. *The LD50 Test—a Statement by FRAME to the Advisory Committee to the Cruelty to Animals Act, 1876.* London: Fund for The Replacement of Animals in Medical Experiments.
———. 1979. *Alternatives to laboratory animals.* London: Fund for the Replacement of Animals in Medical Experiments.
Franchina, J. J. 1979. Animal models of human behavior. Paper given at Conference on Ethics and Animals, May 24–27, 1979, Blacksburg, Va.
Frederickson, D. S. 1978. The National Institutes of Health: yesterday, today and tomorrow. *Public Health Reports* 93: 642–47.
——— . 1981. NIH policy on the use of pound animals. *ILAR NEWS* 25(1): 15–16.
French, R. D. 1975. *Antivivisection and medical science in Victorian society.* Princeton: Princeton University Press.
French, R. D. 1978. Animal experimentation, historical aspects. In *The Encyclopedia of Bioethics.* ed. W. T. Reich, vol. 1, pp. 75–79. New York: Free Press.
Frey, R. G. 1980. *Interest and rights: the case against animals.* Oxford: Clarendon Press.
Gallistel, C. R. 1981. Bell, Magendie and the proposals to restrict the use of animals in neurobehavioral research. *Am. Psychol.* 36: 357–60.
Gallup, G. G. and Suarez, S. D. 1980. On the use of animals in psychological research. *Psychol. Rec.* 30: 211–218.

Gallup, G. G. 1982. Self-awareness and the emergence of mind in primates. *Am. J. Primatol.* 2: 237–48.

Garfield, E. 1977. Citation analysis and the anti-vivisection controversy, Pt. II, An assessment of Lester R. Aronson's citation record. *Current Contents,* No. 48, pp 5–12.

Garfield, E. 1982. To remember Sir Hans Krebs: Nobelist, friend and advisor. *Current contents:* 13(31): 5–11.

Gartner, K.; Buttner, D.; Dohler, K.; Friedle, R.; Lindena, J.; and Trautschold, I. 1980. Stress response of rats to handling and experimental procedures. *Lab Animals* 14: 267–74.

General Accounting Office. 1978. *Lack of authority hampers attempts to increase cosmetic safety.* GAO Report to Congress, HRD–78–139, Washington, D.C.

Gianutsos, J. G. 1975. *Feedback contributions to recovery in the deafferented primate forelimb.* Ph.D. dissertation, Adelphi University, N. Y.

Gibbs, L.; Nace, W.; and Emmons, M. B. 1971. The live frog is dead. *Bioscience* 21: 1027.

Gilmartin, J. E. 1961. The establishment of a dog breeding kennel for pharmaceutical research. *Proc. Animal Care Panel* 11: 222–29.

Goering, H. 1939. *The political testament of Herman Goering,* trans. H. W. Blood–Ryan. London: John Long.

Goodman, L. S., and Gilman, A. 1975. *The Pharmacological Basis of Therapeutics,* 5th Edition. New York: Macmillan.

Goodwin, W. J. and Augustine, J. 1975. The Primate Research Centers program of the National Institutes of Health. *Fed. Proc.* 34: 1641–2.

Gori, G. B. 1980. The regulation of carcinogenic hazards. *Science* 208: 256–61.

Graft, D. A.; Lea, S. E. G.; and Whitworth, T. L. 1977. The matching law in and within groups of rats. *J. Exper. Anal. Behav.* 27: 183–94.

Grafton, T. S. 1977. More on the use of animals. *The Science Teacher* 44: 33.

——— . 1981. The role of alternatives in biomedical research. *Lab Animal* 10(1): 25–30.

Graham, C. E., and Hodgen, G. D. 1979. The use of chimpanzees in reproductive biology. *J. Med. Primatol.* 8: 265–72.

Gray, B. H.; Cooke, R. A.; and Tannenbaum, A. S. 1978. Research involving human subjects. *Science* 201: 1094–1101.

Green, W. R.; Sullivan, J. B.; Hehir, R. M.; Scharpf, J. H.; and Dickinson, A. W. 1978. *A systematic comparison of chemically induced eye injury in the albino rabbit and rhesus monkey.* New York: The Soap and Detergent Association.

Greenberg, J. 1980. Ape talk more than "pigeon" English. *Science News* 117: 298–300.

Greenhouse, D. D. 1980. Trends in primate imports into the United States, 1979. *ILAR News* 23(2/3): 27.

Griffin, D. R. 1976. *The Question of Animal Awareness.* New York: Rockefeller Univ. Press.

——— . 1981. *The question of animal awareness: evolutionary continuity of mental experience.* 2nd ed., New York: Rockefeller University Press.

——— . 1982. *Animal mind—human mind.* Berlin: Springer-Verlag.

Griffith, J. F.; Nixon, G. A.; Bruce, R. D.; Reer, P. J.; and Bannan, E. A. 1980. Dose-response studies with chemical irritants in the albino rabbit eye as a basis for selecting optimum testing conditions for predicting hazard to the human eye. *Toxicol. Appl. Pharmacol.* 55: 501–513.

Grigsby, P., and Maruyama, Y. 1981. Modification of the oral radiation death syndrome with combined WR-2721 and misonidazole. *Br. J. Radiol.* 54: 969–72.

——— . 1982. Letter. *Br. J. Radiol.* 55: 250–51.

Gur, M., and Purple, R. L. 1978. Retinal ganglion cell activity in the ground squirrel under halothane anesthesia. *Vision Res.* 18: 1–14.

Gurney, C. W. 1982. A reviewer's comment on "Biology and the New Age: An Evolutionary and Ethical Assessment. *Pers. Biol. Med.* 25: 194–206.

Guthrie, E. R. and Horton, G. P. 1946. *Cats in a puzzle box.* New York: Rinehart.

Guyton, A. C. 1981. Physiological system modeling as an alternative model procedure. In: *Trends in bioassay methodology: in vivo, in vitro and mathematical approaches,* pp. 247–257. National Institutes of Health, Pub. No. 82–2382, Washington, D. C.

Gyorgy, P., and Pearson, W. M., eds. 1967. *The vitamins*, vol. 7. New York: Academic Press.

Hall, M. 1831. *A critical and experimental essay on the circulation of the blood.* London.

Harless, M. D. 1972. Group operant behavior in free-feeding squirrel monkeys. *Psychol. Rep.,* 30: 572–4.

Harlow, H. F. 1962. Fundamental principles for preparing psychology journal articles. *J. Comp. Physiological Psychol.* 55: 893–6.

Harmison, L. T., ed. 1973. *Research animals in medicine.* National Institutes of Health NIH Publication No. 72–333, Bethesda, Md.

Harrison, R. J., and Harrison, M. J. 1978. Computer simulation as an aid to the replacement of experimentation on animals and humans. *ATLA Abstracts* 62: 22-35.

Harriton, L. 1981. Conversation with Henry Spira: Draize test activist. *Lab Animal* 10(1): 16–22.

Hart, B. L., ed. 1976. *Experimental Psychobiology: a laboratory manual.* San Francisco: W. H. Freeman.

Hartman, C. G. 1932. Studies in the reproduction of the monkey Macacus rhesus with special reference to menstruation and pregnancy. *Contrib. Embryol* 23: 1–167.

Heim, A. W. 1979a. Report of the working party on animal experimentation. *Bull. Br. Psychol. Soc.* 32: 113–14.

——— . 1979b. The proper study of psychology. *New Univ. Quart.* 32(2).

Held, J. R. 1981. Comments on alternatives article. *Lab Animal* 10(4): 10.

Heneson, N. 1980. Live animals in car crash studies. *Int. J. Study Animal Problems.* 1: 214–7.

——— . 1982. Sell us monkeys—or do without aid. *New Scientist* 94: 583–5.

Hennessen, W. 1980. Replacement of animals in manufacture and control of vaccines. *Develop. Biol. Standard.* 45: 163–73.

Hewitt, H. B. 1976. Projecting from animal experiments to clinical cancer. In: *Fundamental aspects of metastasis* (ed. L. Weiss), pp. 343–357. Amsterdam: North Holland.

——— . 1981. The use of animals in experimental cancer research. In *Animals in Research,* ed. D. Sperlinger, pp. 141–174. Chichester: J. Wiley and Sons.

Hewitt, H. B., and Porter, E. H. 1982. Letter. *Br. J. Radiol.* 55: 168.

Hewitt, H. B., and Wilson, C. W. 1959. A survival curve for mammalian leukaemia cells irradiated in vivo (implications for the treatment of mouse leukaemia by whole-body irradiation). *Br. J. Cancer* 13: 69–75.

Heywood, R. 1978. Animal studies in drug safety evaluation. *J. Roy. Soc. Med.* 71: 686–9.

Higginson, J. 1979. Cancer and environment: Higginson speaks out. *Science* 205: 1363–6.

Hillaby, J. 1969. Sanctified torture. *New Scientist.* 41: 69–70.

Hillman, M. 1970. *Scientific undesirability of painful experiments (pamphlet).* Zurich, Switzerland: World Society for the Protection of Animals.

Hinde, R. A. 1970. *Animal behaviour: a synthesis of ethology and comparative psychology.* New York: McGraw-Hill.

Hobbs, K. R., and Bleby J. 1976. *Laboratory non-human primates for biomedical research in the United Kingdom.* London: Medical Research Council Laboratory Animals Centre.

Hoff, C. 1980. Immoral and moral uses of animals. *New England J. Med.* 302: 115–8.

Holden, C. 1974. Beagles: army under attack for research at Edgewood. *Science:* 185: 130–31.

——— . 1982a. NASA student rat project questioned. *Science* 217: 425.

——— . 1982b. New focus on replacing animals in the lab. *Science* 215: 35–38.

Hollstein, M.; McCann, J.; Angelosanto, F. A.; and Nichols, W. W. 1979. Short-term tests for carcinogens and mutagens. *Mutation Res.* 65: 133–226.

Holmberger, F. 1976. In chap. 3. *New concepts in safety evaluation,* ed. M. A. Mehlman, E. R. Shapiro, and H. Blumenthal. New York: Halsted Press.

Holmes, D.; White, G. L.; Elmore, O.; and Prince., M. D. 1976. Stabilization of random source dogs. *Lab Animal* 5(4): 42–46.

Home Office. 1978. *Experiments on Living Animals, Statistics—1977.* Her Majesty's Stationery Office, Cmnd. Paper No. 7333, London.

———. 1979. *Report on the LD50 Test presented to the Secretary of State by the Advisory Committee on the Administration of the Cruelty to Animals Act, 1876.* London: Home Office.

Home Office. 1981. *Statistics of experiments on living animals—Great Britain, 1980.* Her Majesty's Stationery Office, Cmnd. Paper No. 8301, London.

Horenstein, D. 1977. The dynamics and treatment of child abuse: can primate research provide the answers? *J. Clin. Psychol.* 33: 563–5.

Hughes, J. 1975. Isolation of an endogenous compound from the brain with pharmacological properties similar to morphine. *Brain Res.* 88: 295–308.

Hume, C. W. 1957a. *The status of animals in the Christian religion.* Potters Bar, England: Universities Federation for Animal Welfare.

——— . 1957b. The strategy and tactics of experimentation. *Lancet* ii: 1049–52.

——— . 1962. Testimony before the Subcommittee of the Committee on Interstate and Foreign Commerce of the House of Representatives, Sept. 28 and 29. Washington, D. C.: U. S. Government Printing Office.

Humphrey, N. K. 1976. The social function of intellect. In *Growing points of ethology.* ed. P. Bateson and R. A. Hinde. London: Cambridge University Press. pp. 303–317.

Hunt, O. B. 1977. The polio myth. *The AV Magazine* 90(5): 1–2.

Hunter, W. J.; Lingk, W.; and Recht, P. 1979. Intercomparison study on the determination of single administration toxicity in rats. *J. Ass. Off. Anal. Chem.* 62: 864–73.

Hutt, P. B. 1978. Unresolved issues in the conflict between individual freedom and government control of food safety. *Food Drug Cosmetic Law Journal* 33: 558–89.

Illich, I. 1977. *Medical nemesis.* Bantam Books, New York

The Insight Team of the *Sunday Times of London.* 1979. *Suffer the children: the story of thalidomide.* New York: Viking Press.

Institute for Laboratory Animal Resources. 1966–69. *Annual surveys of animals used for research purposes. 1966–1969.* National Academy of Sciences. Washington, D. C.

——— . 1970. Laboratory animal facilities and resources supporting biomedical research, 1967–1968. *Lab Animal Care* 20: 795–869.

——— . 1970–71. *Annual surveys of animals used for research purposes, 1970–1971.* National Academy of Sciences. Washington, D. C.

——— . 1975. *Non-human primates: usage and availability for biomedical programs.* National Academy of Sciences. Washington, D. C.

——— . 1980. *National survey of laboratory animal facilities and resources.* U.S. Department of Health and Human Services (NIH Publc. No. 80–2091), Washington, D. C.

Interagency Regulatory Liaison Group. 1981. *Recommended guidelines for acute eye irritation testing.* Food and Drug Administration. Washington, D. C.

International Committee on Laboratory Animals. 1959. *International survey on the supply, quality and use of laboratory animals,* Supp. 1, 2, 3. Oslo: ICLA.

——— . 1962. International survey on the supply, quality and use of laboratory animals, Supp. 4. Oslo: ICLA.

International Journal for the Study of Animal Problems. 1981a. Dutch figures on animal experiments. 2: 292.

——— . 1981b. Anesthetics for Draize: follow-up 2: 174.

——— . 1982. Alternatives at NIH 3: 191–2.

International Primate Protection League. 1978. High mortality at Washington Primate Center. *Newsletter* 5(1); 14.

——— . 1979. Chimpanzee traffickers denounced in Sierra Leone. *Newsletter* 5(3): 15.

——— . 1979. Armed Forces Radiobiology Research Institute continues radiation experiments. *Newsletter* 6(1): 2–3.

——— . 1980. Psychologist criticizes cruelty to primates at Brooks Air Force Base. *Newsletter* 7(1): 6–7.

International Science and Engineering Fair. 1980. NSTA code on animal use. *ISEF Newsletter* (winter): 2.

Ivy, A. C. 1946. Antivivisectionists. *Clin. Med.* 53: 231–3.

Jacobs, M. 1979. A critical review: will the Ames Salmonella assay system be used as a screen for presumptive carcinogens. *J. Env. Pathol. Toxicol.* 2: 1205–215.

Jaggar, D. H. 1982. Review of Dallas Pratt's *"Alternatives to pain in experiments on animals." Env. Ethics* 4: 273–9.

Jansen, J. D. 1979. The predictive value of tests for carcinogenic and mutagenic activity. In *Toxicology and occupational medicine,* ed. W. B. Deichmann. pp. 71–80. Amsterdam: Elsevier/North Holland.

Jessell, T. M. and Iversen, L. L. 1977. Opiate analgesics inhibit substance P release from rat trigeminal nucleus. *Nature* 268: 549–51.

Johnson, A. W. 1981. Use of small dosage and corneal anaesthetic for eye testing in vivo. In *Proceedings of the CTFA ocular safety testing workshop: in vivo and in vitro approaches, October 6 & 7, 1980.* Washington, D. C.: Cosmetic, Toiletry and Fragrance Association.

Jones, L. M. 1963. Humaniacs threaten research. *J. Am. Med. Ass.* 185: 778–9.

Journal of the American Medical Association. 1951. Defeat for the antivivisectionists 145: 91–92.

———. 1953. Aid to antivivisectionists 153: 1039.

JRB Associates. 1979. *Primate Research Centers Evaluation Study.* Division of Research Resources, NIH Contract no. 1–RR–7–2143). Washington, D. C.

Jukes, T. H. 1982. Animal research is vital to human health. *American Council on Science and Health News and Views* 3(1); 4.

Kaplan, J. E., and Saba, T. M. 1976. Humoral deficiency and reticuloendothelial depression after traumatic shock. *Am. J. Physiol.* 230: 7–13.

Katz, M. 1980. The birth pangs of a new drug. *Drug and Cosmetic Industry* 127(4): 40–44; 138–140.

Keen, W. W. 1917. *Medical Research and human welfare.* Boston: Houghton Mifflin.

Keith, D. A., and Donoff, R. B. 1981. Use of animals questioned. *J. Oral. Surg.* 39: 169.

Kelly, P. J. 1980. Understanding and attitudes derived from the use of animals in schools. In *Animals in education,* ed. H. McGiffin and N. Brownley, pp. 47–59. Washington, D.C.: Institute for the Study of Animal Problems.

Kennedy, D. 1978. Animal testing and human risk. *Human Nature* (May).

Kieffer, G. H. 1979. Can bioethics be taught? *Am. Biol. Teacher* 41: 176.

———. 1980. Should bioethics be taught? *Am. Biol. Teacher* 42: 110–13.

Kitchener, R. 1972. B. F. Skinner—the butcher, the baker, the behavior-shaper. In *Boston Studies in the Philosophy of Science,* ed. R. S. Cohen and M. W. Wartofsky, vol. 20, pp. 87–98. Boston: D. Reidel.

Klein, A. E. 1972. *Trial by fury: the polio vaccine controversy.* New York: Charles Scribner.

Koch, S. 1981. The nature and limits of psychological knowledge. *Am. Psychol.* 36: 257–69.

Kolata, G. B. 1982a. New valiums and anti-valiums on the horizon. *Science* 216: 604–5.

———. 1982b. Brain receptors for appetite discovered. *Science* 218: 460–1.

Kotzwinkle, W. 1976. *Dr. Rat.* London: Knopf.

Krasovskii, G. N. 1976. Extrapolation of experimental data from animals to man. *Env. Hlth. Perspect.* 13: 51.

Krause, L. M. 1980. Student (and animal) welfare. In *Animals in education,* ed. H. McGiffin and N. Brownley, pp. 17–22. Washington, D.C.: Institute for the Study of Animal Problems.

Kuhn, T. S. 1970. *The structure of scientific revolutions.* Chicago: University of Chicago Press.

Laboratory Animal Science Association. 1981. Policy statement on dogs and cats. *Lab. Animals* 15: 405.

Lagoni, N.; Fiebelkorn, J.; and Wormuth, H. J. 1983. Protection of animals and animal experimentation—a survey of scientific experts. *Int. J. Study Animal Problems* 4(3):225–8.

Lamb, R. D. 1936. *American chamber of horrors.* New York: Farrar & Reinhart.

Lapage, G. 1960. *Achievement: some contributions of animal experiments to the conquest of disease.* Cambridge: W. Heffer.

Lea, S. E. G. 1979. Alternatives to the use of painful stimuli in physiological psychology and the study of animal behaviour. *ATLA Abstracts* 7(1): 20–21.

LeCornu, A. P., and Rowan, A. N. 1979. The use of non-human primates in the development and production of poliomyelitis vaccines. *ATLA Abstracts* 7(1): 11–19.

Lederburg, J. 1981. A challenge for toxicologists. *Chemical and Engineering News.* March 2: 5.

Leffingwell, A. 1914. *An ethical problem, or sidelights upon scientific experimentation on man and animals.* London: G. Bell and Sons.

Leighton, J. 1967. *The spread of cancer, pathogenesis, experimental methods, interpretations,* chap. 7. New York: Academic Press.

Leyton, A. S. F. and Sherrington, C. S. 1917. Observations on the excitable cortex of the chimpanzee, orangutan and gorilla. *Quart. J. Exp. Physiol.* 11: 135–222.

Liebeskind, J. C. and L. A. Paul. 1977. Psychological and physiological mechanisms of pain. *Ann. Rev. Psychol.* 28: 41–60.

Lindsey, J. R. 1980. NSMR: Its image, direction and future. *Int. J. Study Animal Problems* 1: 229–33.

Litchfield, J. T., and Wilcoxon, W. F. 1949. A simplified method of evaluating dose-effect experiments. *J. Pharmacol. Exp. Ther.,* 96: 99.

Littlewood Committee. 1965. *Report of departmental committee on experiments on animals.* London: Her Majesty's Stationery Office.

Lockard, R. B. 1968. The albino rat: a defensible choice or bad habit. *Am. Psychol.* 23: 734–42.

Loew, F. M. 1981. Alleviation of pain: the researcher's obligation. *Lab Animal* 10(5): 36–38.

Lowrance, W. W. 1976. *Of acceptable risk.* Los Altos, Ca.: William Kaufman.

McCann, J., and Ames, B. N. 1975. Detection of carcinogens as mutagens in the Salmonella/microsome test: assay of 300 chemicals. *Proceedings of the National Academy of Science, USA* 72: 5135–39.

———. 1976. Detection of carcinogens as mutagens in the Salmonella/microsome test: assay of 300 chemicals: discussion. *Proceedings of the National Academy of Science, USA* 73: 950–54.

McCormack, J. 1981. A procedure for the in vitro evaluation of the eye irritation protential of surfactants. In *Trends in bioassay methodology: in vivo, in vitro and mathematical approaches,* pp. 177–86. NIH Pub. No. 82–2382, Washington, D.C.

McCrea, R. C. 1910. *The humane movement.* New York: Columbia University Press.

McGiffin, H., and Brownley, N. 1980. *Animals in education.* Washington, D.C.: Institute for the Study of Animal Problems.

McGregor, J. C. 1980. The use of the placenta for microsurgical vascular practice. *J. Roy. Coll. Surg.* (Edin). 25: 233–6.

McGrew, W. C. 1981. Social and cognitive capabilities of nonhuman primates: lessons from the wild to captivity. *Int. J. Study of Animal Problems,* 2: 138–49.

McKinney, W. T. and Bunney, W. F. 1969. Animal model of depression. *Arch. Gen. Psychiatry* 21: 240–47.

Manuel, D. E. 1981. Antivivisection and physiology—Victorian influences. *Biologist* 28: 202–206.

Manufacturing Chemists Association 1975. *Study of the potential economic impacts of the proposed Toxic Substances Control Act as illustrated by Senate Bill S. 776.* Florham Park, N.J.: Foster D. Snell, Inc.

Marcuse, F. L. and Pear J. J. 1979. Ethics and animal experimentation: personal views. In *Psychopathology in animals: research and clinical implications,* ed. J. D. Keehn, pp. 305–329. New York: Academic Press.

Markowitz, H. 1975. Analysis and control of behavior in the zoo. In *Research in zoos and aquariums,* pp 77–90. Washington, D.C.: National Academy of Sciences.

Marks, J. 1972. Ending the routine guinea-pig test. *Tubercle* 53: 31–34.

Marten, M. 1981a. International coalition to abolish LD50. *The Beast* (Summer): 10.

———. 1981b. The price of polio vaccine. *Lab Animal* 10(7): 20–25.

Martyn, J. 1964. Unintentional duplication of research. *New Sci.* 21: 338.

Marzulli, F. N., and Simon, M. E. 1971. Eye irritation from topically applied drugs and cosmetics: preclinical studies. *Amer. J. Optom. Arch. Amer. Acad. Optom.* 48: 61–78.

Marzulli, F. N., and Ruggles, D. I. 1973. Rabbit eye irritation test: collaborative study. *J. Assc. of Anal. Chem* 56: 905–914.

Maser, J. D. and Seligman, M. E. P., eds. 1977. *Psychopathology: experimental models.* San Francisco: W. H. Freeman.

Mason, J. 1981. The politics of animal rights: making the human connection. *Int. J. Study Animal Problems* 2: 198–202.

Mason, W. A. 1976. Environmental models and mental modes: representational processes in great apes and man. *Am. Psychol.* 31: 284–94.

Masson, D. R. 1970. Apartheid for whom. *Nature* 228: 193.

Maugh, T. H. 1978a. Chemicals: how many are there? *Science* 199: 162.

———. (1978b) Chemical carcinogens: the scientific basis for regulation. *Science* 201: 1200–1205.

———. (1978c) Chemical carcinogens: how dangerous are low doses? *Science* 202: 37–41.

Mayer, W. V. 1973. Biology: study of the living or the dead? *The Am. Biology Teacher* 35: 27–30.

———. 1980. Objectives of animal use in biology courses. In *Animals in education,* ed. H. McGiffin and N. Brownley, pp. 11–16. Washington, D.C.: Institute for the Study of Animal Problems.

———. 1982. *Guidelines for educational priorities and curricular innovations on issues in human/animal interactions.* Boulder: Biological Sciences Curriculum Study.

Medawar, P. B. 1969. *The art of the soluble.* London: Pelican Books.

———. 1972. *The hope of progress.* London: Methuen.

———. 1981. Research with animals. *Lancet* i: 1308–1309.

Meier-Ewert, H. 1977. The use of experimental animals and in vitro systems for proving virus diagnosis. In *International symposium on experimental animals and in vitro systems in medical microbiology,* pp. 236–42. Munich: WHO Collaborating Center for Collection and Evaluation of Data on Comparative Virology.

Melmon, K. L. 1976. The clinical pharmacologist and scientifically unsound regulations for drug development. *Clin. Pharmacol. Ther.* 20: 125–9.

Menzel, E. W. 1967. Naturalistic and experimental research on primates. *Human Dev.* 10: 170–86.

Merchant, C. 1980. *The death of nature.* Berkeley: University of California Press.

Mered, B.; Albrecht, P.; Hopps, E. H.; Petricciani, J. C.; and Salk, J. 1981. Propagation of poliovirus in microcarrier cultures of three monkey kidney cell lines. *J. Biol. Standard.* 9: 137–45.

Merton, R. K. 1973. The normative structure of science. In *The sociology of science: theoretical and empirical observations,* ed. Storer, N. W., pp. 221–78. Chicago: University of Chicago Press.

Meselson, M., and Russell, K. 1977. Comparisons of carcinogenic and mutagenic potency. In *Origins of human cancer, Book C. Human risk assessment,* ed. H. H. Hiatt, J. D. Watson and J. A. Winstein, pp. 1473–81. Cold Spring Harbor, NY: Cold Spring Harbor Laboratory.

Midgley, M. 1981. Why knowledge matters. In *Animals in research,* ed. D. Sperlinger, pp. 319–336. Chichester: J. Wiley & Sons.

Mikhail, A. A.; Kamaya, V. A.; and Glavin, G. B. 1978. Stress and experimental ulcer: critique of psychological literature. *Can. Psychol. Review* 19: 296–303.

Miller, R. I.; Johnson, R. P.; Ryan, D. E.; and Chilton, R. J. 1980. Cardiopulmonary resuscitation: a teaching aid. *J. Oral Surg.* 38: 513–15.

Mitruka, B. M.; Rawnsley, H. M.; and Vadehra, D. V. 1976. *Animals for medical research: models for the study of human diseases.* New York: J. Wiley & Sons.

Molinengo, L. 1979. The curve doses vs survival time in the evaluation of acute toxicity. *J. Pharm. Pharmacol.* 31: 343–4.

Moore, B. R., and Stuttard, S. 1979. Dr. Guthrie and Felis domesticus or: tripping over the cat. *Science* 205: 1031–33.

Moran, G. 1975. Severe feed deprivation: some thoughts regarding its exclusive use. *Psychol. Bull.* 82: 543–57.

Morgan, C. L. 1894. *An introduction to comparative psychology.* London: Scott.

Morgan, M. J.; Fitch, M. D.; Holman, J. G.; and Lea, S.E.G. 1976. Pigeons learn the concept of an 'A'. *Perception* 5: 57–66.

Morgan, R. 1980. *Love and anger: an organizing handbook.* Westport, Conn.: Animal Rights Network.
Morris, M. E. 1980. Patterns of carcinogenicity. *Food & Cosmetics Toxicol.* 18: 437–8.
Morrison, J. K.; Quinton, R. M.; and Reinert, H. 1968. The purpose and value of LD50 determinations. In *Modern trends in toxicology* ed. E. Boyland and R. Goulding, vol. 1, pp. 1–17. London: Butterworths.
Morrison, M. 1981. Legislation and practice in the United States. In *Animals in Research,* ed. D. Sperlinger, pp. 63–77. Chichester: J. Wiley & Sons.
Mulder, J. B. 1979. Who is right about animal rights? *Lab. Animal Sci.* 29: 435–6.
Munn, N. L. 1950. *Handbook of psychological research on the rat.* Boston: Houghton-Mifflin.
Murphy, D. H. 1982. The problem of pain: what do animals really feel? *Int. J. Study Animal Problems* 3: 275–82.
Muul, I.; Hegyeli, A. F.; Dacre, J. C.; and Woodard, G. 1976. Toxicological testing dilemma. *Science* 193: 834.
Nader. R. 1974. The regulation of the safety of cosmetics. In *The legislation of product safety: consumer health and product safety: consumer health and product hazards cosmetics and drugs, pesticides, food additives,* ed. S. S. Epstein and R. D. Grundy, vol. 2, pp. 73–141. Boston: M.I.T. Press.
Nardone, R. M. 1977. Toxicity testing in vitro. In *Growth, nutrition and metabolism of cells in culture,* ed. R. H. Rothblatt and V. J. Christofala, vol. 3, pp. 471–96. New York: Academic Press.
———. 1980. The interface of toxicology and tissue culture and reflections on the carnation test. *Toxicology* 17: 105–111.
National Academy of Sciences. 1977. *The future of animals, cells, models and systems in research, development, education and testing.* Washington, D.C.
———. 1978. *Saccharin: technical assessment of risks and benefits.* Committee for a Study of Saccharin and Food Safety Policy, National Academy of Sciences, Washington, D.C.
National Commission for the Protection of Human Subjects of Biomedical and Behavioral Research. 1978. *Ethical guidelines for the protection of human subjects of research.* DHEW Publication No. (05) 78–0012. Washington, D.C.: U.S. Government Printing Office.
National Institutes of Health. 1978a. *In-house report,* Interagency Primate Steering Committee, April 21. Washington, D.C.
———. 1978b. *Report of the task force on the use of and need for chimpanzees.* Interagency Primate Steering Committee. Washington, D.C.
———. 1981a. *Report on the allegations of noncompliance with Public Health Service policy governing the care of laboratory animals at The Institute for Behavioral Research.* The Office for Protection from Research Risks, October 7. Washington, D.C.
———. 1981b. *Trends in bioassay methodology: in vivo, in vitro and mathematical approaches.* NIH Pub. No. 82-2382. Washington, D.C.
———. 1982. NIH moving to tighten animal research controls. *NIH Week* (June 18): 3–4.
National Opinion Polls. 1974. *Report to Annual General Meeting of the Royal Society for the Prevention of Cruelty to Animals,* 28, June, 1974.

National Primate Plan. 1980. U.S. Department of Health, Education and Welfare (Publication No. (NIH) 80–1520), Washington, D.C.

National Science Teachers Association. 1980. Code of practice on animals in schools. *The Science Teacher* 47(6): 57–58.

Nature. 1981. Protection for laboratory animals? 293: 173–4.

Neal, R. 1981. Panel Discussion. In: *Trends in bioassay methodology: in vivo, in vitro and mathematical approaches,* pg. 118. National Institutes of Health, (NIH, Publ. No. 82–2382), Washington, D.C.

Nerem, R. M.; Levesque, M. J.; and Cornhill, J. F. 1980. Social environment as a factor in diet-induced atherosclerosis. *Science* 208: 1475–6.

New Scientist. 1981. Animal crankers 91:2.

Newton, C. M. (1977) Biostatistical and biomathematical methods of efficient animal experimentation; In *The future of animals, cells, models and systems in research, development, education and testing,* pp. 152–164. Washington, D.C., National Academy of Sciences.

Nielsen, M.; Braestrup, C.; and Squires, R. F. 1978. Evidence for a late evolutionary appearance of brain-specific benzodiazepine receptors: an investigation of 18 vertebrate and 5 invertebrate species. *Brain Res.* 141: 342–6.

Nishigaki, I.; Hagihara, M.; Hiramatsu, M.; Izawa, Y.; and Yagi, K. 1980. Effect of thermal injury on lipid peroxide levels of rat. *Biochem. Med.* 24: 185–9.

Niven, C. D. 1967. *History of the humane movement.* New York: Transatlantic Arts.

Noguchi, P. D. 1981. Alternatives to animals in cancer research: a personal experience. In *Nonanimal research methodologies,* ed. A. Posner, pp. 14–22. Washington, D.C. George Washington University Ethics and Animals Society.

Noguchi, P. D.; Johnson, J. B.; O'Donnell, R.; and Petricciani, J. C. 1978. Chick embryonic skin as a rapid organ culture assay for cellular neoplasia. *Science* 199: 980–3.

Nordin, M. 1981. Trends in primate exports from Malaysia. *Lab. Primate Newsletter* 20(3): 9–11.

Office of Technology Assessment. 1977. *Cancer testing technology and saccharin.* U.S. Congress, OTA, Washington, D.C.

Official Journal of The European Communities. 1976. Proposal for a directive relating to the notification, packaging and labelling of dangerous products. *OJC* Nov. 5: 260.

Orlans, F. B. 1972a. High school students continue cruel experiments despite "supervision." *AWI Info. Report* 21(3): 1–6.

———. 1972b. New rules for old problems. *AWI Information Report* 24(1): 1.

Paget, G. E. 1970. Introduction. In *Methods in toxicology,* ed. G. E. Paget, p. 4. Oxford: Blackwell Scientific Publications.

Pain. 1981. Editorial 9: 141–3.

Palmer, A. E. 1973. Diseases encountered during the conditioning of random source dogs and cats. In *Research animals in medicine,* ed. L. T. Harmison, pp. 981–9. Washington, D.C.: NIH, U.S. Dept. of Health, Education and Welfare.

Passmore, J. 1975. The treatment of animals. *J. Hist. Ideas* 36: 195–218.

Paton, W. M. D. 1979. Animal experiment and medical research: a study in evolution. *Conquest* 169: pp. 1–14.

Paul, S. M. 1977. Models of madness: animal models of schizophrenia. In *Psychopathology: experimental models,* ed. J. D. Maser and M. E. P. Seligman, p. 384. San Francisco: W. H. Freeman.

Payton, N. 1981. *Testimony in support of H. 1245,* February, Boston: Massachusetts Society for the Prevention of Cruelty to Animals.

Pelling, D.; Sharratt, M.; and Hardy, J. 1973. The safety testing of medical plastics. I., An assessment of methods. *Fd. Cosmet. Toxicol.* 11: 69–83.

Perry, D. R.; Calloner, D. R.; and Oberst, R. J. 1981. Research advances and resource constraints. *New Eng. J. Med.* 305: 320–4.

Peters, D. P., and Ceci, S. J. 1982. Peer-review practices of psychological journals: the fate of published articles submitted again. *Behav. & Brain Sciences* 5: 187–255.

Peters, I. T. 1969. Vivisection: the rational alternatives. *Humanist* 84(9): 15–20.

Petricciani, J. D.; Hopps, H. E.; Elisberg, B. L.; and Early, E. M. 1977. Application of in vitro systems to public health. In *The future of animals cells, models and systems in research, development education and testing,* pp. 240–54. Washington, D.C.: National Academy of Sciences.

Petricciani, J. C.; Hopps, H. E.; and Chapple, P. J., eds. 1979. Cell substances: their use in the production of vaccines and other biologicals. *Advances in Experimental Medicine,* vol. 118. New York: Plenum Press.

Pharmaceutical Manufacturers Association. 1982. The role of the LD50 determination in drug safety evaluation. Research and Development Section, Pharmaceutical Manufacturer's Association, Washington, D.C.

Plaa, G. L. 1976. Animal models in the safety evaluation process. *Austr. J. Pharmac. Sci.* 5: 57–63.

Pomerat, C. M., and Leake, C. D. 1954. Short-term cultures for drug assays. *Ann. N.Y. Acad. Sci.* 58: 1110–28.

Ponten, J. 1976. The relationship between in vitro transformation and tumor formation in vivo. *Biochem. Biophys. Acta.* 458: 397–422.

Potkay, S. and Bacher, J. D. 1973. The research dog: random source or colony reared? In *Research animals in medicine,* ed. L. T. Harmison, pp. 1061–65. Washington, D.C.: NIH, U.S. Department of Health, Education and Welfare.

Pratt, D. 1976. *Painful experiments on animals.* New York: Argus Archives.

———. 1980. *Alternatives to pain in experiments on animals.* New York: Argus Archives.

Prince, A. M. 1981. The use of chimpanzees in biomedical research. In *Trends in bioassay methodology: in vivo, in vitro and mathematical approaches,* pp. 81–97. National Institutes of Health Pub. No. 82–2382, Washington, D.C.

Pritchard, W. R. 1968. Animal research in the new biology. *Lab Animal Care* 18: 230.

Procter and Gamble Company. 1979. *Comments on draft IRLG guidelines for acute toxicity tests.* Interagency Research Liaison Group, Washington, D.C.

Quastler, H.; Austin, M. R.; and Miller, M. 1956. Oral radiation death. *Radiation Res.* 5: 338–53.

Quinton, R. M., and Reinert, H. 1968. The mutability of LD50 values in animals with differing nutritional status. Cited by J. K. Morrison, R. M. Quinton, and Reinert, H. 1968. In *Modern Trends in Toxicology,* pp. 1–18. ed. E. Boyland and R. Goulding, London: Butterworths.

Raettig, H. 1977. Bacteria: the use of experimental animals and in vitro systems in investigating scientific diagnostic problems. In *International symposium on experimental animals and in vitro system in medical microbiology,* pp. 214–20. Munich: WHO Collaborating Center for Collection and Evaluation of Data on Comparative Virology.

Reese, W. G. 1979. A dog model for human psychopathology. *Am. J. Psychiatry* 136: 1168–72.

Regan, T. 1982. *All that dwell therein.* Berkeley: University of California Press.

Regan, T., and Singer, P., eds. 1976. *Animal rights and human obligations.* Englewood Cliffs, N.J.: Prentice-Hall.

Reines, B. K. 1982. *Psychology experiments on animals: a critique of animal models of human psychopathology.* Boston: New England Anti-vivisection Society.

Rekker, R. F. 1980. LD50 values: are they about to become predictable. *Trends in Pharm. Sci.* 1: 383–4.

Richards, C. D., and Webb, A. C. 1975. The effect of nitrous oxide on cats anesthetized with Brietal. *J. Physiol. Lond.* 245: 72p–73p.

Riley, V. 1981. Psychoneuroendocrine influences on immunocompetence and neoplasia. *Science* 212: 1100–1109.

Roberts, C. 1980. *Science, animals and evolution: reflections on some unrealized potentials of biology and medicine.* Westport, Conn.: Greenwood Press.

Robinson, H. J. 1967. Animal experimentation leading to the development of drugs benefiting human beings and animals. *Am. J. Publ. Hlth.* 57: 1613–20.

Rimbach, J. A. 1982. The Judeo-Christian tradition and the human/animal bond. *Int. J. Study Animal Problems* 3: 198–207.

Rodman, J. 1977. The liberation of nature. *Inquiry* 20: 83–145.

Rofe, P. C. 1971. Tissue culture and toxicology. *Food & Cosmetic Toxicology* 9: 683–96.

Rollin, B. E. 1981. *Animal Rights and Human Morality.* Buffalo: Prometheus.

Rosenfeld, A. 1981. Animal rights versus human health. *Science 81* 2(5): 18, 22.

Ross, M. W. 1978. The ethics of animal experimentation: control in practice. *Australian Psychol.* 13: 375–8.

Ross, W. P. D. 1963. Monkeys and apes as laboratory animals. Coll. Papers of Lab. An. Centre *12:* 29–40.

Rowan, A. N. 1981a. Can alternatives be integrated with animal models? *Lab Animal* 10(2): 38–45.

———. 1981b. Regulation of biomedical research. *Int. J. Study of Animal Problems.* 2: 227–9.

———. 1982a. The Silver Spring seventeen. *Int. J. Study of Animal Problems.* 3: 219–27.

———. 1982b. The LD50 test. *Int. J. Study Animal Problems* 3: 54–56.

———. 1982c. The issue of science and the issue of care. *Int. J. Study Animal Problems* 3: 177–8.

Rowan, A. N., and Stratmann, C. J. eds. 1980. *The use of alternatives in drug research.* London: Macmillan.

Rowsell, H. C. 1980. High school science fairs: evaluation of live animal experimentation—the Canadian experience. In *Animals in Education,* ed. H. McGiffin and N. Brownley, pp. 85–98. Washington, D.C.: Institute for the Study of Animal Problems.

Royal Society for the Prevention of Cruelty to Animals. 1980. *Report of the panel of enquiry into shooting and angling.* Horsham, U.K.: RSPCA.

Rubin, H. 1976. Carcinogenicity testing. *Science* 191: 241.

Ruesch, H. 1978. *Slaughter of the innocents.* New York: Bantam Books.

Rush, R. I. 1981. Memorandum on repeal of Section 53. 11(h) of the Los Angeles Municipal Code, City of Los Angeles, January 2.

Russell, G. K. 1978. *Laboratory investigations in human physiology.* New York: Macmillan.

Russell, W. J. 1973. Nitrous oxide—is it an adequate anesthetic? *J. Physiol. Lond.* 231: 20p–21p.

Russell, W. M. S. 1957. The increase of humanity in experimentation: replacement reduction and refinement. *Lab. Animals Bureau Collected Papers* 6: 23–25.

Russell, W. M. S., and Burch, R. L. 1959. *The principles of humane experimental technique.* London: Methuen.

Rust, J. H. 1982. Animal models for human diseases. *Perspect. Biol. Med.* 25: 662–72.

Ryder, R. 1975. *Victims of Science.* London: Davis-Poynter.

Rynearson, E. K. 1978. Humans and pets and attachment. *Br. J. Psychiat* 133: 550–55.

Sachs, B. D. (1976) Letter, *Science,* 184: 860.

Saffioti, U. 1976. Validation of short-term bioassays as predictive screens for chemical carcinogens. In: *Screening tests in Chemical carcinogenesis,* eds. R. Montesano, H. Bartsch & L. Tomatis, pp 3–13. International Agency for Research on Cancer, Lyon.

Salk, J. and Salk, D. 1977. Control of influenza and poliomyelitis with killed virus vaccines. *Science* 195: 834–847.

Salsburg, D. 1983. The lifetime feeding study in mice and rats—an examination of its validity as a bioassay for human carcinogens. Fund. Appl. Toxicol. 3: 63–7.

Salt, H. S. 1892. *Animals' rights.* London (New edition issued by Society for Animals Rights, Clarks Summit, PA, 1980).

Santamarina, E. 1976. *Animal science techniques.* A course at Cook College, Rutgers University, New Jersey.

Saunders and Company Market Survey. 1966. *Information Lab. Animals for Research* 9(3): 10.

Saxen, L. 1976. Advantages of organ culture techniques in teratology. In *Tests of teratogenicity in vitro,* ed. J. Ebert and M. Marois, pp. 262–84. Amsterdam: North Holland.

Scala, R. A. 1981. Eye irritation testing in animals: the present situation. In *Proceedings of the CTFA Ocular Safety Testing Workshop: in vivo and in vitro approaches, October 6 & 7, 1980.* Washington, D.C.: Cosmetic, Toiletry and Fragrance Association.

Schabel, F. M. 1981. In vitro and in vivo systems for detection and development of anticancer drugs. In *Trends in bioassay methodology: in vivo, in vitro and mathematical approaches,* pp. 43–61. Washington, D.C.: National Institutes of Health Pub. no. 82–2382.

Scharff, M. D.; Roberts, S.; and Thammana, P. 1981. Hybridomas as a source of antibodies. In *Trends in bioassay methodology: in vivo, in vitro and mathematical approaches,* pp. 187–98. National Institutes of Health Pub. No. 82–2382, Washington, D.C.

Schiller, J. 1967. Claude Bernard and vivisection. *J. Hist. Med.* 22: 246–60.

Shultz, W. J. 1968. *The humane movement in the United States, 1910–1922.* New York: AMS Press.

Schumacher, H. J. 1975. Chemical structure and teratogenic properties. In *Methods for detection of environmental agents that produce congenital defects,* ed. T. H. Shepard, J. R. Miller, and M. Marois, pp. 65–77. Amsterdam: North Holland.

Scientists Center for Animal Welfare. 1982. NAS backs rules on animal use. *SCAW Newsletter* 4(2): 1–4.

Seay, B.; Alexander, B. K.; and Harlow, H. F. 1964. Maternal behavior of socially deprived rhesus monkeys. *J. Abnormal and Social Psychol.* 69: 345–54.

Secord, D. C., and Russell, J. D. 1973. A clinical laboratory study of conditioned mongrel dogs and labrador retrievers. *Lab Animal Science* 23: 567–71.

Segal, E. 1982. Editorial. *J. Exp. Analysis Behav.* 38: 116.

Select Committee. 1980. *Report of the Select Committee on the Laboratory Animals Protection Bill,* vols. 1 and 2. London: Her Majesty's Stationary Office.

Selye, H. 1973. The evolution of the stress concept. *Am. Sci.* 61: 692–99.

Shanahan, A. J. 1978. *Formation and management of an expert toxicological review team for literaure search, evaluation and organization of currently available rapid toxicological tests,* vol. 1. U.S. Army Medical Research and Development Command, Contract No. DAMD—17–77–C–75–6, Fort Detrick, MD.

Shugg, W. 1968. Humanitarian attitudes in the early experiments of the Royal Society, *Annals of Science* 24: 227–38.

Shuster, S. 1978. The antivivisectionists—a critique. *New Scientist* 77: 80–82.

Silverman, A. P. 1978. *Animal behavior in the laboratory.* New York: Pica Press.

Simons, P. J. 1980. An alternative to the Draize Test. In *The use of alternatives in drug research,* ed. A. N. Rowan and C. J. Stratmann, pp. 147–51. London: Macmillan.

Singer, P. 1975. *Animal liberation.* New York: Random House.

Smyth, D. H. 1978. *Alternatives to animal experiments.* London: Scolar Press.

Soave, O. A. 1981. The cost of domestic breeding of rhesus monkeys. *Lab. Primate Newsletter* 20(3): 1–4.

Solomon, M., and Lovenheim, P. 1982. Reporting requirements under the Animal Welfare Act: their inadequacies and the public's right to know. *Int. J. Study Animal Problems.* 3: 210–18.

Solomon, R. C. 1982. Has not an animal organs, dimensions, senses, affections, passions? *Psychol. Today* 16(3): 36–47.

Somers, G. F. 1962. Thalidomide and congenital abnormalities. *Lancet* i: 912–913.

Sperling, F. 1981. Bioassay conference. *Bioscience* 31: 480–81.

Sperling, F., and McLaughlin, J. L. 1976. Biological parameters and the acute LD50 test. *J. Assoc. Off. Anal. Chem.* 59: 734–6.

Sperlinger, D. 1981. Natural relations—contemporary views of the relationship between humans and other animals. In *Animals in research,* ed. D. Sperlinger, pp. 79–101. Chichester: John Wiley & Sons.

Spink, J. D. 1977. Drug testing. In *The welfare of laboratory animals: legal, scientific and humane requirements,* pp. 44–50. Potters Bar, England: Universities Federation for Animal Welfare.

Spitz, R. A. 1945. Hospitalism: an inquiry into the genesis of psychiatric conditions in early childhood. *Psychoanal. Stud Child* 1: 53–74.

Squire, R. A. 1981. Ranking animal carcinogens: a proposed regulatory approach. *Science* 216: 877–80.

Stammati, A. P.; Silano, V.; and Zucco, F. 1981. Toxicology investigations with cell culture systems. Toxicology *20:* 91–153.

Stara, J. F. and Kello, D. 1979. Relationship of long-term animal studies to human disease. In: *Assessing Toxic effects of environmental pollutants,* eds. S. D. Lee & J. B. Mudd, pp. 43–76. Ann Arbor: Ann Arbor Science Publishers.

Sternbach, R. A. 1976. The need for an animal model of chronic pain. *Pain* 2: 2–4.

Stevens, C. 1978. Laboratory animal welfare. In: *Animals and their legal rights*, ed. Leavitt, E. S., pp 46–58. Animal Welfare Institute, Washington.

Stevenson, D. E. 1979. Current problems in the choice of animals for toxicity testing. *J. Tox. Env. Hlth.* 5: 9–15.

Stevenson, L. G. 1955. Science down the drain. *Bull. Hist. Med.* 29: 1–26.

———. 1956. Religious elements in the background of the British antivivisection movement. *Yale J. Biol. Med.* 29: 125–57.

Storz, J.; Moore, K. A.; and Spears, P. 1977. The use of experimental animals and in vitro systems for the detection and identification of chlamydial and rickettsial agents. In *International symposium on experimental animals and in vitro systems in medical microbiology,* pp. 221–35. Munich: WHO Collaborating Center for Collection and Evaluation of Data on Comparative Virology.

Straight, W. 1962. Man's debt to laboratory animals. *Miami University Med. School Bull.* 16: 106.

Sudak, H. M. 1981. Animal research in psychology. *Am. Psychol.* 36: 312.

Sun, M. 1980. Primate center attempts bailout through Congress. *Science* 210: 1333.

Sunshine, I., ed. 1979. *CRC handbook of analytical toxicology.* Boca Raton, Fla.: CRC Press.

Tajima, Y. 1975. Present status of experimental animals in Japan. *Exp. Animals* 24: 67–77.

Tamir, P., and Hamo, A. 1980. Attitudes of secondary school students in Israel toward the use of living organisms in the study of biology. *Int. J. Study of Animal Problems* 1: 299–311.

Task Force of Past Presidents. 1982. Animal data in hazard evaluation: paths and pitfalls. *Fund. Appl. Toxicol.* 2: 101–107.

Taub, E. 1982. Letter. *Pavlovian J. Biol. Sci.* 17: 106.

Technical Committee on Poliomyelitis Vaccine. 1956. The monkey safety test for poliomyelitis vaccine. *Am. J. Hyg.* 64: 104–137.

Tennov, D. 1980. Pain infliction in animal research. In *Animals in Education,* ed. H. McGiffin and N. Brownley, pp. 35–40. Washington, D.C.: Institute for the Study of Animal Problems.

Thompson, W. R. 1947. Use of moving averages and interpolation to estimate median-effective dose. I. Fundamental formulas, estimation of error, and relation to other methods. *Bacteriol. Rev.* 11: 115–145.

Thorpe, W. H. 1974. *Animal nature and human nature.* Garden City: Doubleday.

Tinbergen, N., and Perdeck, A. C. 1950. On the stimulus situation releasing the begging response in the newly hatched herring gull chick *Behavior* 3: 1–39.

Trevan, J. W. 1927. The error of determination of toxicity. *Proc. R. Soc. Lond. (Biol.)* 101: 483.

Turner, J. 1980. *Reckoning with the beast: animals, pain and humanity in the Victorian mind.* Baltimore: Johns Hopkins University Press.

Ulrich, R. E., and Azrin, N. W. 1962. Reflexive fighting in response to aversive stimulation. *J. Exp. Anal. Behav.* 5: 511–520.

Underwood, P. C., and Durbin, C. G. 1963. Beagles for pharmacological studies. *Lab Animal Care* 13: 525–9.

U.S., Congress. 1979. House, Subcommittee of the Committee on Appropriations, Pt. 4, National Institutes of Health. 96th Cong., p. 486.

———. 1981. House, Congressional Record, 97th Cong., June 15, E 2953.

U.S. Dept. of Agriculture. 1979. Code of Federal Regulations, Title 9. *Animals and animal products.* chap. 1, sec. 113.99(c)4. Washington, D.C.

U.S. Dept. of Health, Education and Welfare. 1954. *Minimum requirements—poliomyelitis vaccine.* Public Health Service. Washington, D.C.

U.S. Dept. of State. 1977. Telegram No. 172141, July.

———. 1978. Telegram No. 2615372, May.

Universities Federation for Animal Welfare. 1977. *Report and accounts, 1977–1978.* Potters Bar.

———. 1982. Humane experimental techniques. UFAW Annual Report, 1981–1982. Potters Bar.

Van Abbe, N. J. 1973. Eye irritation studies relating to responses in man and laboratory animals. *J. Soc. Cosmetic Chemists* 24: 685–692.

Van Citters, R. 1973. The role of animal research in clinical medicine: In *Research animals in medicine.* L. T. Harmison, ed., pp. 3–8. Washington: U.S. Dept. of Health, Education and Welfare.

Vierck, C. J. 1976. Extrapolations from the pain research literature to problems of adequate veterinary care. *J. Am. Vet. Med. Ass.* 168: 510–513.

Visscher, M. B. 1973. Commentary on laws relating to the scientific use of unclaimed impounded animals. *J. Am. Vet. Med. Ass.* 163: 78–79.

———. 1979. Animal rights and alternative methods—two new twists in the antivivisection movement. *The Pharos* Fall: 11–19.

Vyvyan, J. 1969. *In pity and in anger: a study of the use of animals in science.* London: Michael Joseph.

———. 1971. *The dark face of science.* London: Michael Joseph.

Waddell, H. 1946. *Beasts and saints,* trans. London: Constable.

Waddington, C. H. 1960. *The ethical animal.* Chicago: University of Chicago Press.

Wade, N. 1976. Animal rights: NIH cat sex study brings grief to New York Museum. *Science* 194: 162–7.

———. 1978a. India bans monkeys export: US may have breached accord. *Science* 199: 280–81.

———. 1978b. New vaccine may bring man and chimpanzee into tragic conflict. *Science* 200: 1027–1030.

———. 1980. Does man alone have language? Apes reply in riddles and a horse says neigh. *Science* 208: 1349–51.

———. 1981. *The Noble duel: two scientists' 21-year race to win the world's most coveted research prize.* Garden City: Anchor Press/ Doubleday.

Waksman, B. H. 1980. Information overload in immunology: possible solutions to the problem of excessive publication. *J. Immunology* 124: 1009–1015.

Wall, P. D. 1975. Editorial. *Pain* 1: 1–2.

Wall, P. D. 1976. Editorial. *Pain* 2: 1.

Walsh, J. 1982. Public attitude towards science is yes, but. . . . *Science* 215: 270–72.

Waters, R. H.; Rethlingshafter, D. A.; and Cladwell, W. E. 1960. *Principles of comparative psychology.* New York: McGraw-Hill.

Watson, J. D. 1968. *The double helix.* New York: Atheneum.

Weatherall, M. 1982. An end to the search for new drugs? *Nature* 296: 387–90.

Weil, C. S. 1952. Tables for convenient calculation of median-effective dose (LD50 or ED50) and instructions in their use. *Biometrics* 8: 249–63.

Weil, C. S., and Scala, R. A. 1971. Study of intra- and inter-laboratory variability in the results of rabbit eye and skin irritation test. *Toxicol Appl. Pharmacol.* 19: 276–360.

Weisburger, J. H., and Williams, G. M. 1981. Carcinogen testing: current problems and new approaches. *Science* 214: 401–407.

Whipple, G. H. 1921. Value of animal experimentation to mankind. *Am. J. Public Health* 11: 105–107.

Whitehair, L. A., and Gay, W. J. 1981. The seven NIH primate research centers. *Lab Animal* 10(7): 26–34.

Wiggins, R. A. 1976. Replacement of biological methods by chemical and physical methods. II. Chemical analysis of vitamins, A, D. and E. *Proceedings of the Analytical Division of the Chemical Society* 13: 133–7.

Wilk, A. L.; Greenberg, J. H.; Horigan, E. A.; Pratt, R. M.; and Martin, G. R. 1980. Detection of teratogenic compounds using differentiating embryonic cells in culture. *In Vitro* 16: 269–76.

Wilson, J. G. 1975. Reproduction and teratogenesis: current methods and suggested improvements. *J. Ass. Off. Anal. Chem.* 58: 657–67.

———. 1978. Review of in vitro system with potential for use in teratogenicity screening. *J. Env. Pathol. Toxicol* 2: 149–67.

Wilson, J. R. 1963. *Margins of Safety.* London: Collins.

Winterscheid, L. C. 1967. Animal experimentation leading to the development of advanced surgical technics. *Am. J. Public Hlth.* 57: 1604–1612.

Wisconsin Regional Primate Research Center. 1982. *Policy statement on principles for the ethical uses of animals.* Madison, Wisc.

Wood, J. R.; Ansbacher, R.; Castro, R. J.; Marshall, W.; and Trabal, J. R. 1980. Animal surgery: an adjunct to training in obstetrics and gynecology. *Obstet. Gynecol.* 56: 373–4.

Woodcock, I. 1972. In *Systematic Fungicides,* ed. R. W. March, pp. 86–91. London: Longmans.

Worden, A. N. 1974. Tissue culture. In *Modern trends in toxicology,* vol. 2. Ed. E. Boyland and R. Goulding, pp. 216–49. London: Butterworth.

World Health Organization. 1967. *Principles for the testing of drugs for teratogenicity.* Technical Report Series, No. 364. World Health Organization, Geneva.

Yaffe, S. J. 1980. Summary: pediatrician's view. In *Drug and chemical risks to the fetus and newborn* ed. R. H. Schwarz and S. J. Yaffe, pp. 157–61. New York: Alan R. Liss.

Yalow, R. S. 1981. Radioactivity in the service of man. *Bioscience* 31: 23–28.

——— . 1982. The role of technology in creative biologic research. *Perspect. Biol. Med.* 25: 573–82.

Yelton, D. E., and Scharff, M. D. 1980. Monoclonal antibodies. Am. Sci. 68: 510.

Yoxall, A. T. 1978. Pain in small animals: its recognition and control. *J. Small Anim. Pract.* 19: 423–38.

Zbinden, G. 1963. Experimental and clinical aspects of drug toxicity. In *Advances in pharmacology,* ed. S. Garattini and P. A. Shore, vol. 11, pp. 1–12. London: Academic Press.

——— . 1973. *Progress in toxicology.* Berlin: Springer-Verlag.

——— . 1976. A look at the world from inside the toxicologist's cage. *Eur. J. Clin. Pharmacol.* 9: 333–8.

Zbinden, G., and Flury-Roversi, M. 1981. Significance of the LD50-test for the toxicological evaluation of chemical substances. *Arch. Toxicol.* 47: 77–79.

Zinn, R. D. 1968. The research dog. *J. Am. Vet. Med. Ass.* 153: 1883–6.

Index

Index

Index